The Little Book of
BIG
FEELINGS

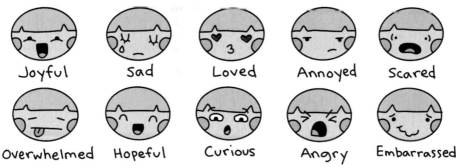

Joyful   Sad   Loved   Annoyed   Scared

Overwhelmed   Hopeful   Curious   Angry   Embarrassed

An Illustrated Exploration of Life's *Many* Emotions

by Maureen "Marzi" Wilson

ADAMS MEDIA

NEW YORK LONDON TORONTO SYDNEY NEW DELHI

Adams Media
An Imprint of Simon & Schuster, Inc.
57 Littlefield Street
Avon, Massachusetts 02322

First Adams Media hardcover edition November
2019

ADAMS MEDIA and colophon are trademarks of
Simon & Schuster.

For information about special discounts for bulk
purchases, please contact Simon & Schuster
Special Sales at 1-866-506-1949 or
business@simonandschuster.com.

The Simon & Schuster Speakers Bureau can bring
authors to your live event. For more information
or to book an event contact the Simon & Schuster
Speakers Bureau at 1-866-248-3049 or visit our
website at www.simonspeakers.com.

Interior illustrations by Maureen Wilson

Manufactured in the United States of America

10 9 8 7 6 5 4 3 2 1

ISBN 978-1-5072-1208-0
ISBN 978-1-5072-1209-7 (ebook)

For Dad,

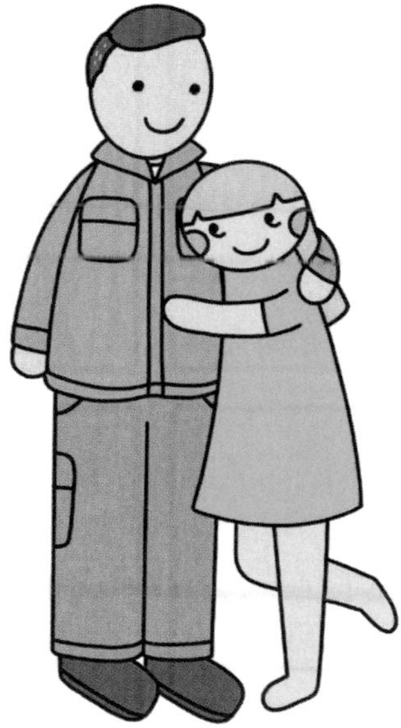

who always shows up.

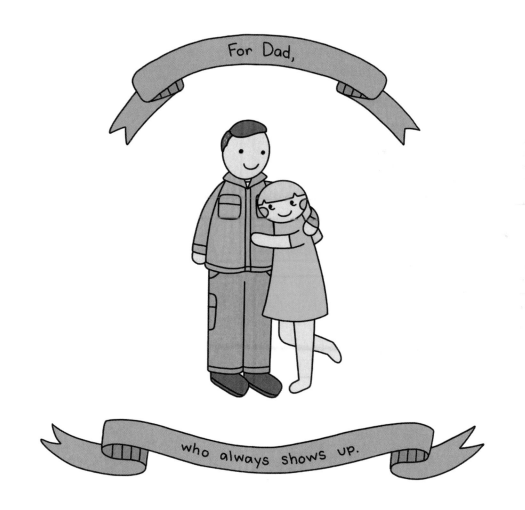

TABLE OF CONTENTS

INTRODUCTION

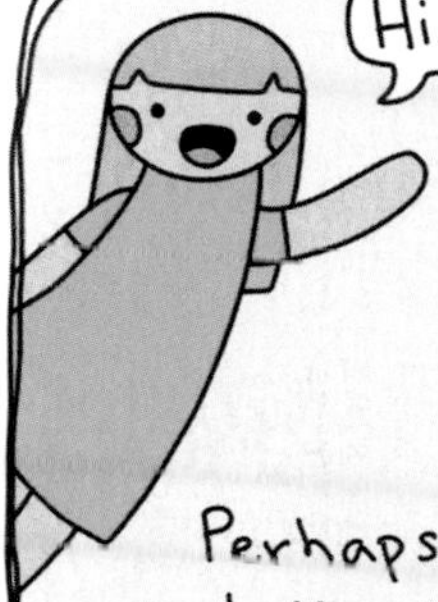
Hi. How are you?

Many of us have been conditioned to believe that "Fine, thanks" is the only appropriate response. But really:

How are you?

Perhaps you're feeling overwhelmed, angry, or sad. Maybe you're too embarrassed or ashamed to admit that you aren't "fine"?

I've come to believe that there's no such thing as a "bad" emotion. Our feelings simply offer us feedback on our experiences. What would happen if we acknowledged our emotions instead of ignoring them? Perhaps if we stopped pretending to be "fine," we could discover what it is that our emotions are trying to teach us.

Joy, sadness, hope, anger—these feelings are natural and normal. It's time to stop stifling our feelings and start celebrating and validating the diverse beauty of human emotion.

CHAPTER 1

TODAY I'M FEELING:

CURIOUS

I spend a lot of my time feeling curious; I think curiosity is my default state. For me, curiosity isn't limited to fact-finding. It's also intertwined with fantasy and imagination. Curiosity breeds creativity! I love dreaming up possibilities and exploring the "why." I always have questions!

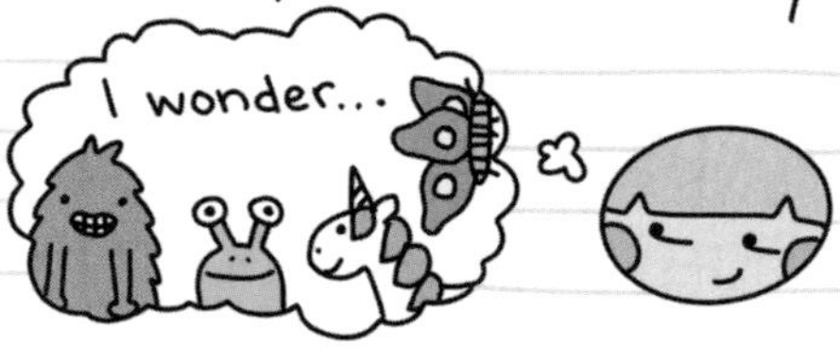
I wonder...

But I've learned the hard way that it's important to be respectfully curious. I once asked a friend a question about her religion that was unintentionally rude. Although my query came from a place of genuine curiosity, it was based on an incorrect assumption that I learned was offensive.

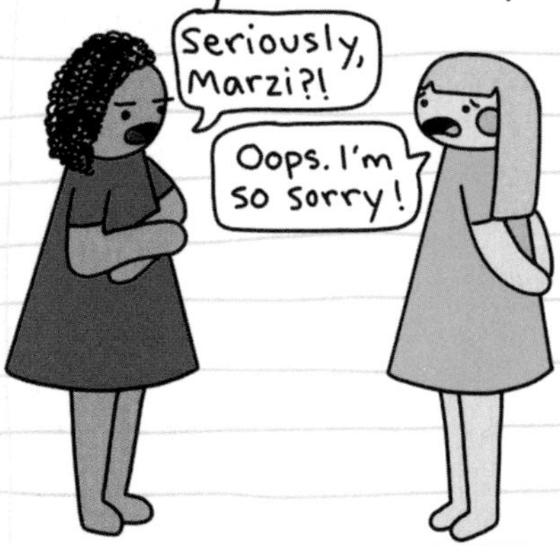
Seriously, Marzi?!
Oops. I'm so sorry!

I apologized and then did what I should have done in the first place:

I studied books about her religion
I Googled specific questions

I utilized my curiosity to lay a groundwork of knowledge so I could communicate more thoughtfully.

I've learned that although feeling curious can be a good thing, it's unfair for me to expect my friends to be responsible for educating me. I'm capable of researching and learning on my own!

HISTORY of BELIEF
documentaries
blogs
books
news sites
TIMES

CURIOUS MIND

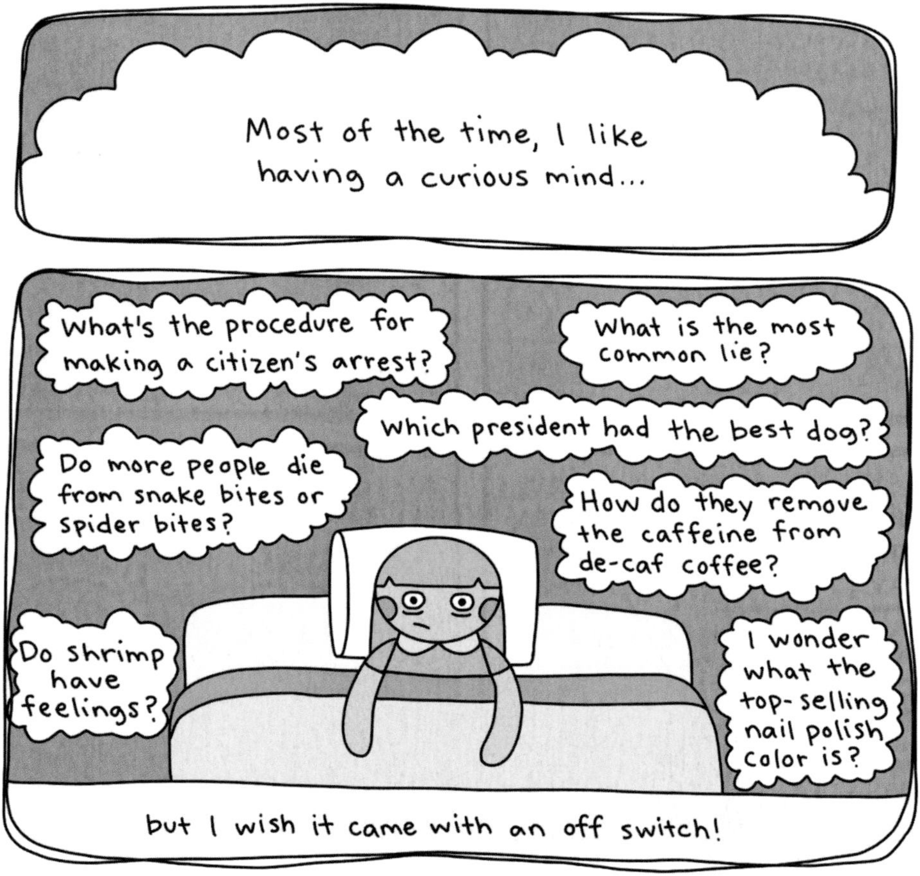
Most of the time, I like having a curious mind...
What's the procedure for making a citizen's arrest?
What is the most common lie?
Which president had the best dog?
Do more people die from snake bites or spider bites?
How do they remove the caffeine from de-caf coffee?
Do shrimp have feelings?
I wonder what the top-selling nail polish color is?
but I wish it came with an off switch!

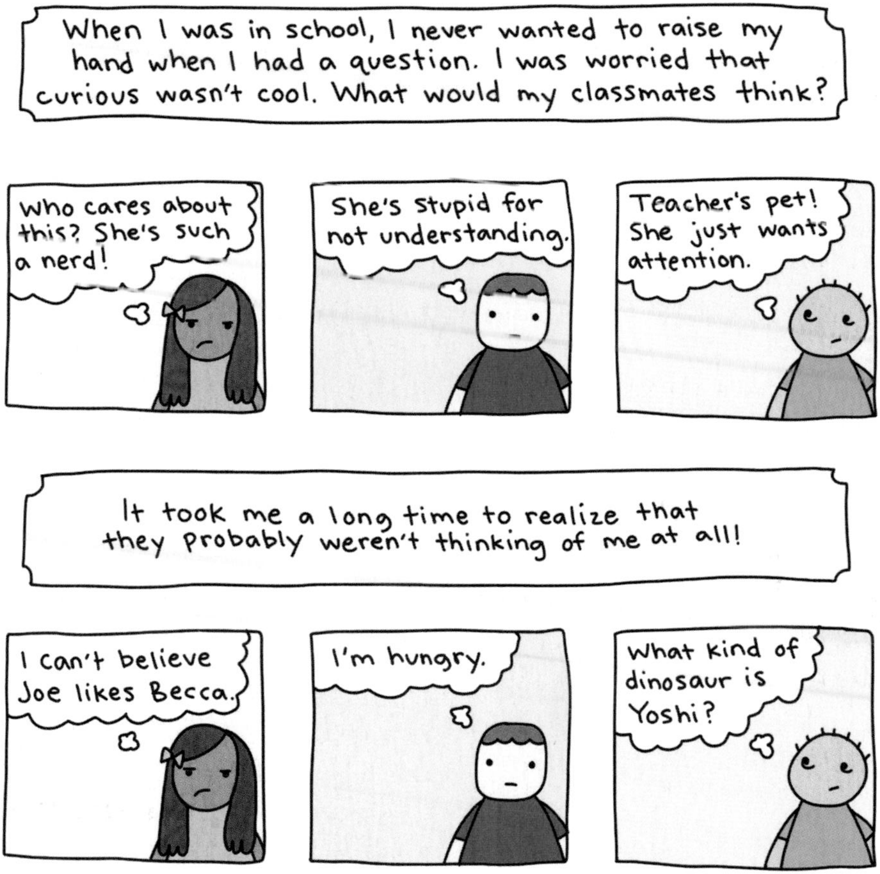
When I was in school, I never wanted to raise my hand when I had a question. I was worried that curious wasn't cool. What would my classmates think?
Who cares about this? She's such a nerd!
She's stupid for not understanding.
Teacher's pet! She just wants attention.
It took me a long time to realize that they probably weren't thinking of me at all!
I can't believe Joe likes Becca.
I'm hungry.
What kind of dinosaur is Yoshi?

UNSOLVED MYSTERIES

Where does my paycheck go?

stolen by leprechauns?

How do I _always_ manage to wear the wrong thing?

I thought this was a pool party...?

Why don't restaurants have play land zones for grownups?

I'm taking steps to diversify my portfolio.

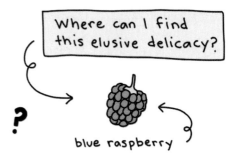

Where can I find this elusive delicacy?

blue raspberry

I'M CURIOUS WHY THIS ISN'T CALLED THAT

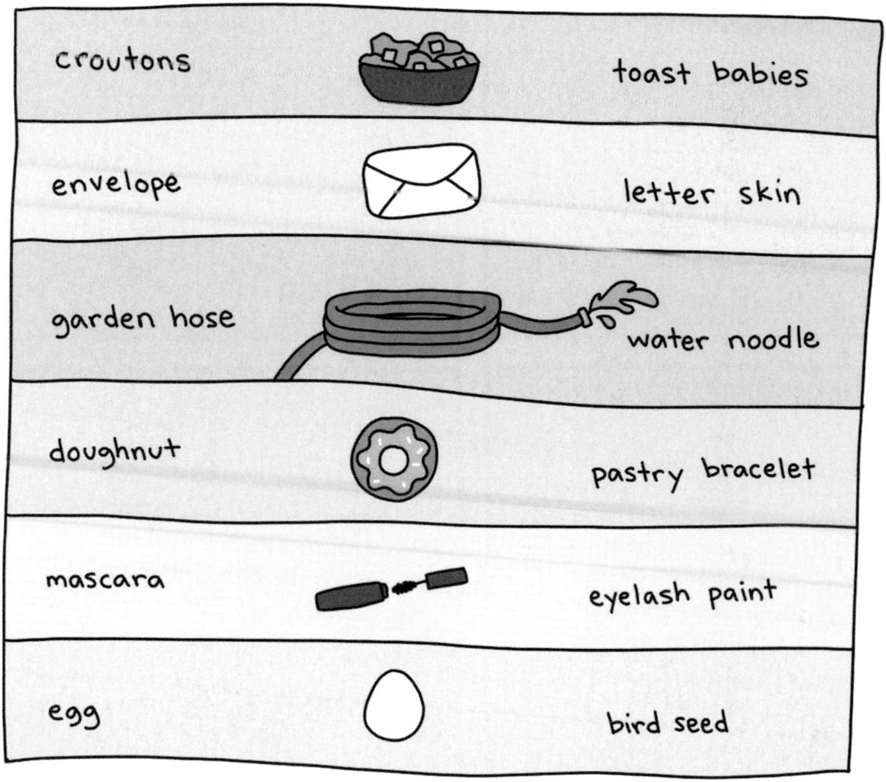

croutons		toast babies
envelope		letter skin
garden hose		water noodle
doughnut		pastry bracelet
mascara		eyelash paint
egg		bird seed

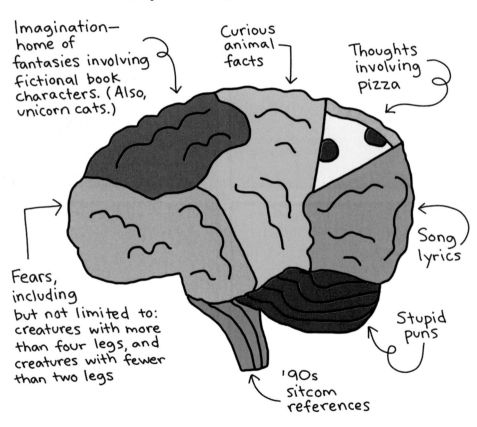

A VERY SCIENTIFIC

DIAGRAM OF MY BRAIN

Imagination— home of fantasies involving fictional book characters. (Also, unicorn cats.)

Curious animal facts

Thoughts involving pizza

Fears, including but not limited to: creatures with more than four legs, and creatures with fewer than two legs

Song lyrics

Stupid puns

'90s sitcom references

CURIOUS WHY THESE DON'T EXIST...

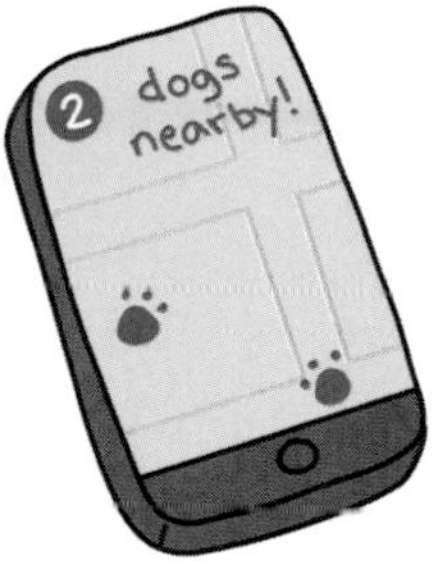
2 dogs nearby!

An app that utilizes pets' microchip technology to locate nearby dogs.

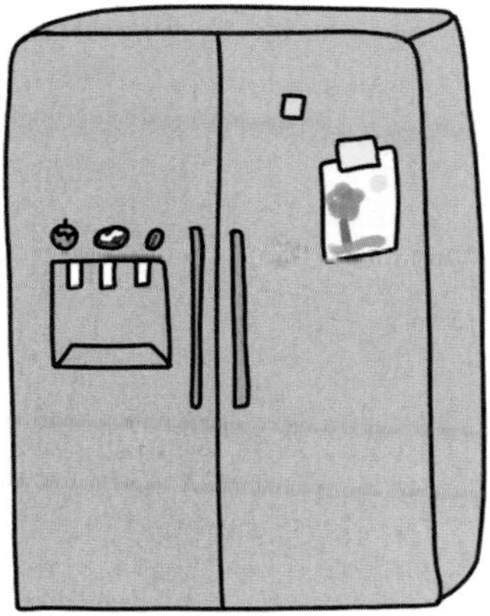

A restaurant-style drink dispenser built into my fridge door.

A self-tanning spray that also dissolves body hair on contact.

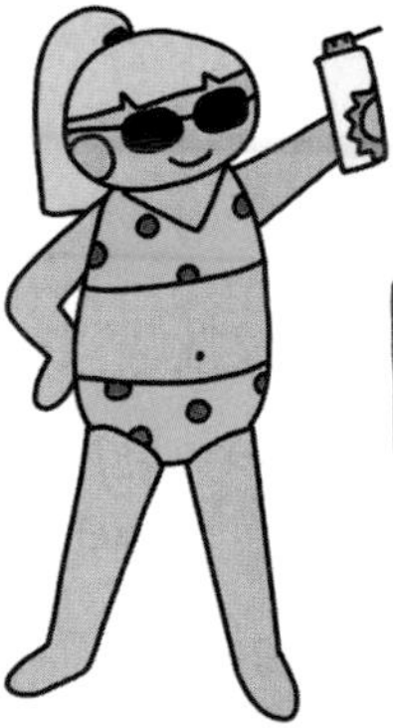

A backpack that instantly inflates into a bed when the ripcord is pulled.

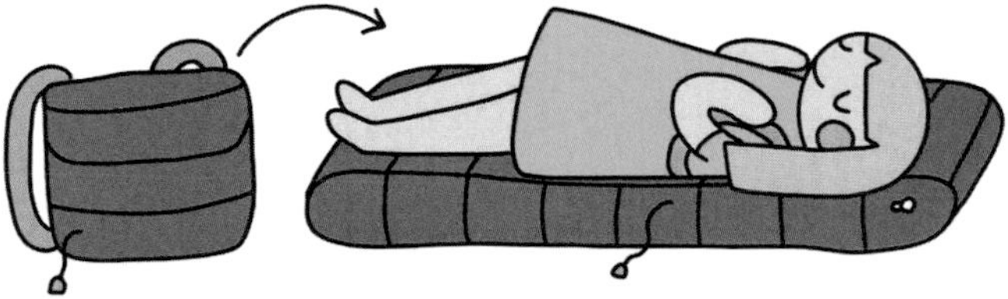

WONDER

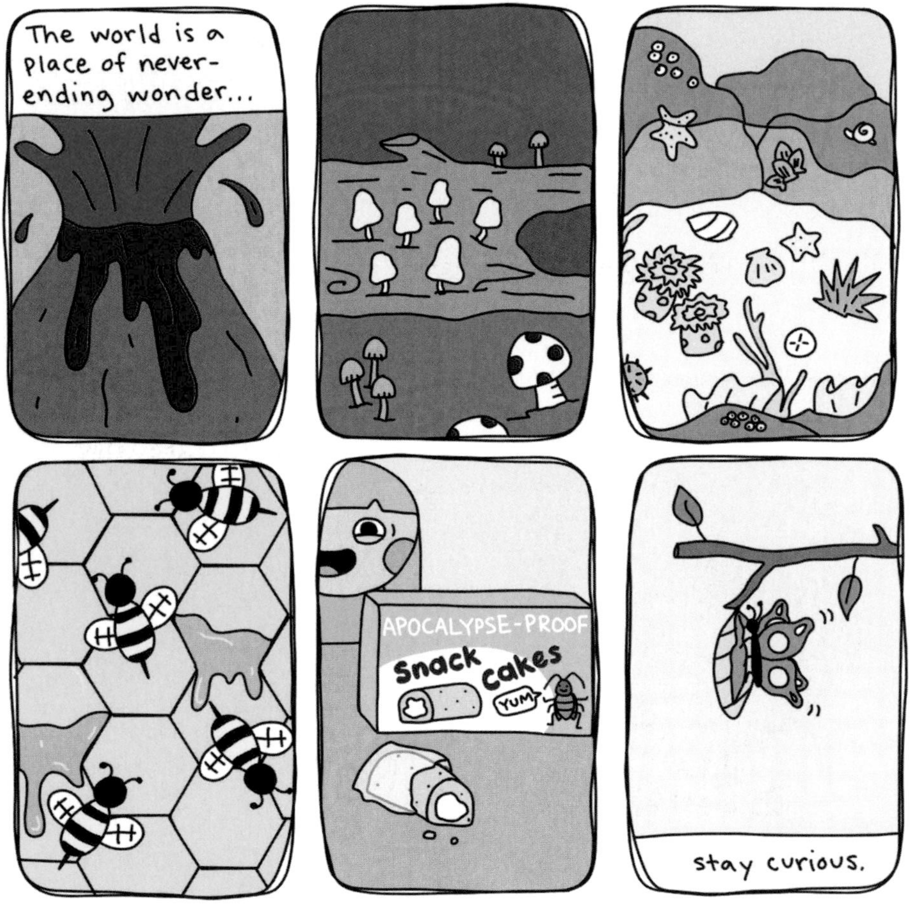
The world is a place of never-ending wonder...
APOCALYPSE-PROOF
Snack cakes
YUM
stay curious.

STUFF I'VE RESEARCHED THIS MONTH

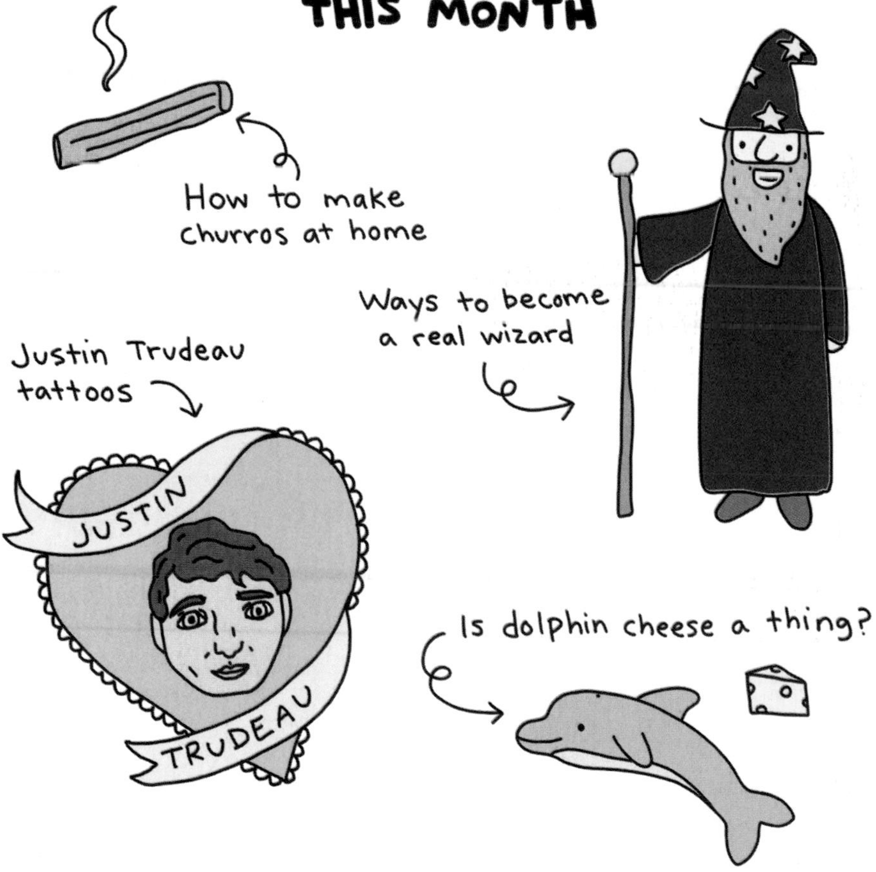
How to make churros at home
Ways to become a real wizard
Justin Trudeau tattoos
JUSTIN
TRUDEAU
Is dolphin cheese a thing?

FOCUS

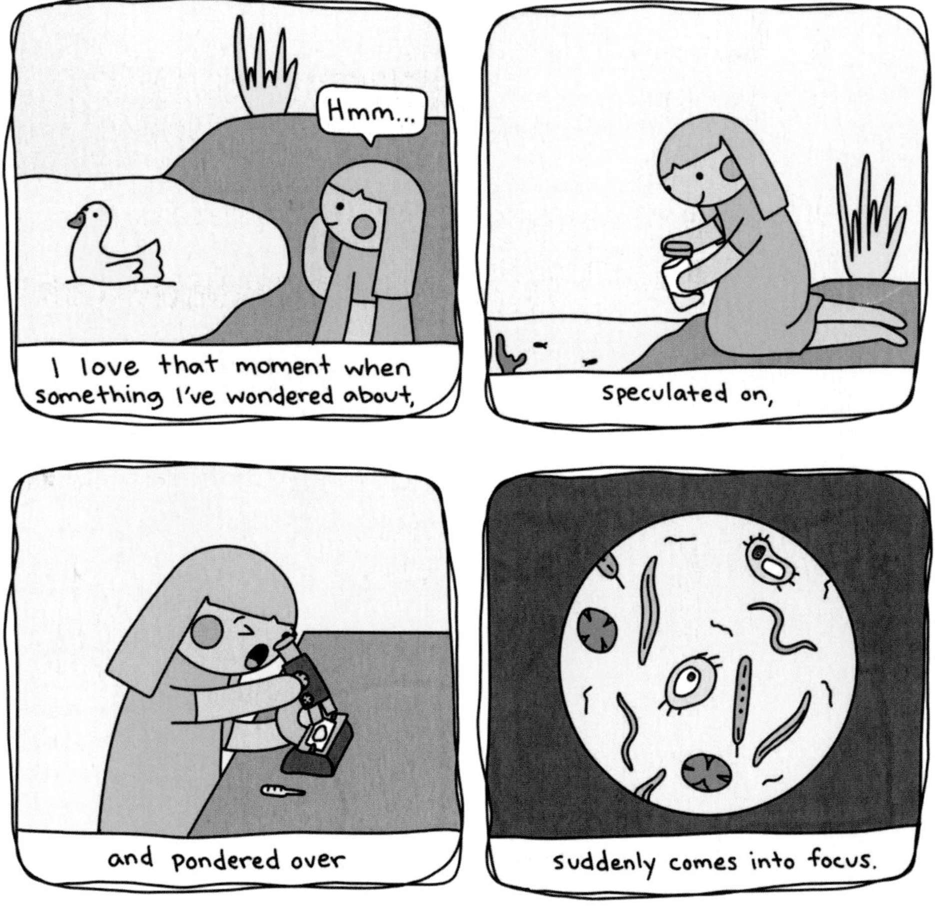

Hmm...
I love that moment when something I've wondered about,
speculated on,
and pondered over
suddenly comes into focus.

Questions lead to more questions.

I will never be done learning.
And that's okay.

TODAY I'M FEELING:

ANNOYED

Arggh! I spend a lot of time feeling annoyed. I think working in a busy office is irritating. I find parties obnoxious. Grocery stores, with their bright lights and long lines, make me feel frazzled. But why do those things annoy me so much?

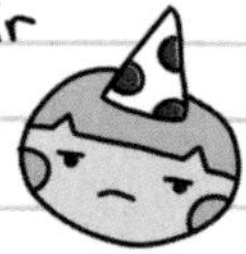

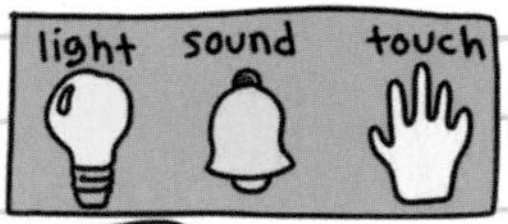
light
sound
touch

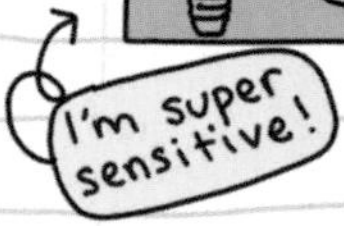
I'm super sensitive!

I've learned that introverts (like me!) are naturally more sensitive to stimuli. Lights, sounds, the physical touch in a crowd of people— they affect me strongly, overwhelming my brain and making me feel on edge.

Things go more smoothly for me if I change my focus from the external source of irritation to the internal reason for my annoyance. I've learned that annoyance is my brain's way of telling me my body needs something: quiet, space, or maybe a nap!

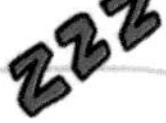
ZZZ

INFRACTION

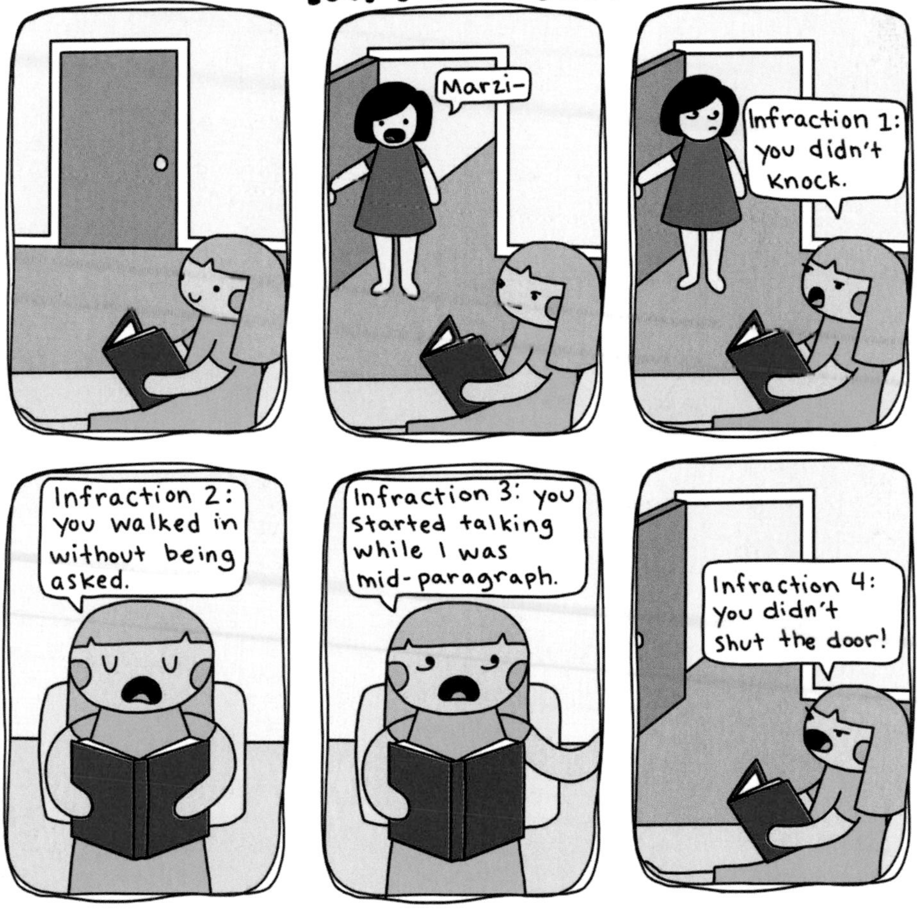
Marzi-
Infraction 1: you didn't knock.
Infraction 2: you walked in without being asked.
Infraction 3: you started talking while I was mid-paragraph.
Infraction 4: you didn't shut the door!

TODAY I WANT TO RUN AWAY

Places I want to run away to

Lisbon

Paris

Cancún

Rome

Places I can afford to run away to

Who am I kidding, I always overspend here!

The mall

The library

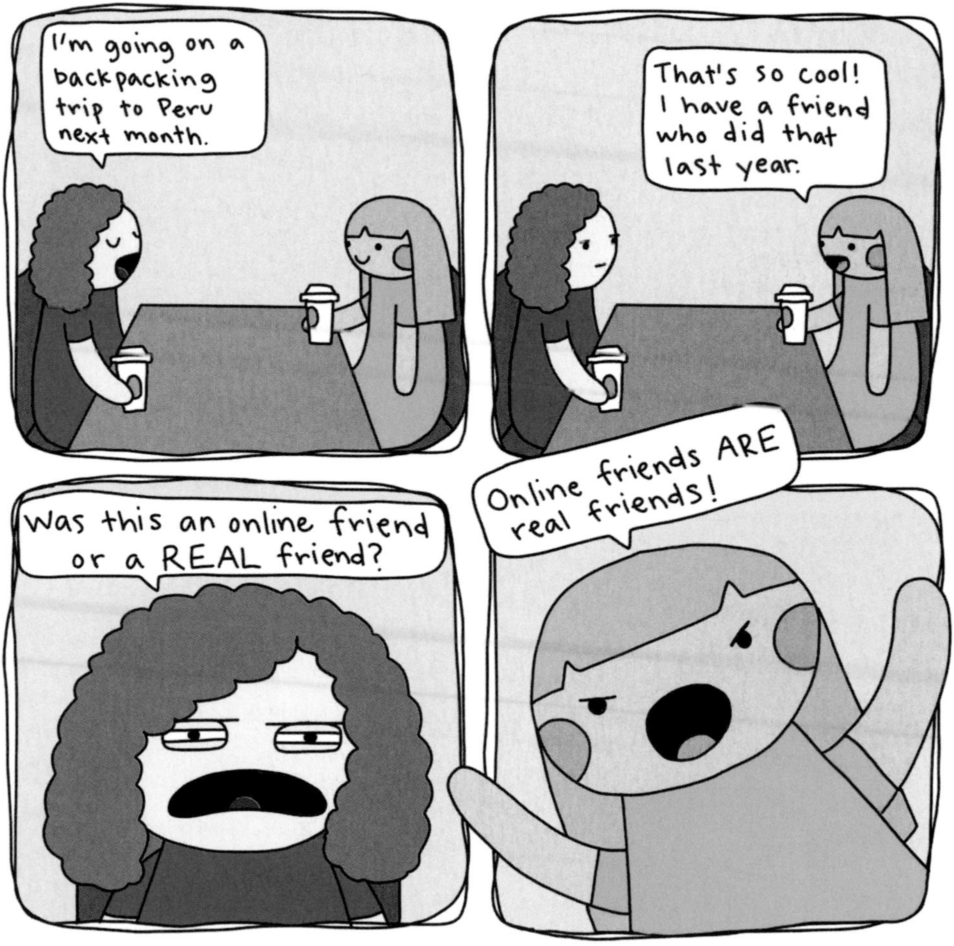
I'm going on a backpacking trip to Peru next month.
That's so cool! I have a friend who did that last year.
Was this an online friend or a REAL friend?
Online friends ARE real friends!

LITTLE THINGS THAT ANNOY ME

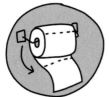

when the toilet paper roll is like this

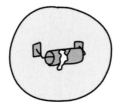

or this

Can I help you? How about now?

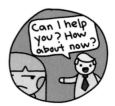

sales clerks who follow me

buffering

SCREECH

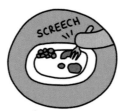

silverware scraping

seriously?!

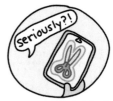

packaging that requires scissors to open

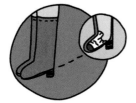

when my sock bunches up in my shoe

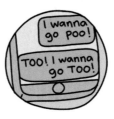

I wanna go poo!
TOO! I wanna go TOO!

autocorrect

PROTECTS AGAINST LEAKS

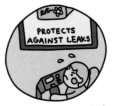

when I have to watch commercials like it's 1995

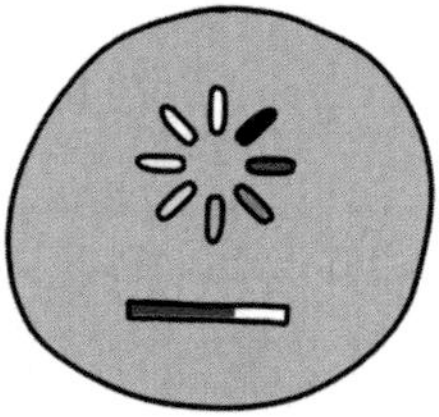

PEOPLE I HATE WHEN I'M GRUMPY

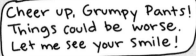

Cheer up, Grumpy Pants! Things could be worse. Let me see your smile!

People who don't think I should feel this way.

Oh, I know EXACTLY how you feel, I've been in the SAME situation (except totally different).

People who think they know how I feel.

It's your own fault you're in this mess. I don't want to say "I told you so," but...

People who don't care how I feel.

OPINIONS!

Everyone else.

COWORKER CEASE & DESIST ORDER

You, _____, have been charged with the following infraction(s) under the Employee Pet Peeve Penal Code 136.4.

- ☐ "Borrowing" office supply items from coworkers (i.e., scissors, notepads, staplers), and misplacing said items due to negligence.

- ☐ Failure to respect headphones as a nonverbal request to be left alone.

- ☐ Consuming refrigerated items that do not belong to you, including but not limited to: leftover pizza, Diet Coke, and yogurt cups.

- ☐ Playing obnoxious *YouTube* videos on high volume. Playing them again.

- ☐ Unnecessary physical touch, including documented instances of "shoulder squeezing," "arm rubbing," "hair ruffling," and "side hugs."

- ☐ Forwarding subpar or dead memes to fellow staff in group emails.

- ☐ Persistent demands to "hang out," "get together," or "chill" on weekends and/or holidays.

We request that you immediately cease the aforementioned activities to preserve the sanctity of the workplace.

Signed, _____

NOVEL ANNOYANCE

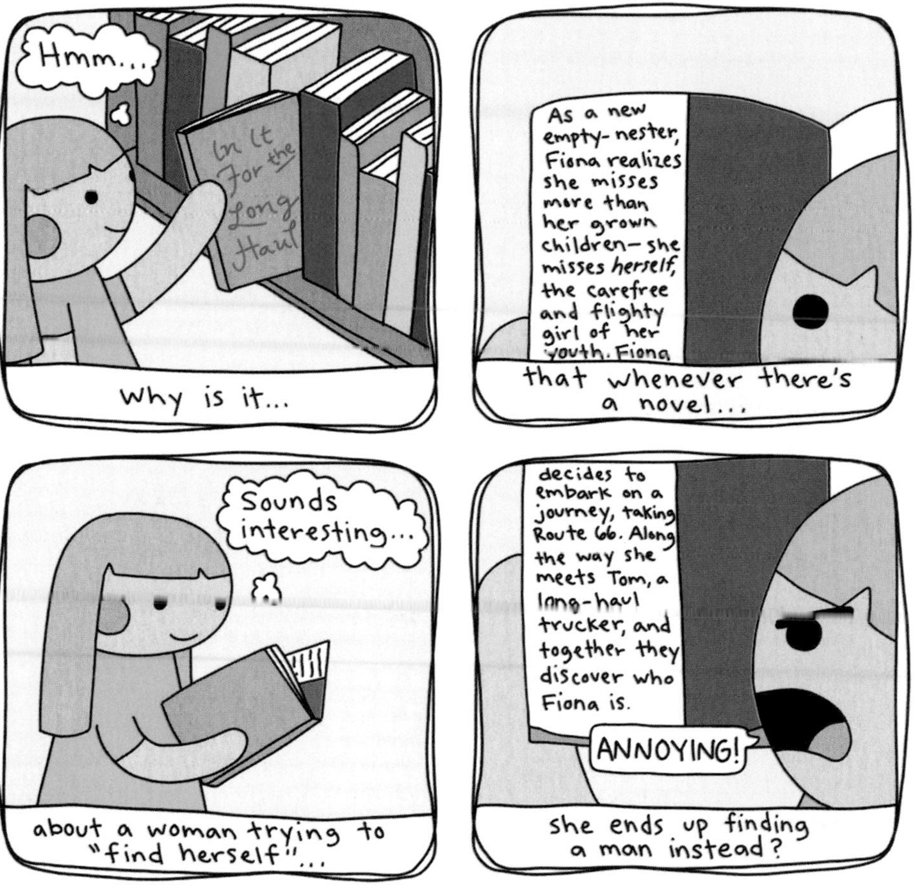
Hmm...
In it For the Long Haul
Why is it...
As a new empty-nester, Fiona realizes she misses more than her grown children—she misses *herself*, the carefree and flighty girl of her youth. Fiona
that whenever there's a novel...
Sounds interesting...
about a woman trying to "find herself"...
decides to embark on a journey, taking Route 66. Along the way she meets Tom, a long-haul trucker, and together they discover who Fiona is.
ANNOYING!
she ends up finding a man instead?

MANAGING ANNOYANCES

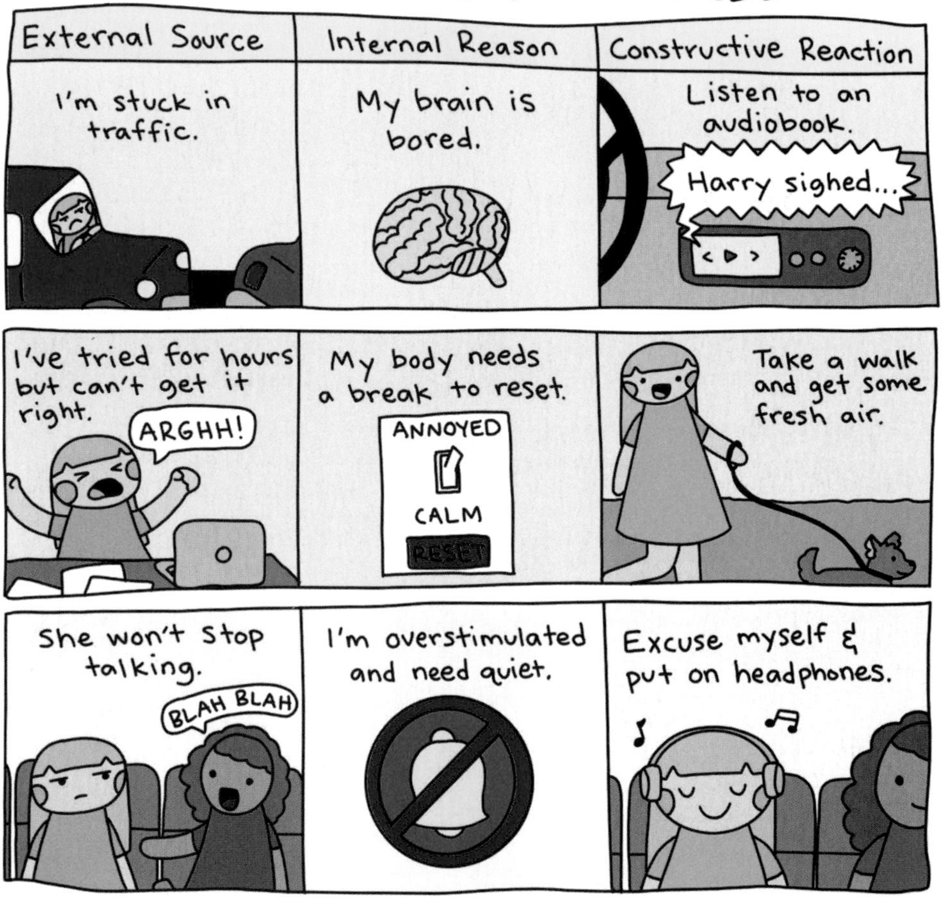

External Source
Internal Reason
Constructive Reaction
I'm stuck in traffic.
My brain is bored.
Listen to an audiobook.
Harry sighed...
I've tried for hours but can't get it right.
ARGHH!
My body needs a break to reset.
ANNOYED
CALM
RESET
Take a walk and get some fresh air.
She won't stop talking.
BLAH BLAH
I'm overstimulated and need quiet.
Excuse myself & put on headphones.

NIGHT OUT

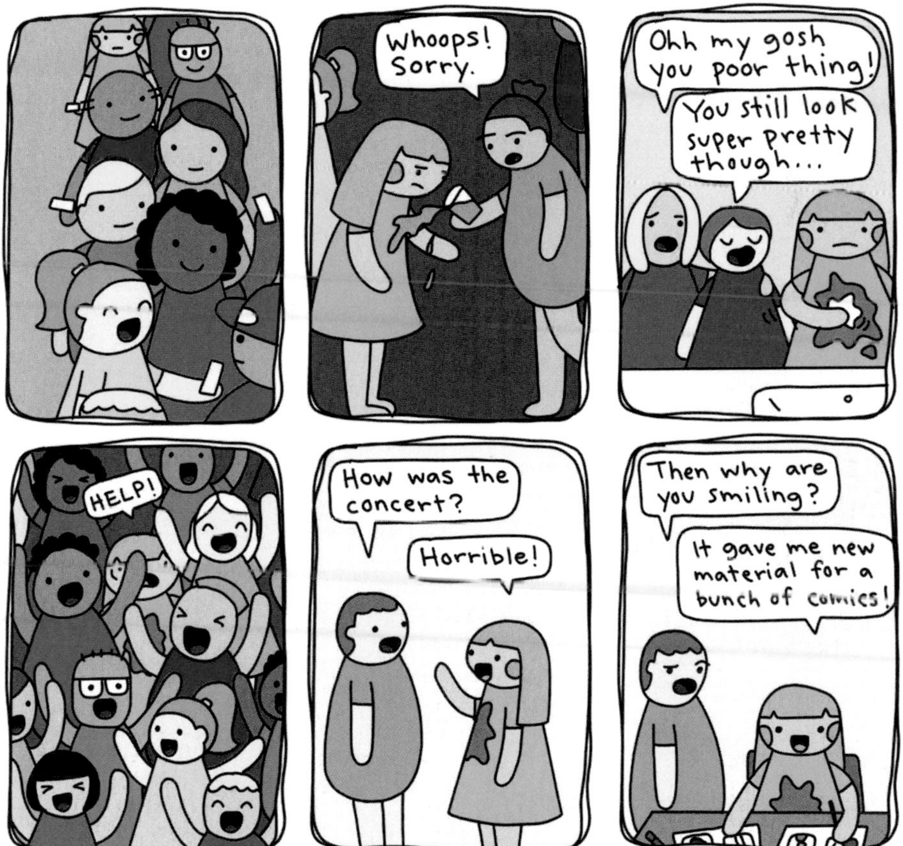

Whoops! Sorry.
Ohh my gosh you poor thing!
You still look super pretty though...
HELP!
How was the concert?
Horrible!
Then why are you smiling?
It gave me new material for a bunch of comics!

STUFF THAT HELPS WHEN I'M ANNOYED

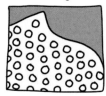

Popping
bubble wrap

My favorite
playlist

Ripping up
junk mail

Aggressively
chewing gum

Venting to
a friend

Drawing
mustaches
on magazine
models

Scrolling
through
memes

Deep
breathing

Squeezing
a squishy

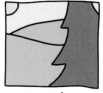

Stepping
outside

Doodling

Puppy
kisses

CHAPTER 3

TODAY I'M FEELING:

EMBARRASSED

Embarrassment seems to go hand-in-hand with my social anxiety. I tend to hold tightly to my embarrassing moments, replaying those scenes over and over in my head.

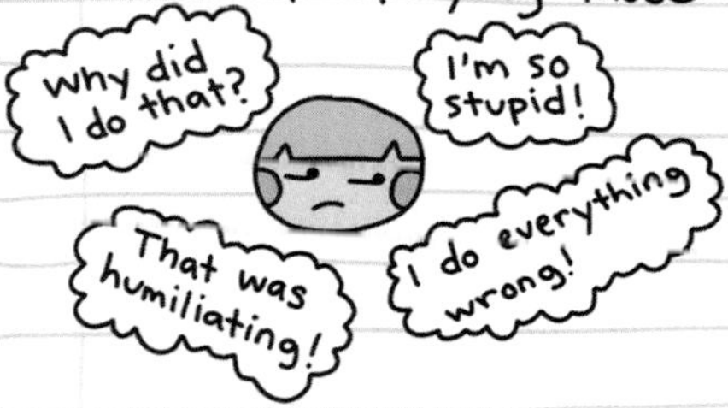
Why did I do that?
I'm so stupid!
That was humiliating!
I do everything wrong!

Every time I do, it's accompanied by self-judgment. The embarrassment settles into something heavy and shameful.

I try to remind myself that everyone feels embarrassed sometimes. I had an *Introvert Doodles* feature called "Introvert Escapades," in which folks would share their most embarrassing moments, and I'd turn them into comics. It was reassuring to know I wasn't the only person on the planet slipping up. And even though these people were sharing totally cringe-worthy moments, they could laugh about them!

There's a lesson for me in that. I can mess up, feel embarrassed, and still move forward...

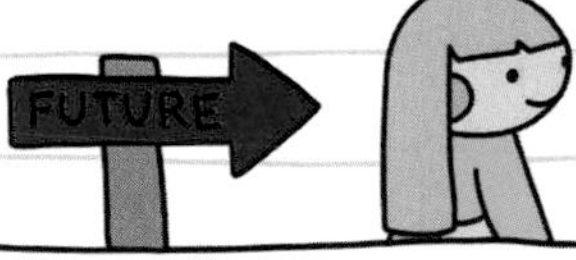
FUTURE

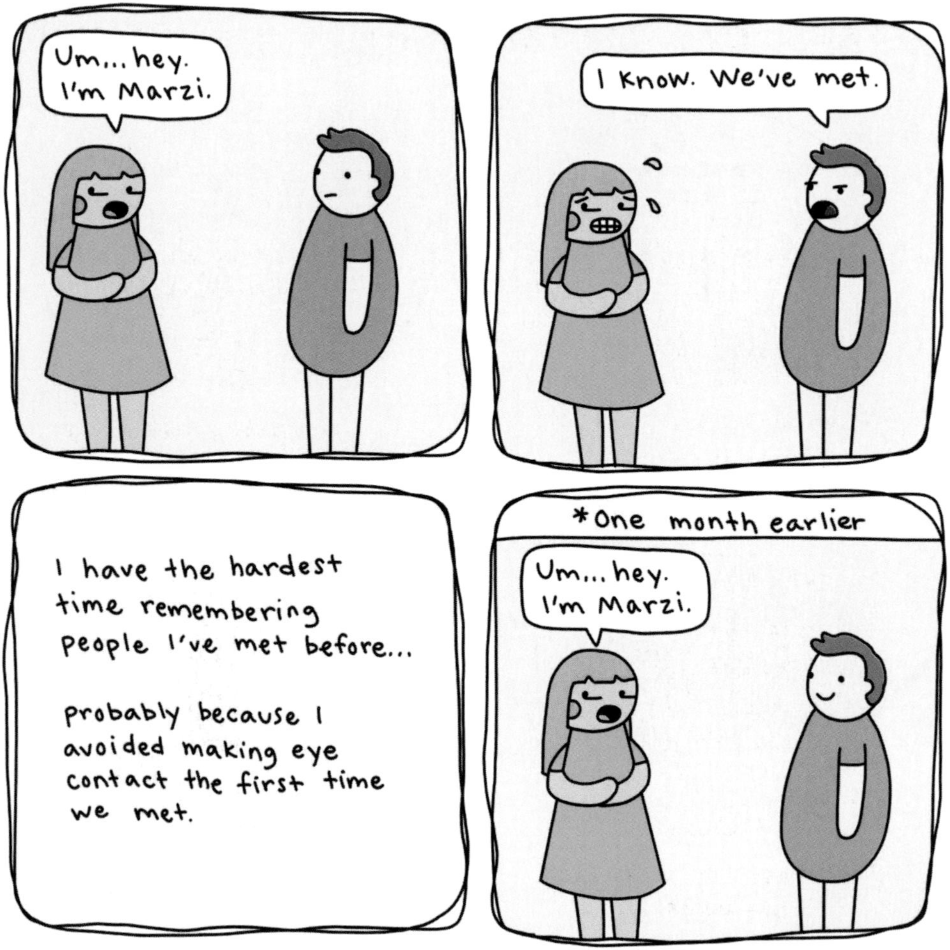
Um... hey. I'm Marzi.
I know. We've met.
I have the hardest time remembering people I've met before...
probably because I avoided making eye contact the first time we met.
*One month earlier
Um... hey. I'm Marzi.

SMALL THINGS THAT MAKE ME BLUSH

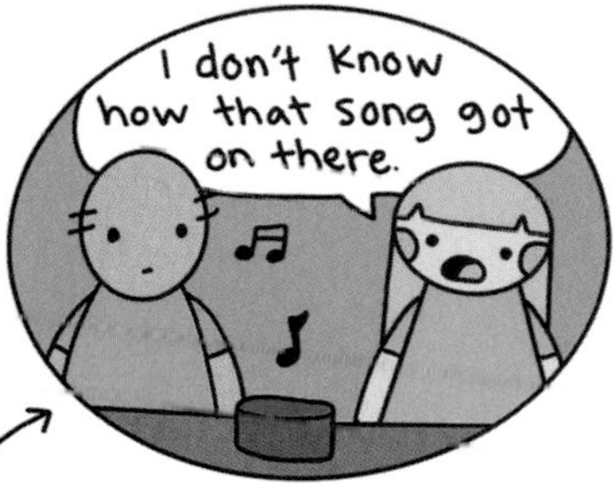
I don't know how that song got on there.

Someone else listening to my playlists.

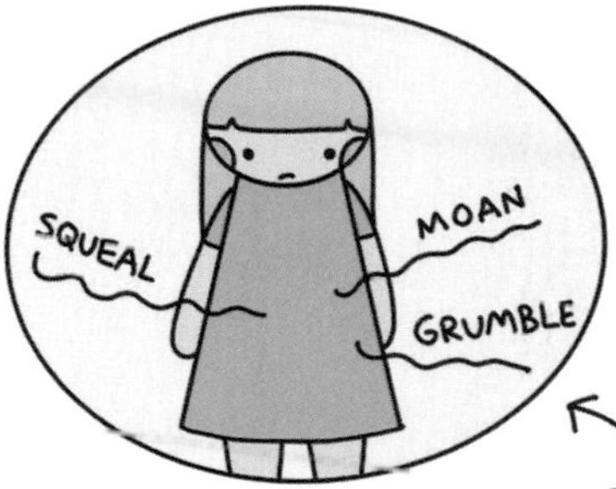
SQUEAL
MOAN
GRUMBLE

My stomach rumbling like a forlorn orca whale.

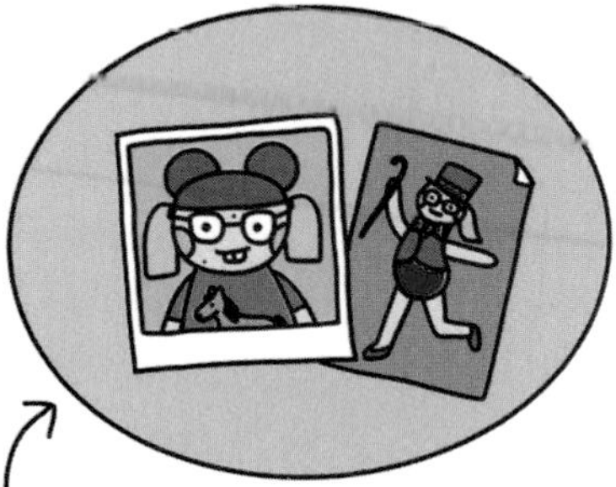

Photos of myself from ages 12-15.

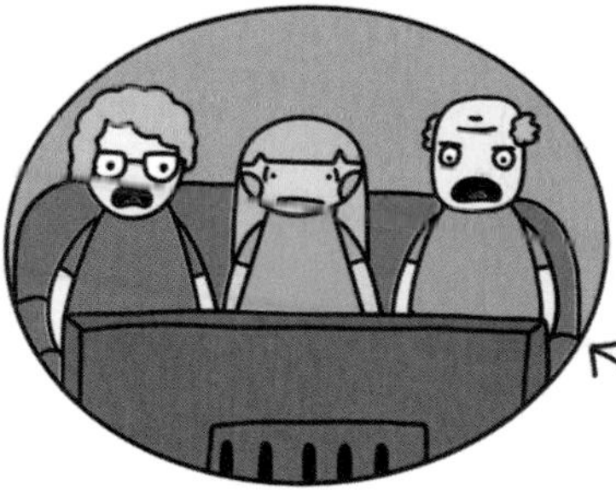

Watching a movie with my parents and there's a love scene.

RECENT EMBARRASSING MOMENTS

I ordered a pizza and was upset that the delivery was taking so long. They finally called to ask why I wasn't answering the door. I'd accidentally sent it to my previous address in a different city.

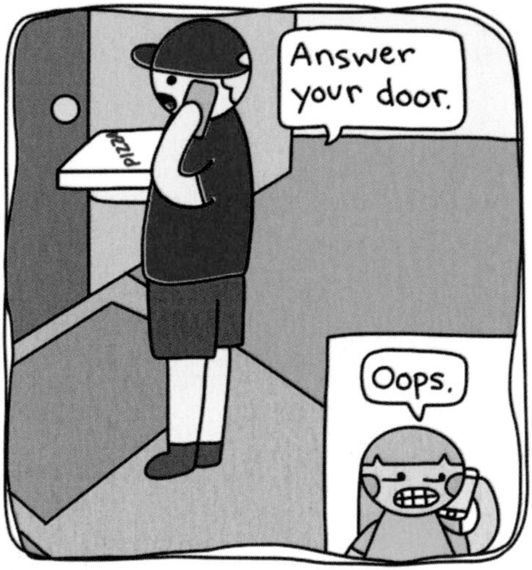
Answer your door.
Oops.

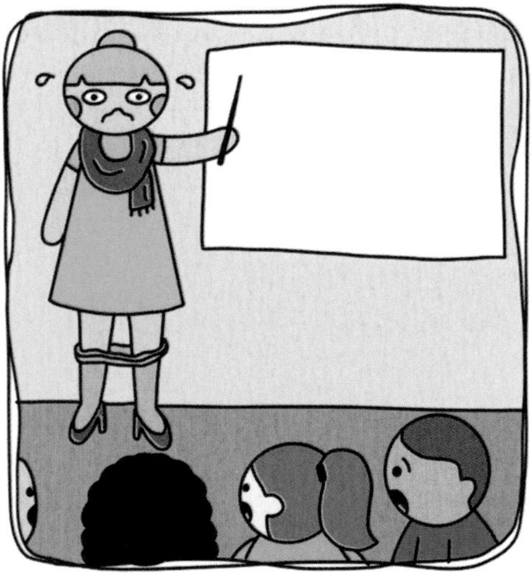

I dressed up to give a presentation. I thought I looked nice, until suddenly my nylons rolled down to my knees.

THERE'S MORE

I was car shopping and found a vehicle I liked on the lot. I sat in it and was dismayed by the poor detailing job. There was even a coffee cup in the cupholder! It finally dawned on me that I was sitting in another customer's car. Oops.

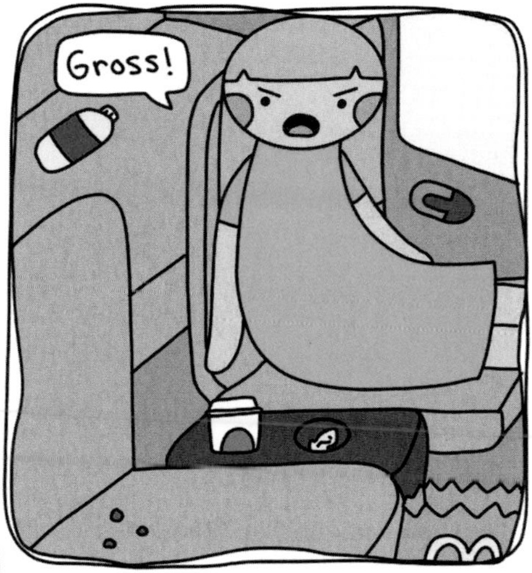
Gross!

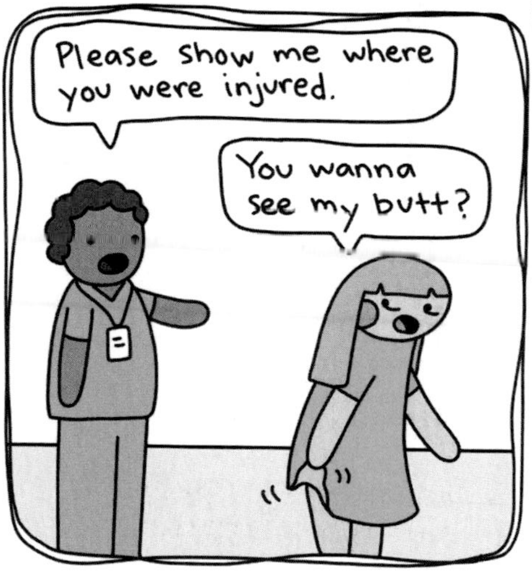
Please show me where you were injured.
You wanna see my butt?

I was going to visit a relative in the hospital when I slipped on an icy patch in the parking lot. Concerned that someone else might fall, I told a staff member that I'd fallen and gotten a bit bruised. She asked me to show her exactly where. I thought she meant where on my BODY. She meant where in the parking lot.

BARBECUE EMBARRASSMENT

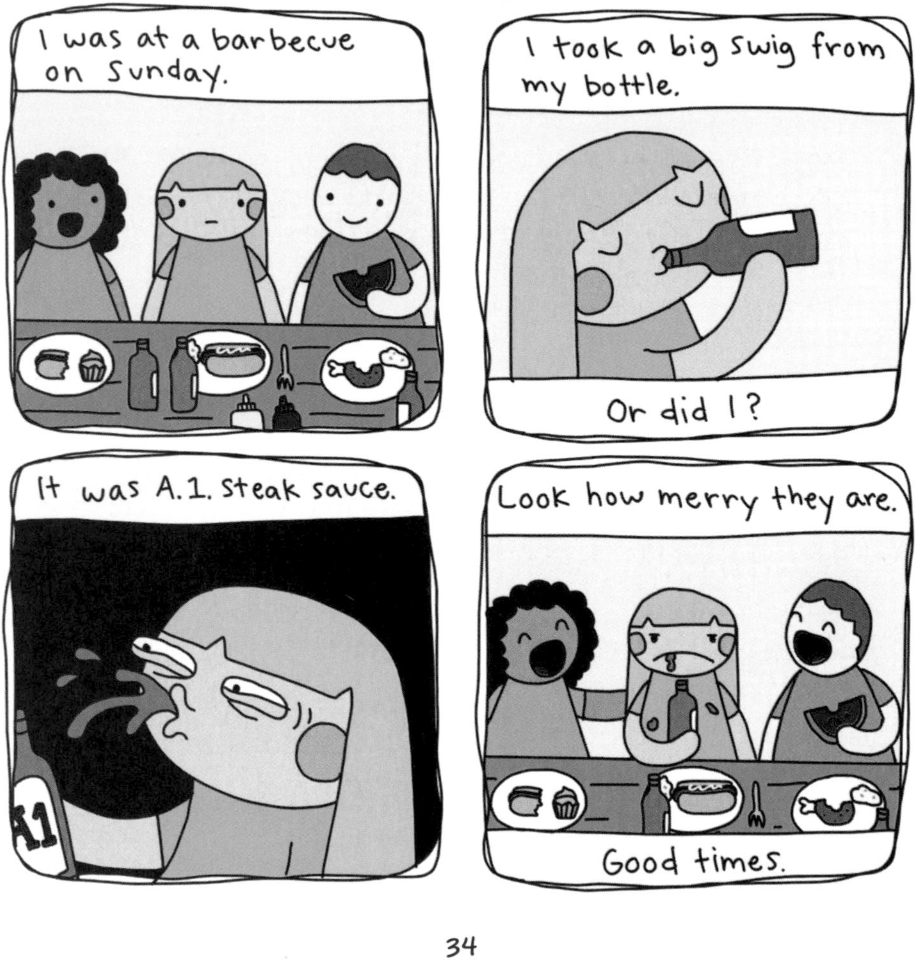
I was at a barbecue on Sunday.
I took a big swig from my bottle.
Or did I?
It was A.1. Steak sauce.
A1
Look how merry they are.
Good times.

GUILTY AS CHARGED

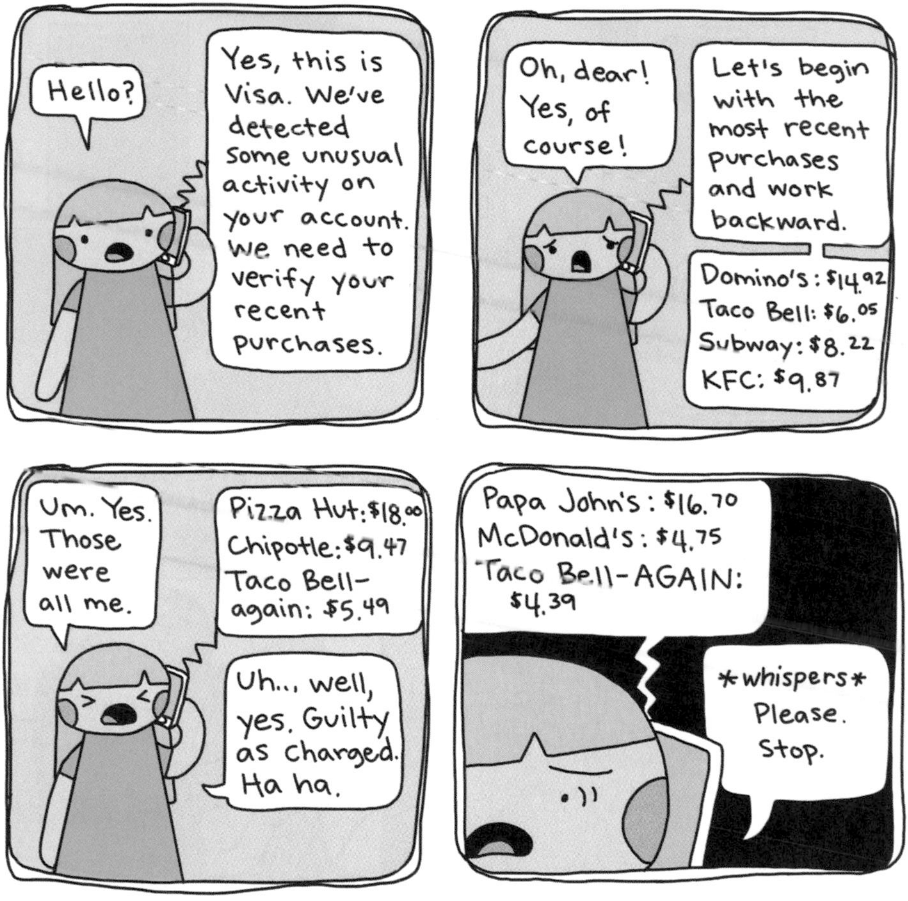

Hello?
Yes, this is Visa. We've detected some unusual activity on your account. We need to verify your recent purchases.
Oh, dear! Yes, of course!
Let's begin with the most recent purchases and work backward.
Domino's: $14.92
Taco Bell: $6.05
Subway: $8.22
KFC: $9.87
Um. Yes. Those were all me.
Pizza Hut: $18.00
Chipotle: $9.47
Taco Bell-again: $5.49
Uh..., well, yes. Guilty as charged. Ha ha.
Papa John's: $16.70
McDonald's: $4.75
Taco Bell-AGAIN: $4.39
whispers Please. Stop.

EMBARRASSING THINGS I KEEP DOING

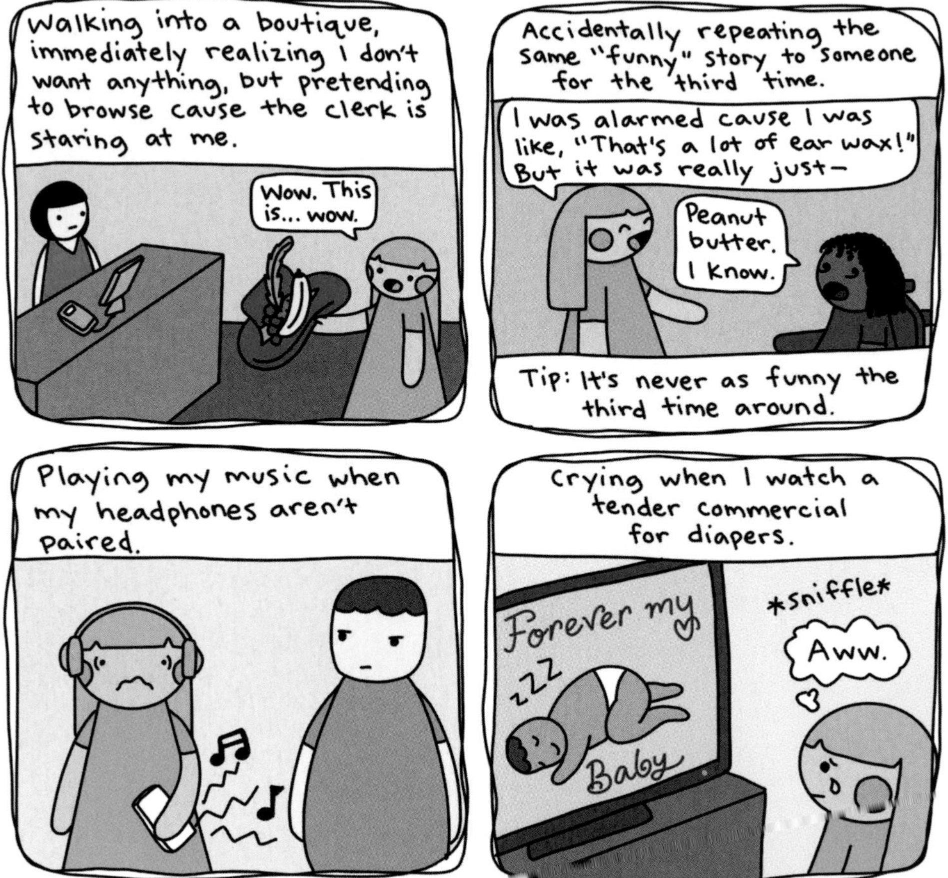

Walking into a boutique, immediately realizing I don't want anything, but pretending to browse cause the clerk is staring at me.
Wow. This is... wow.
Accidentally repeating the same "funny" story to someone for the third time.
I was alarmed cause I was like, "That's a lot of ear wax!" But it was really just—
Peanut butter. I know.
Tip: It's never as funny the third time around.
Playing my music when my headphones aren't paired.
Crying when I watch a tender commercial for diapers.
Forever my ♡
zZZ
Baby
sniffle
Aww.

EMBARRASSMENT BINGO

How many of these situations have you been in?

Snorted while laughing	Realized you smell funny	Caught picking nose	"Liked" a crush's pic from 3 years ago	Ordered food & then realized you forgot your wallet
Couldn't hear, so just smiled & nodded	Spilled water on pants	Pulled on a "PUSH" door	Really bad haircut	Made a joke no one got
Public wedgie	Broke something that wasn't yours	TOTAL FREE SPACE HUMILIATION	Forgot where you parked	Jeans unzipped
Caught in a white lie	Tripped over nothing	Visibly sweaty armpits	Called your teacher "mom"	Food stuck in teeth
Runny nose, no tissue	Crashed your shopping cart into a display	Forgot someone's name	Super squeaky shoes	Asked a question with an obvious answer

(Don't worry, you aren't the only one!)

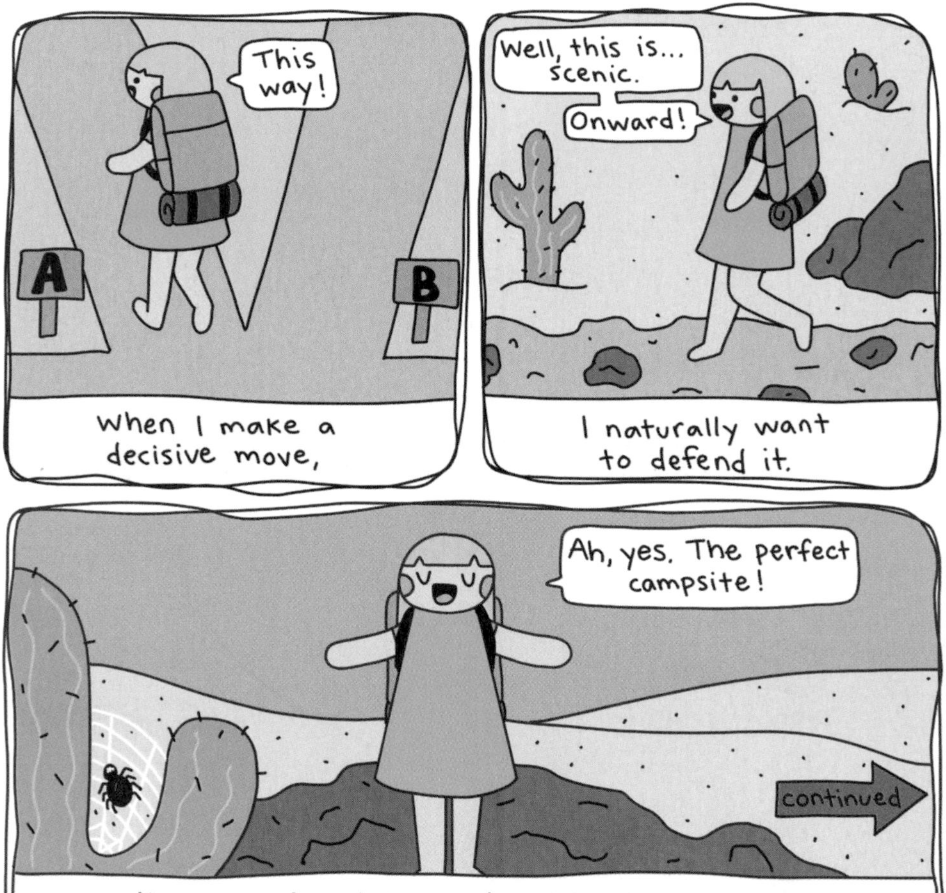
This way!
when I make a decisive move,
Well, this is... scenic.
Onward!
I naturally want to defend it.
Ah, yes. The perfect campsite!
continued
I'm committed to holding my ground...

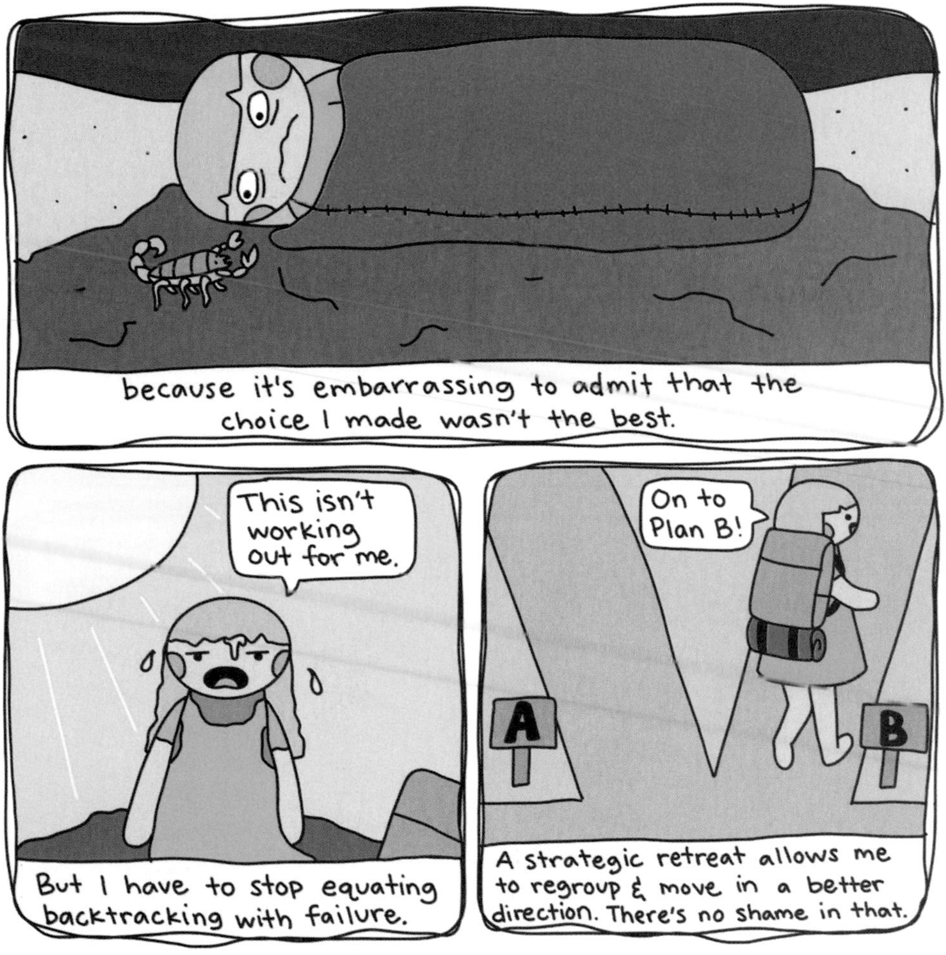
because it's embarrassing to admit that the choice I made wasn't the best.
This isn't working out for me.
But I have to stop equating backtracking with failure.
On to Plan B!
A
B
A strategic retreat allows me to regroup & move in a better direction. There's no shame in that.

CHAPTER 4

TODAY I'M FEELING:
LOVED

Everyone wants to feel loved. I always assumed that love would look like it does in the movies: Boy falls for girl. Boy pursues girl with escalating displays of affection. Hijinks and misunderstandings ensue, but then: A grand, romantic gesture, and girl lives happily ever after, adored—nay, worshipped—by boy forevermore.

Acceptable Romantic Gestures

Balcony serenade

Gifting me a library

Mob flashdance

So is it any wonder that I'd feel a bit disappointed when things didn't play out that way?

It's taken time for me to realize that there are many variations of love, and all of them are valid. When I let go of the movie stereotypes, I began to notice people all around me demonstrating love in different, beautiful ways:

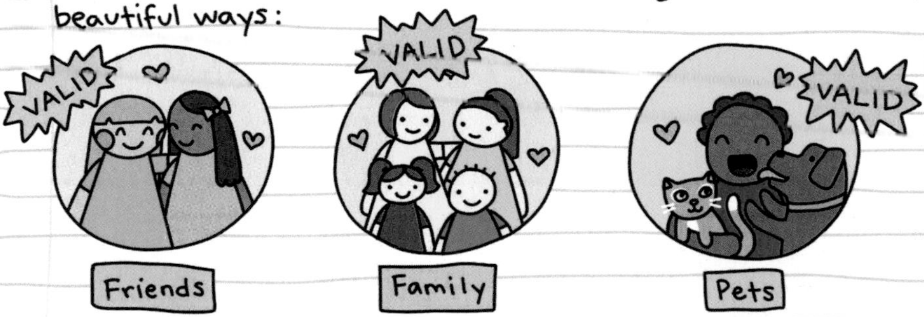
VALID
VALID
VALID
Friends
Family
Pets

I don't need to wait around for the perfect person to worship me. "But Marzi," you say, "Why lower your standards? You deserve love!" Yes, I know I'm worthy of love. I'm simply adjusting my perspective and letting go of unreasonable expectations. The truth is, I <u>am</u> loved, by many people, in many ways. It may not look the way Hollywood told me it would, but it's every bit as special.

SOMETHING SIMPLER

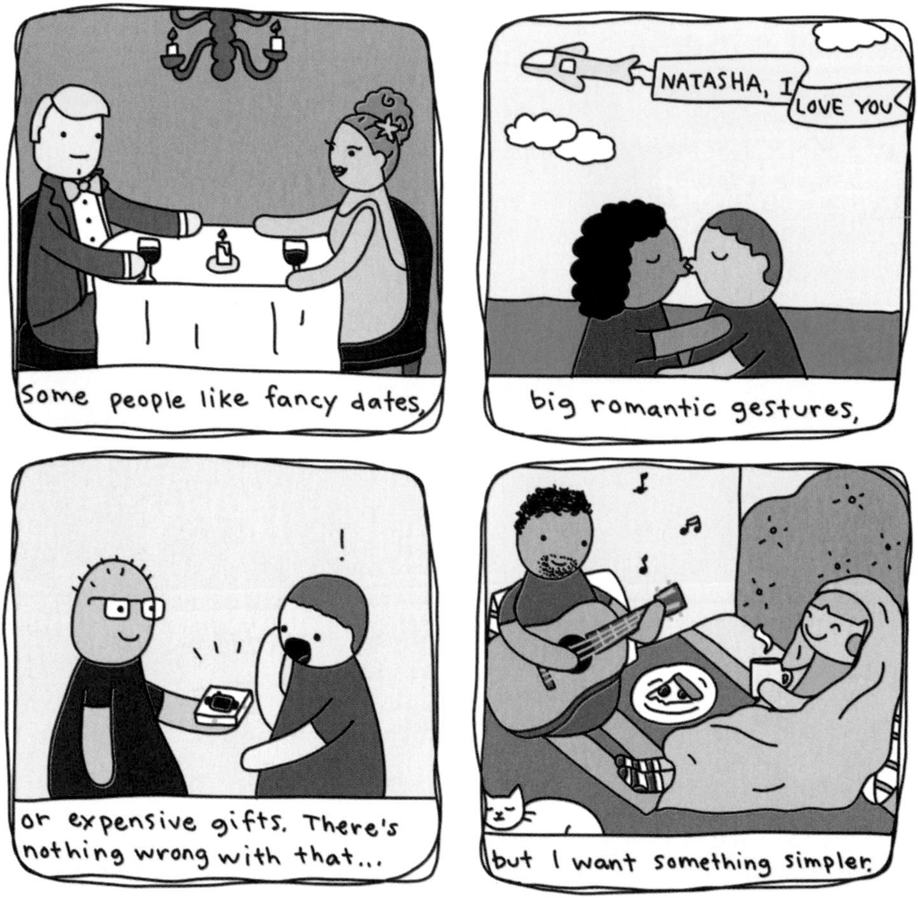
Some people like fancy dates,
NATASHA, I LOVE YOU
big romantic gestures,
!
or expensive gifts. There's nothing wrong with that...
but I want something simpler.

ALL I HAVE

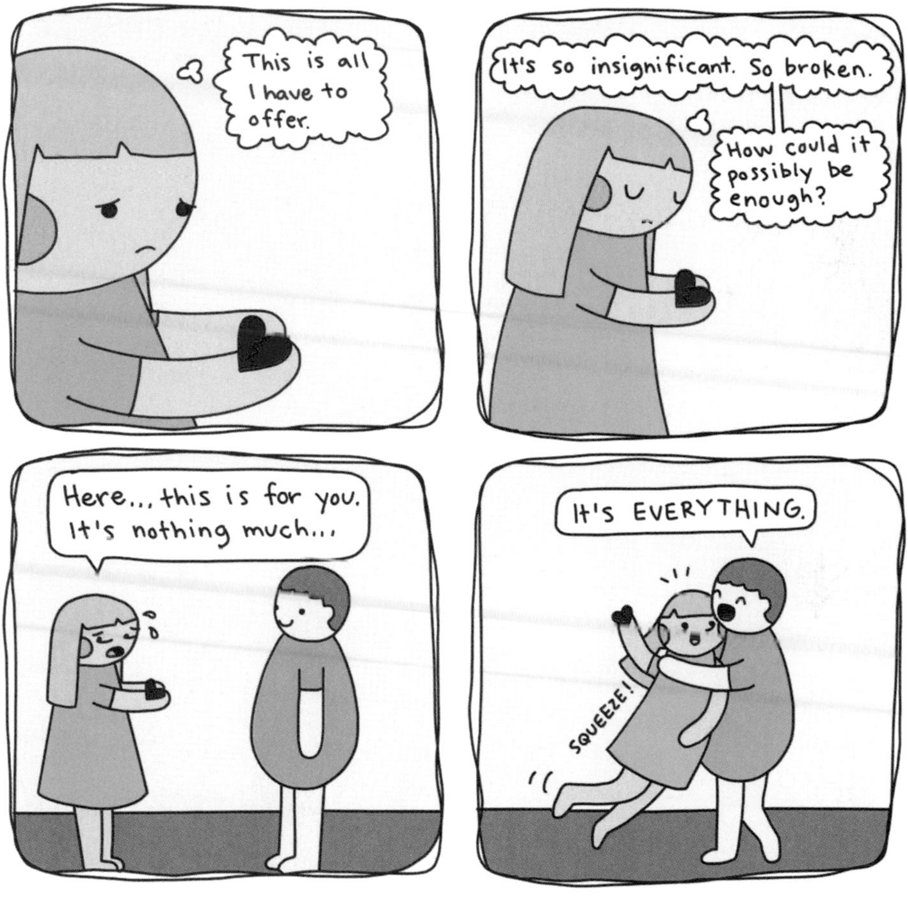
This is all I have to offer.
It's so insignificant. So broken.
How could it possibly be enough?
Here... this is for you. It's nothing much...
It's EVERYTHING.
SQUEEZE!

HOW WE MET

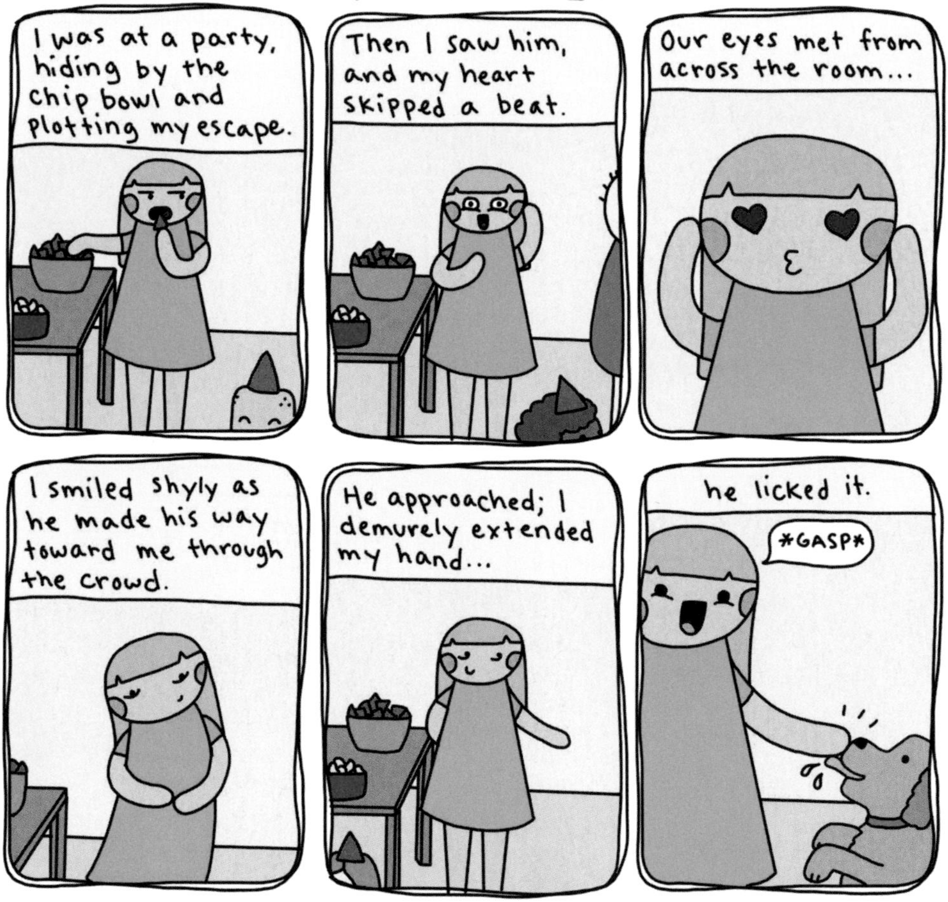
I was at a party, hiding by the chip bowl and plotting my escape.
Then I saw him, and my heart skipped a beat.
Our eyes met from across the room...
I smiled shyly as he made his way toward me through the crowd.
He approached; I demurely extended my hand...
he licked it.
GASP

YOU KNOW I ♥ YOU IF...

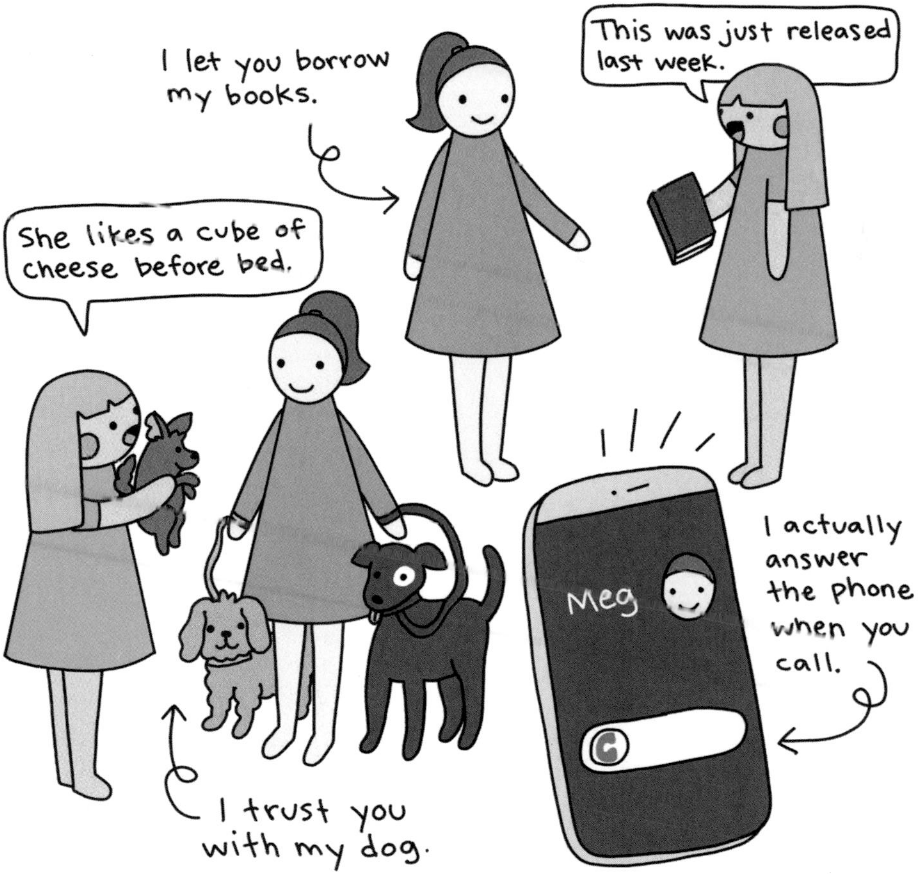
I let you borrow my books.
This was just released last week.
She likes a cube of cheese before bed.
I trust you with my dog.
Meg
I actually answer the phone when you call.

MAGICAL

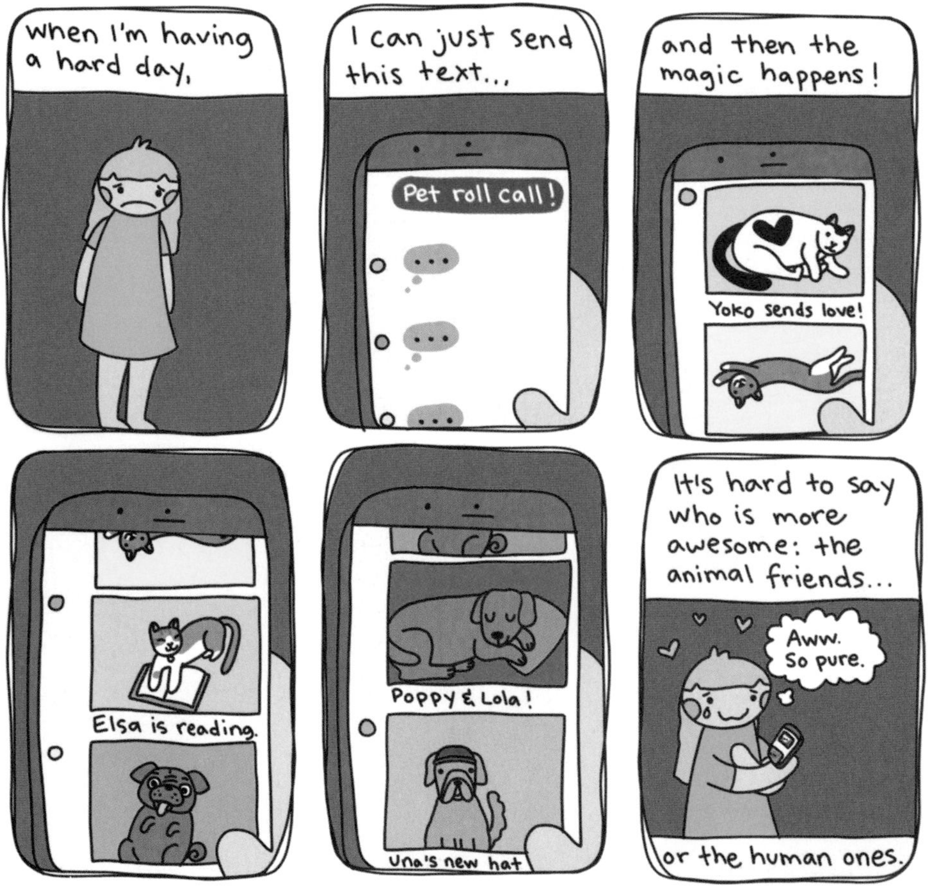

when I'm having a hard day,
I can just send this text...
Pet roll call!
...
...
...
and then the magic happens!
Yoko sends love!
Elsa is reading.
Poppy & Lola!
Una's new hat
It's hard to say who is more awesome: the animal friends...
Aww. So pure.
or the human ones.

STRANGE LOVE

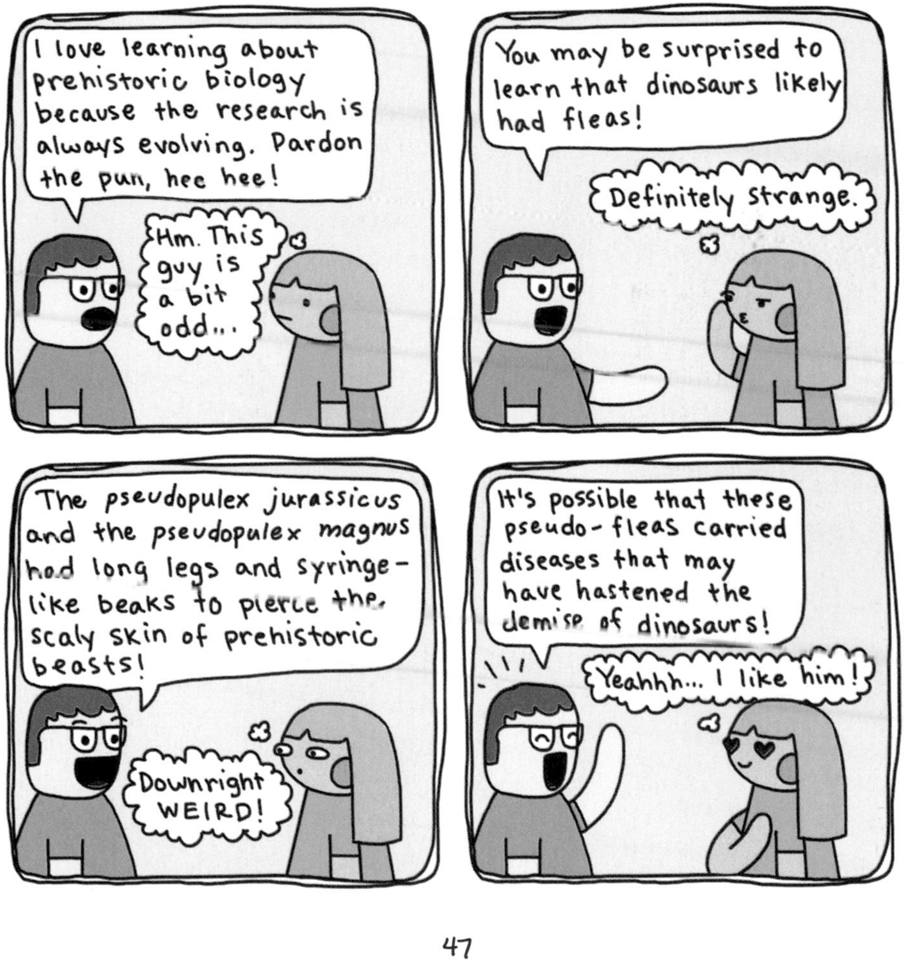
I love learning about prehistoric biology because the research is always evolving. Pardon the pun, hee hee!
Hm. This guy is a bit odd...
You may be surprised to learn that dinosaurs likely had fleas!
Definitely strange.
The pseudopulex jurassicus and the pseudopulex magnus had long legs and syringe-like beaks to pierce the scaly skin of prehistoric beasts!
Downright WEIRD!
It's possible that these pseudo-fleas carried diseases that may have hastened the demise of dinosaurs!
Yeahhh... I like him!

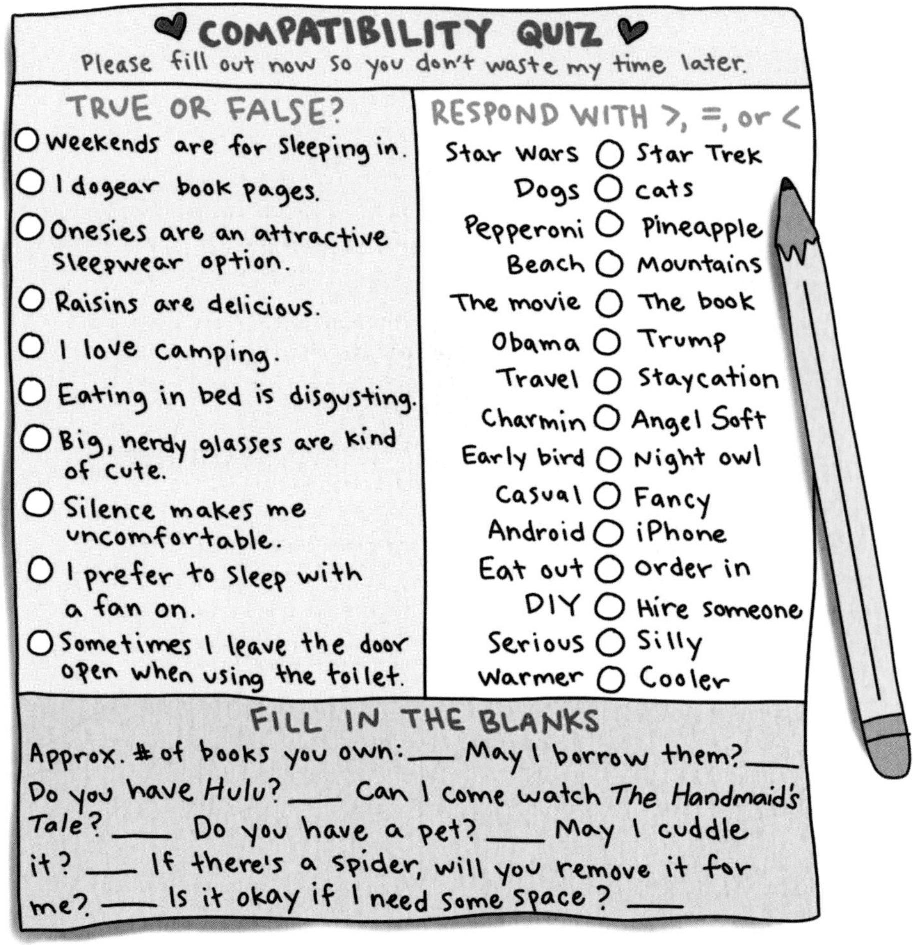
COMPATIBILITY QUIZ
Please fill out now so you don't waste my time later.
TRUE OR FALSE?
Weekends are for sleeping in.
I dogear book pages.
Onesies are an attractive sleepwear option.
Raisins are delicious.
I love camping.
Eating in bed is disgusting.
Big, nerdy glasses are kind of cute.
Silence makes me uncomfortable.
I prefer to sleep with a fan on.
Sometimes I leave the door open when using the toilet.
RESPOND WITH >, =, or <
Star Wars Star Trek
Dogs cats
Pepperoni Pineapple
Beach Mountains
The movie The book
Obama Trump
Travel Staycation
Charmin Angel Soft
Early bird Night owl
Casual Fancy
Android iPhone
Eat out Order in
DIY Hire someone
Serious Silly
Warmer Cooler
FILL IN THE BLANKS
Approx. # of books you own: ___ May I borrow them? ___
Do you have Hulu? ___ Can I come watch The Handmaid's Tale? ___ Do you have a pet? ___ May I cuddle it? ___ If there's a spider, will you remove it for me? ___ Is it okay if I need some space? ___

I LIKE YOU

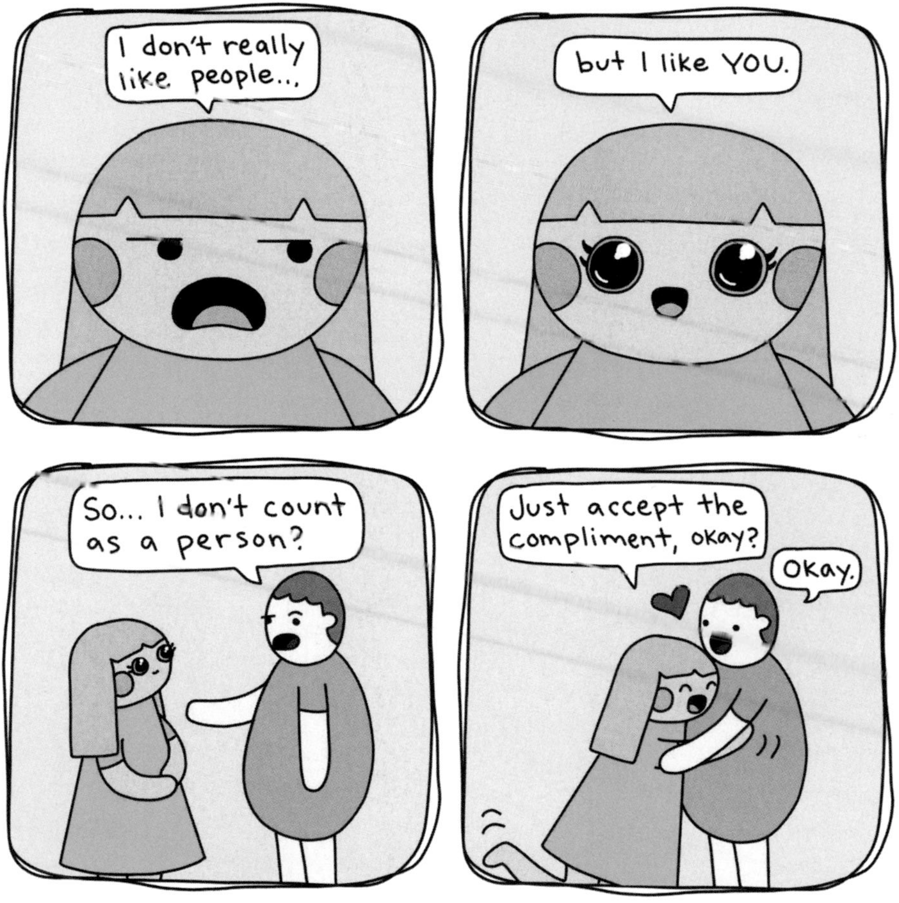
I don't really like people...
but I like YOU.
So... I don't count as a person?
Just accept the compliment, okay?
Okay.

ROMANTIC

People think it's so special & romantic when a couple can finish each other's sentences.

We should order—

CHINESE!

But I like not knowing what you'll say next.

Guess what I got?

Um, Milk?

Two copies of the same book! I thought we might like to have our own little book club?

I love how you make me laugh in surprise,

How do I look?

Well, light passes through your corneas, and is then refracted—

You're a nerd.

giggle

Yep. P.S.: You're lovely.

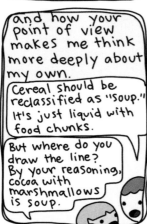

and how your point of view makes me think more deeply about my own.

Cereal should be reclassified as "soup." It's just liquid with food chunks.

But where do you draw the line? By your reasoning, cocoa with marshmallows is soup.

Your ideas astonish me, and, well...

Do you think we could build a big, shallow tray & fill it with sod so we can have a rug made of grass this winter?

Only if YOU mow it.

I think that's pretty special and romantic.

Whatcha thinkin'?

Ha, do you really wanna know?

Always.

WORTHY

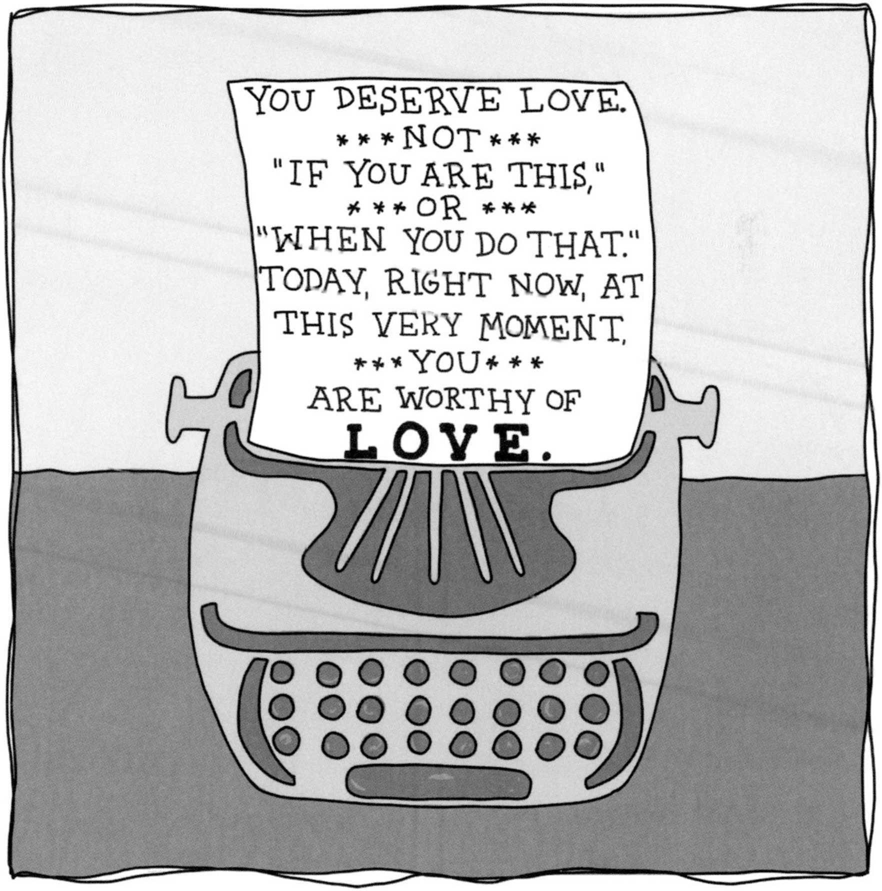
YOU DESERVE LOVE.
NOT
"IF YOU ARE THIS,"
OR
"WHEN YOU DO THAT."
TODAY, RIGHT NOW, AT
THIS VERY MOMENT,
YOU
ARE WORTHY OF
LOVE.

CHAPTER 5

TODAY I'M FEELING:

OVERWHELMED

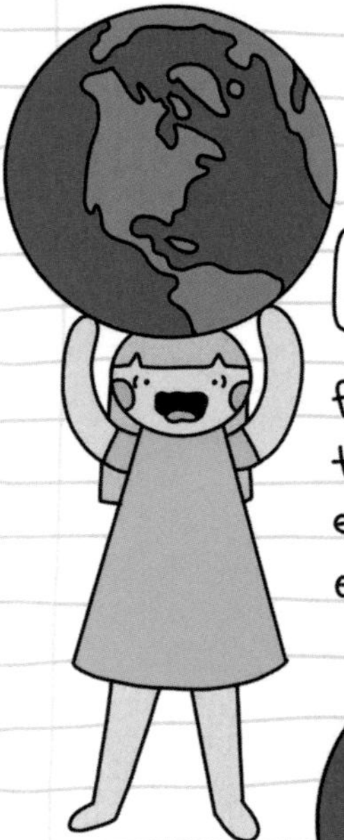
I can keep this up!

Whenever I felt overwhelmed, I'd repeat this mantra: "I'm going to do this for as long as I can, until I know that I can't."

I applied this thinking to work, church, and relationships. Even though I constantly felt frazzled, I continued to push myself. I thought that if I wasn't giving it everything I had, I wasn't trying hard enough. Then, inevitably, I'd collapse.

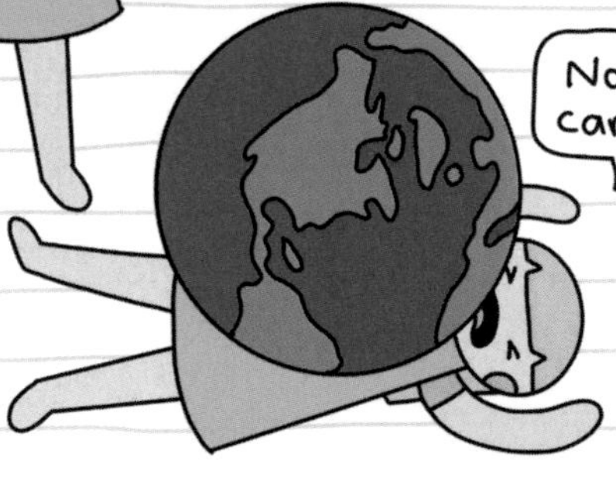
No, I can't.

The problem with giving everything I had was that I had nothing left for myself. I felt crushed, burned out, and broken.

I interpreted those feelings of inadequacy and exhaustion as signs:

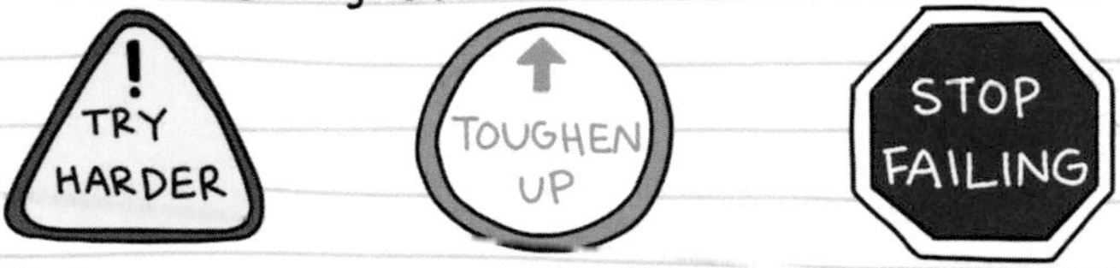
TRY HARDER
TOUGHEN UP
STOP FAILING

Therapy helped me realize that my emotions were trying to tell me the opposite:

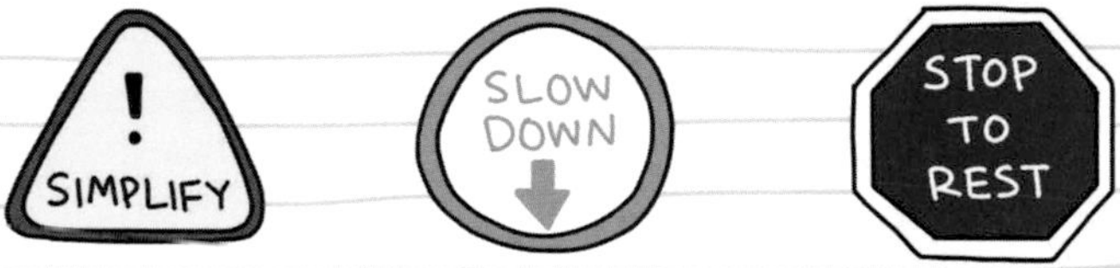
SIMPLIFY
SLOW DOWN
STOP TO REST

When I feel overwhelmed, my body is signaling that I need to reassess my priorities, simplify my approach, or take a break. As I've begun to heed that message, I've gained a greater sense of control in my life.

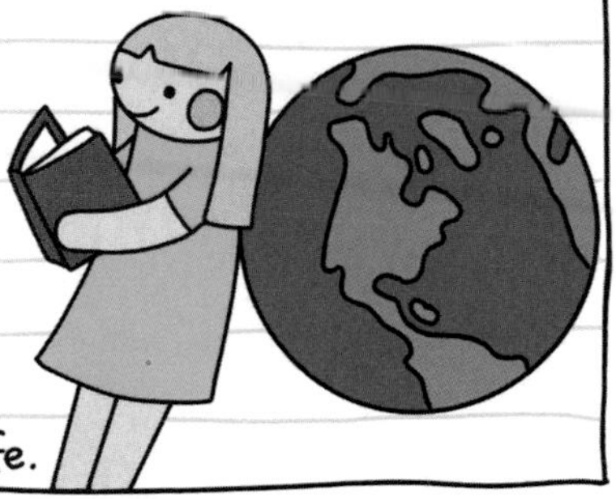

WORST WORKSHOP

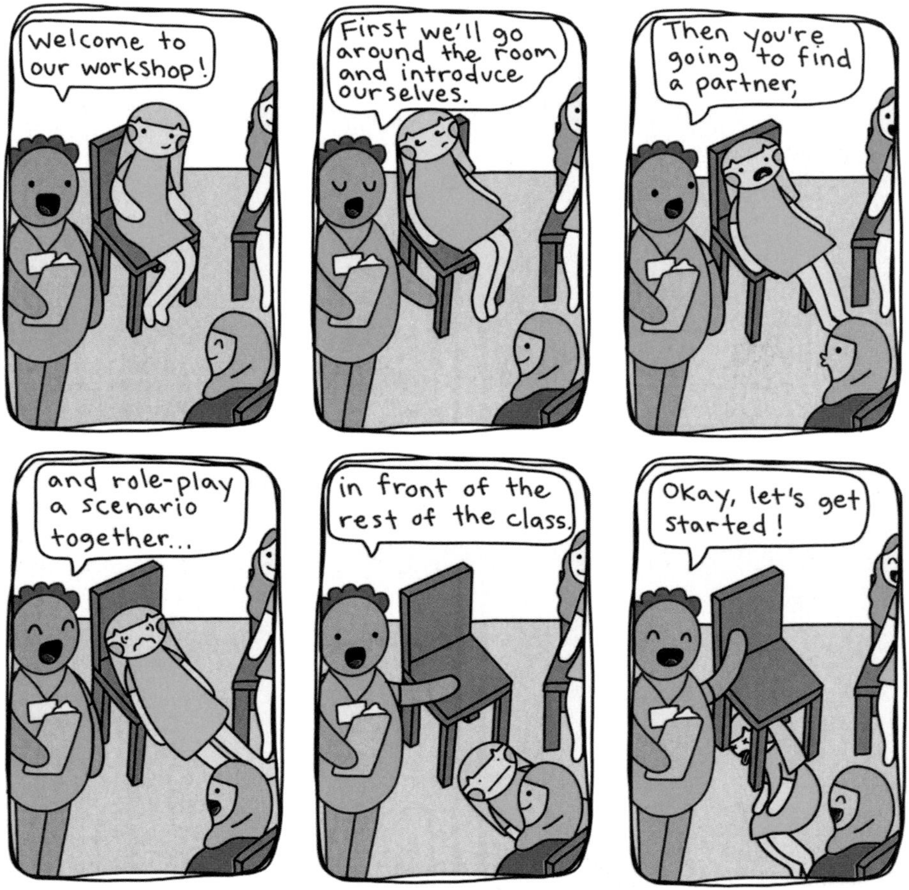
Welcome to our workshop!
First we'll go around the room and introduce ourselves.
Then you're going to find a partner,
and role-play a scenario together...
in front of the rest of the class.
Okay, let's get started!

WHEN THERE'S A SOCIAL EVENT

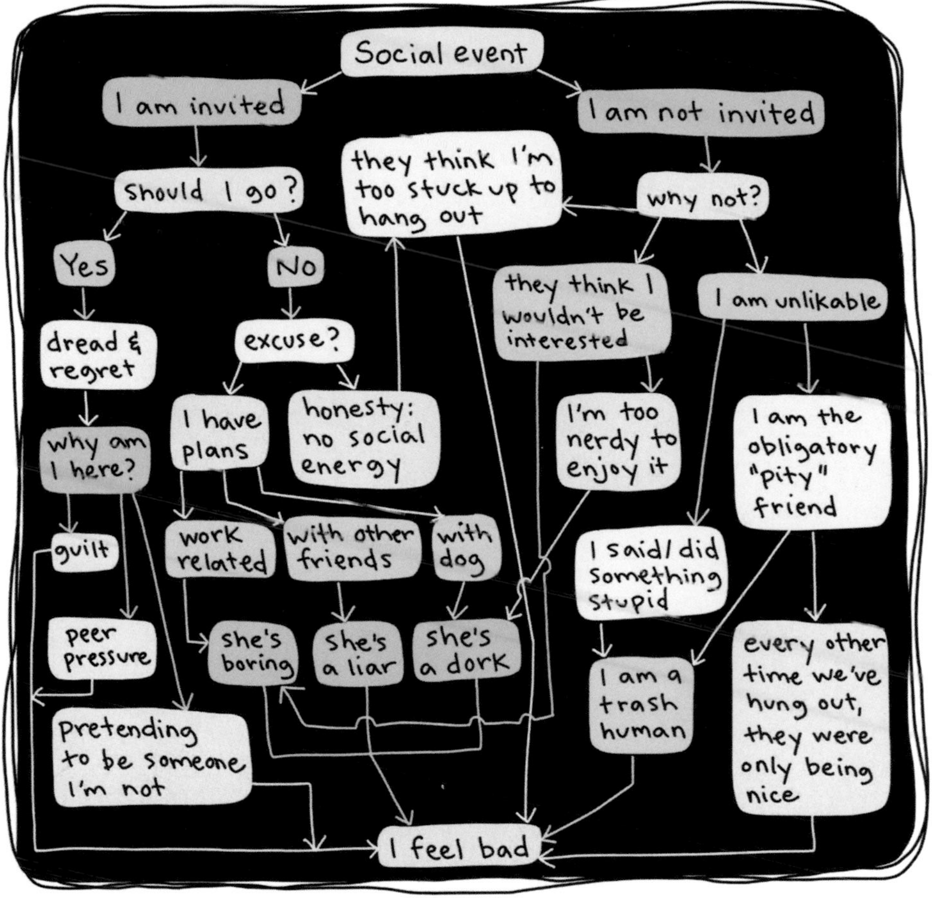
Social event
I am invited
I am not invited
should I go?
they think I'm too stuck up to hang out
why not?
Yes
No
they think I wouldn't be interested
I am unlikable
dread & regret
excuse?
why am I here?
I have plans
honesty: no social energy
I'm too nerdy to enjoy it
I am the obligatory "pity" friend
guilt
work related
with other friends
with dog
I said/did something stupid
peer pressure
she's boring
she's a liar
she's a dork
I am a trash human
every other time we've hung out, they were only being nice
pretending to be someone I'm not
I feel bad

DOWNHILL

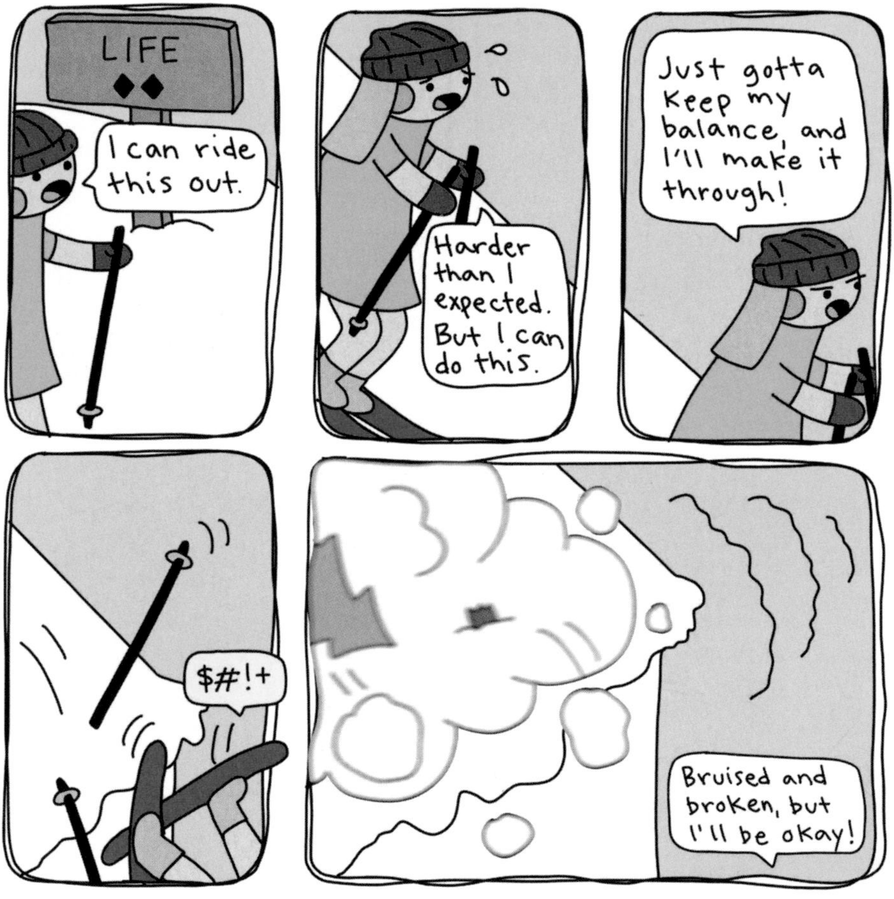
LIFE
I can ride this out.
Harder than I expected. But I can do this.
Just gotta keep my balance, and I'll make it through!
$#!+
Bruised and broken, but I'll be okay!

NON-INSPIRATIONAL POSTERS

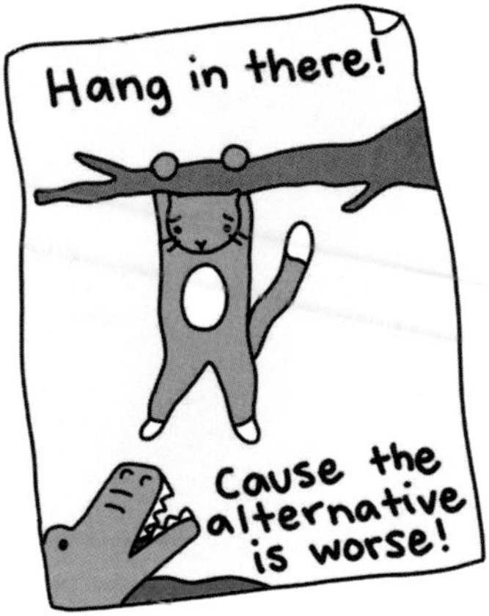

Hang in there!
Cause the alternative is worse!

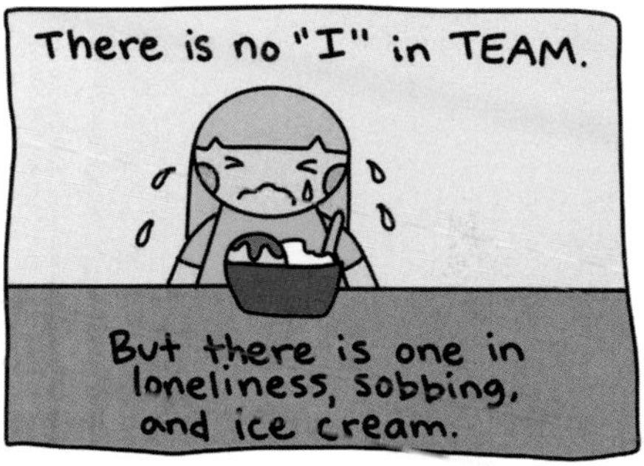

There is no "I" in TEAM.
But there is one in loneliness, sobbing, and ice cream.

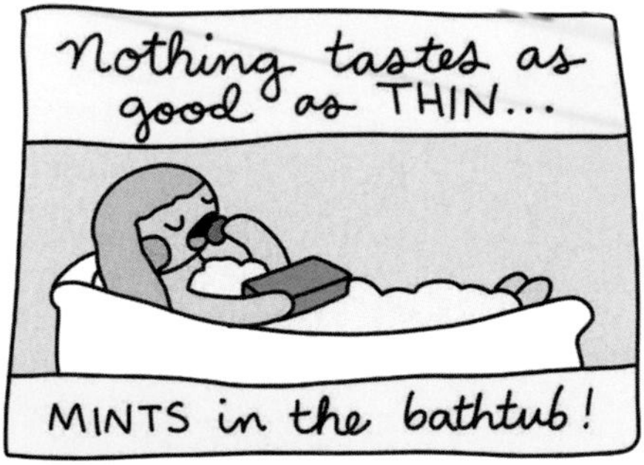

Nothing tastes as good as THIN...
MINTS in the bathtub!

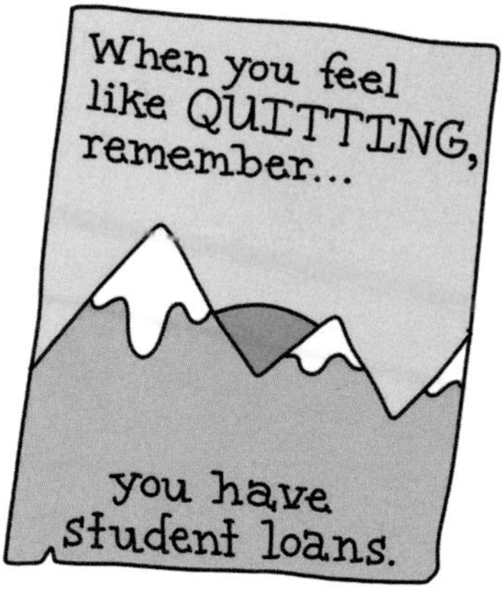

When you feel like QUITTING, remember...
you have student loans.

WORKING

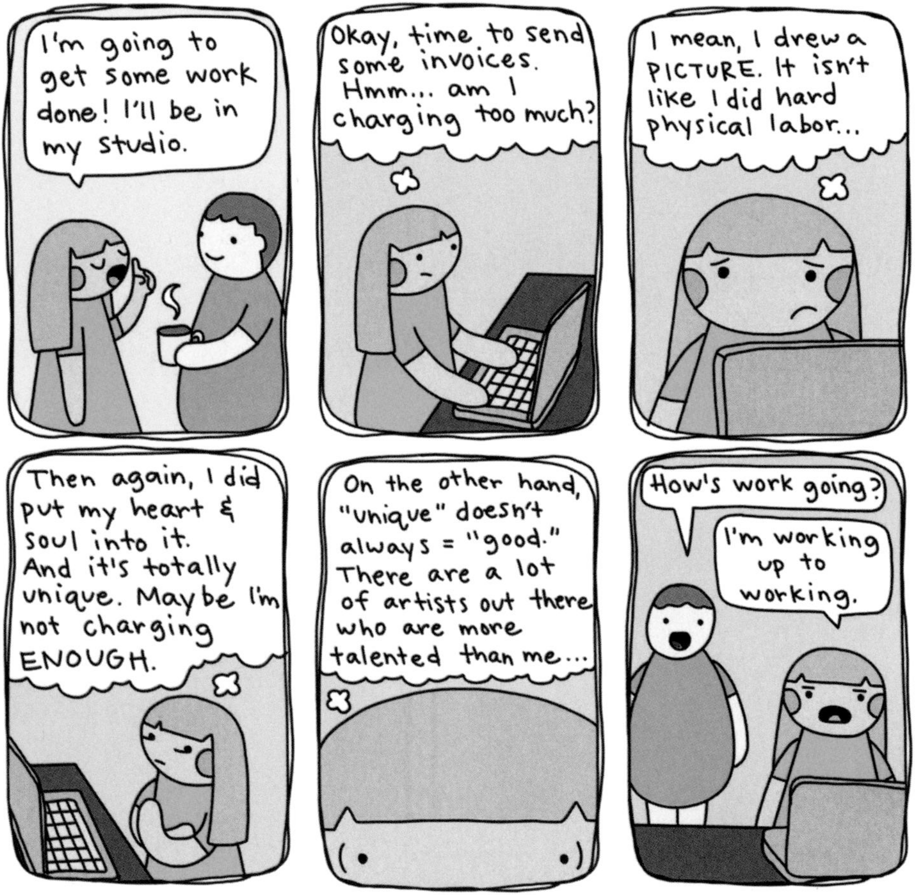
I'm going to get some work done! I'll be in my studio.
Okay, time to send some invoices. Hmm... am I charging too much?
I mean, I drew a PICTURE. It isn't like I did hard physical labor...
Then again, I did put my heart & soul into it. And it's totally unique. Maybe I'm not charging ENOUGH.
On the other hand, "unique" doesn't always = "good." There are a lot of artists out there who are more talented than me...
How's work going?
I'm working up to working.

Saying "yes" in the past doesn't forfeit your right to say "no" in the future.*

*Including but not limited to:

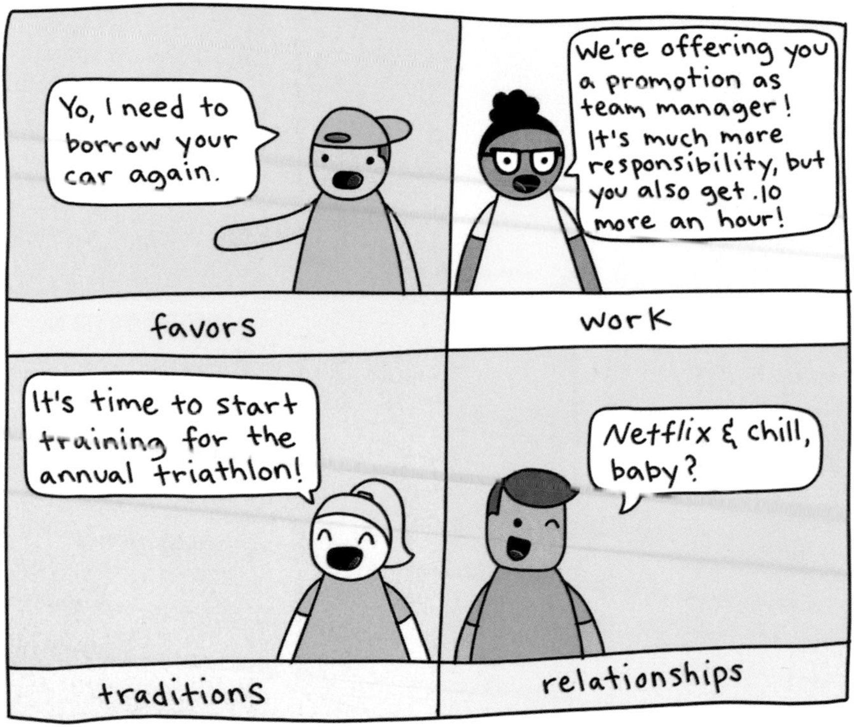
Yo, I need to borrow your car again.
favors
We're offering you a promotion as team manager! It's much more responsibility, but you also get .10 more an hour!
work
It's time to start training for the annual triathlon!
traditions
Netflix & chill, baby?
relationships

PRESSURE

This little balloon has the potential to stretch & grow.

Add a little helium and it can soar to new heights!

But what if the pressure is increased...

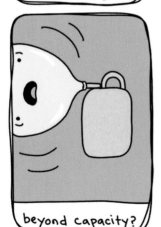

beyond capacity?

GRAPHIC IMAGE*

Oh.

A little pressure = growth.

A lot of pressure = explosion.

*Simulated special effects. No balloons were harmed in the making of this doodle.

HOW CAN I PUT THIS...?

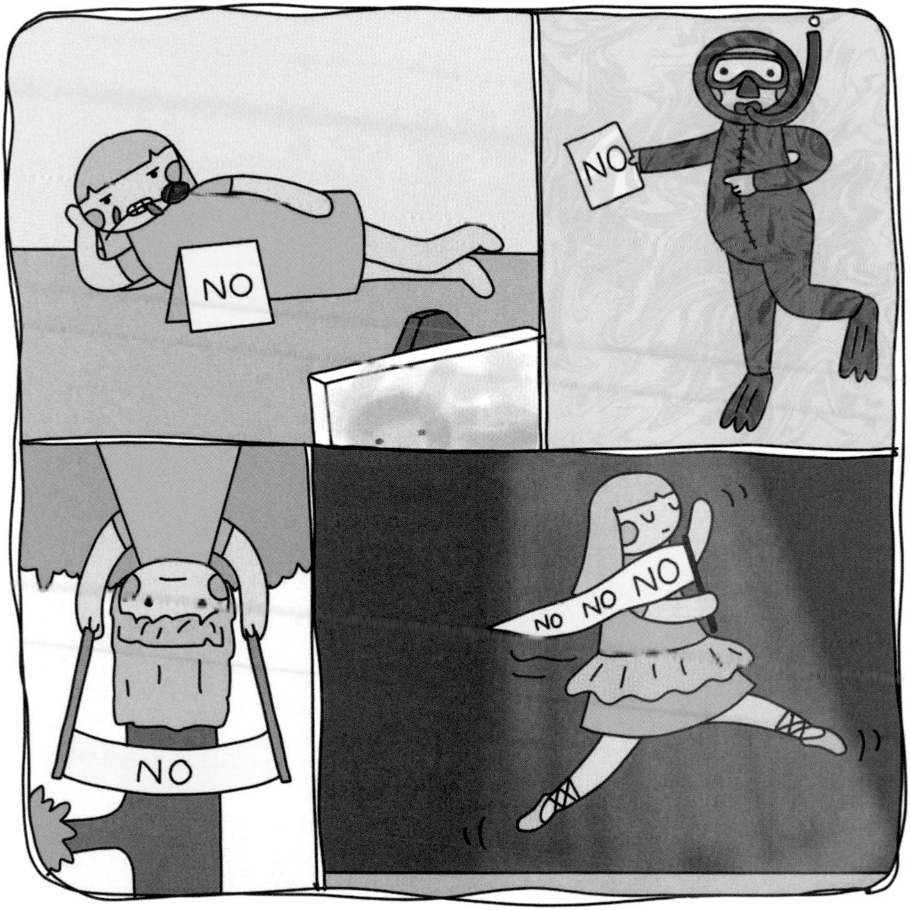

NO
NO
NO
NO NO NO

ESTABLISH ORDER

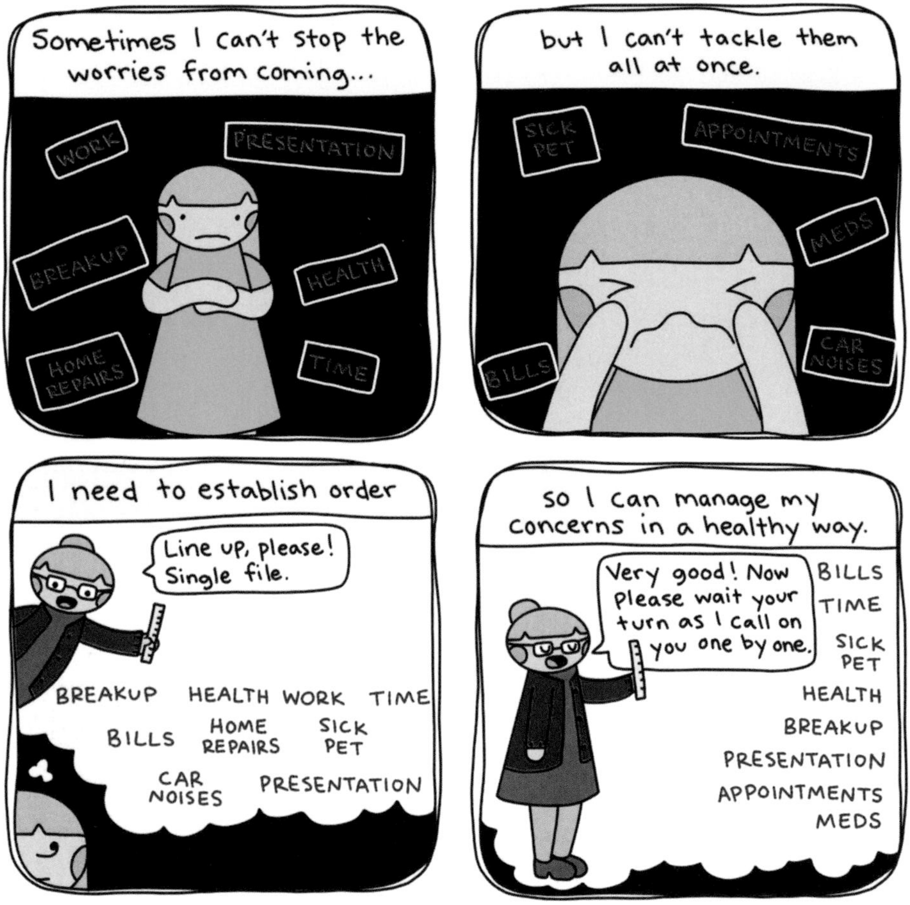
Sometimes I can't stop the worries from coming...
WORK
PRESENTATION
BREAKUP
HEALTH
HOME REPAIRS
TIME
but I can't tackle them all at once.
SICK PET
APPOINTMENTS
MEDS
BILLS
CAR NOISES
I need to establish order
Line up, please! Single file.
BREAKUP
HEALTH
WORK
TIME
BILLS
HOME REPAIRS
SICK PET
CAR NOISES
PRESENTATION
so I can manage my concerns in a healthy way.
Very good! Now please wait your turn as I call on you one by one.
BILLS
TIME
SICK PET
HEALTH
BREAKUP
PRESENTATION
APPOINTMENTS
MEDS

IDEAS FOR COPING WHEN OVERWHELMED

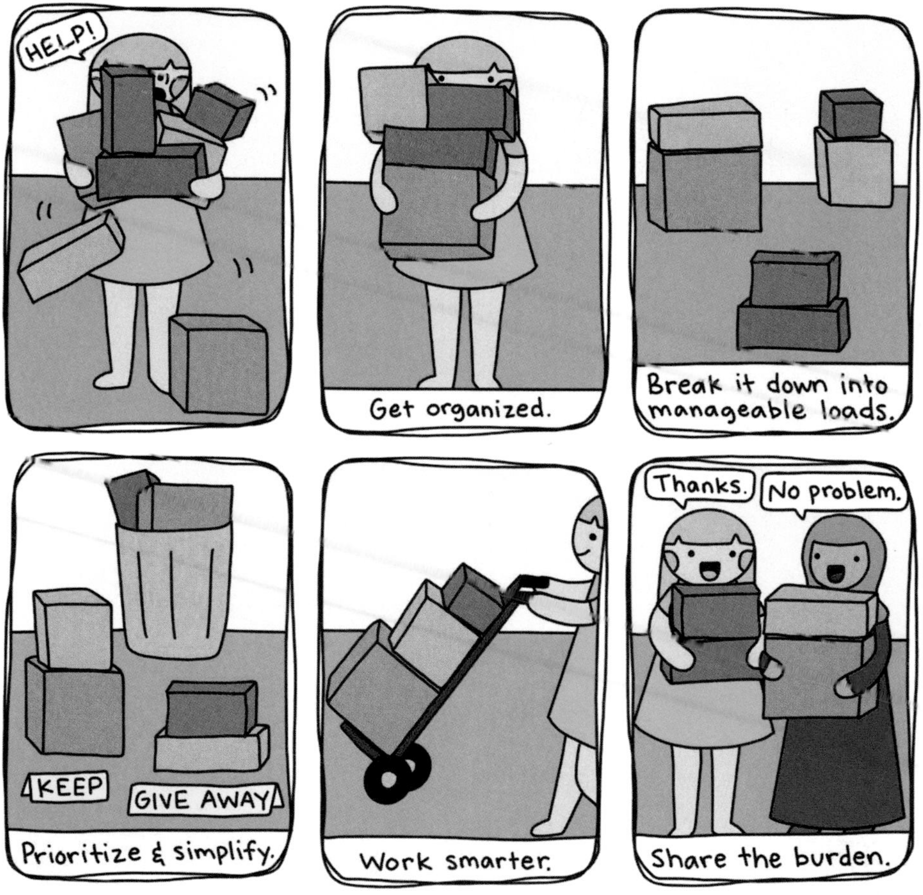
HELP!
Get organized.
Break it down into manageable loads.
KEEP
GIVE AWAY
Prioritize & simplify.
Work smarter.
Thanks.
No problem.
Share the burden.

CHAPTER 6

TODAY I'M FEELING:

ANTICIPATION

I love the feeling of anticipation – that tingly sensation like champagne in my veins. I enjoy the dreamy warmth of imagining, again and again, the moment I've been waiting for. I revel in the growing excitement as I count down days and minutes!

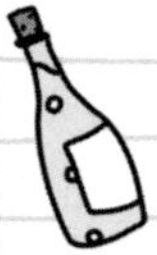

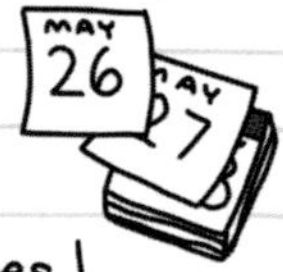
MAY
26
MAY
27

I've found that I appreciate the anticipation of an event almost as much as the event itself. There's pleasure in planning, in talking about the upcoming day, and in fantasizing about every detail.

The tricky part for me is trying to stay fluid in my expectations. I can become so enthralled by the daydream, so committed to the fantasy script, that I'm disappointed when things don't go exactly as I'd planned.

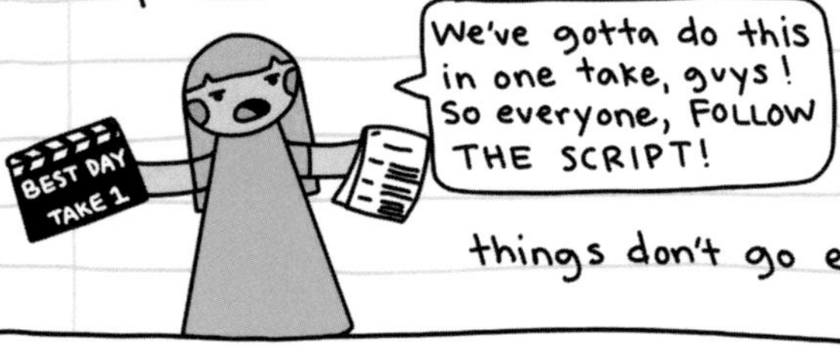
BEST DAY
TAKE 1
We've gotta do this in one take, guys! So everyone, FOLLOW THE SCRIPT!

Does that mean I should try to squash that anticipatory thrill? Lessen it so I won't get hurt? Would it be wise to forego the feeling of anticipation altogether?

I've discovered that I can do the 🔆opposite🔆: Instead of shooing away the daydreams, I choose to imagine 🔆more🔆 variations of the event. Instead of one script, there are many possibilities. When the big day arrives, I'm prepared to experience it with an open mind!

JUNE CAMPING TRIP   we might...

catch lots of fish   -or-   swim if the fish aren't biting   -or-   read while listening to the rain

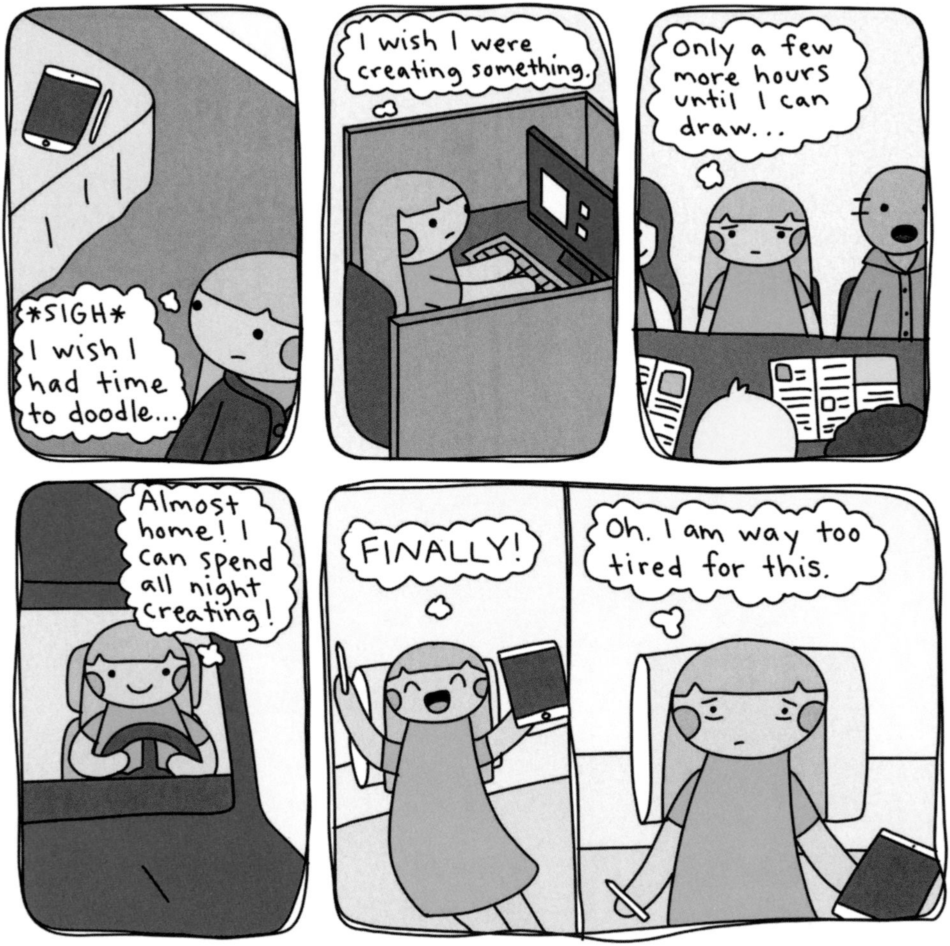
SIGH I wish I had time to doodle...
I wish I were creating something.
Only a few more hours until I can draw...
Almost home! I can spend all night creating!
FINALLY!
Oh. I am way too tired for this.

DREAM

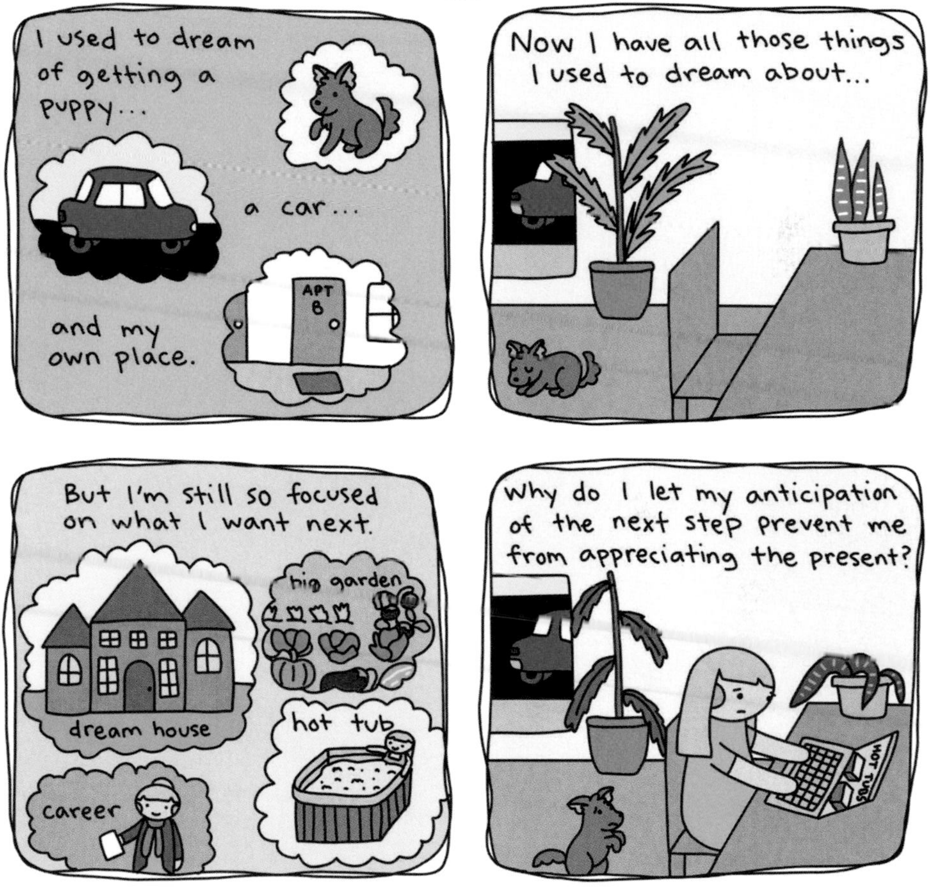

I used to dream of getting a puppy...
a car...
APT 8
and my own place.
Now I have all those things I used to dream about...
But I'm still so focused on what I want next.
big garden
dream house
hot tub
career
Why do I let my anticipation of the next step prevent me from appreciating the present?
HOT TUBS

REMEMBER THAT FEELING OF GOING BACK TO SCHOOL?

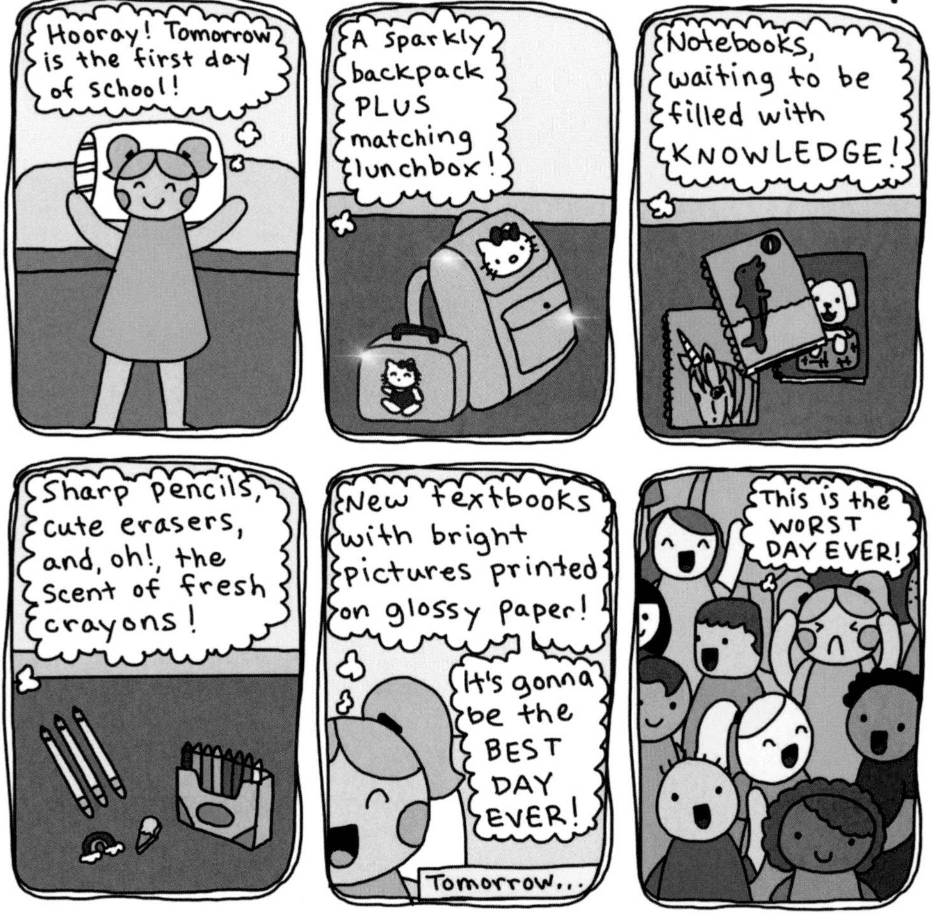
Hooray! Tomorrow is the first day of school!
A sparkly backpack PLUS matching lunchbox!
Notebooks, waiting to be filled with KNOWLEDGE!
Sharp pencils, cute erasers, and, oh!, the scent of fresh crayons!
New textbooks with bright pictures printed on glossy paper!
It's gonna be the BEST DAY EVER!
Tomorrow...
This is the WORST DAY EVER!

PLANS

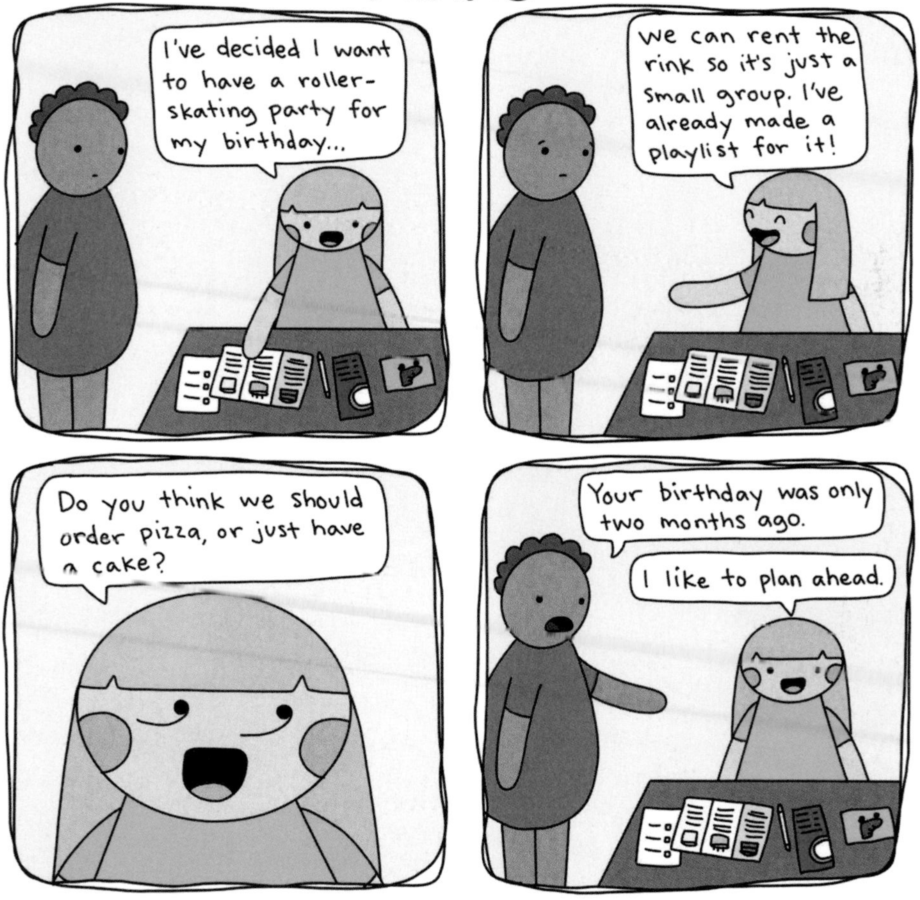
I've decided I want to have a roller-skating party for my birthday...
We can rent the rink so it's just a small group. I've already made a playlist for it!
Do you think we should order pizza, or just have a cake?
Your birthday was only two months ago.
I like to plan ahead.

When I was little, I'd anticipate life as a sophisticated adult...

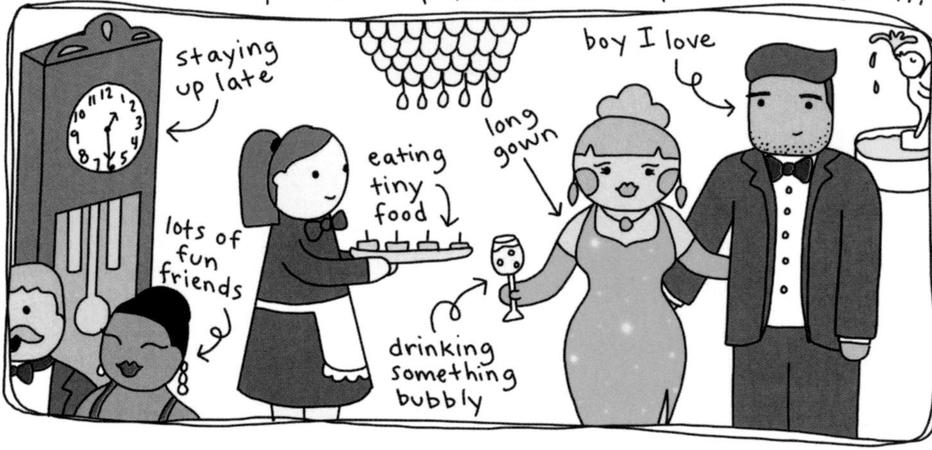
staying up late
boy I love
long gown
eating tiny food
lots of fun friends
drinking something bubbly

close enough.

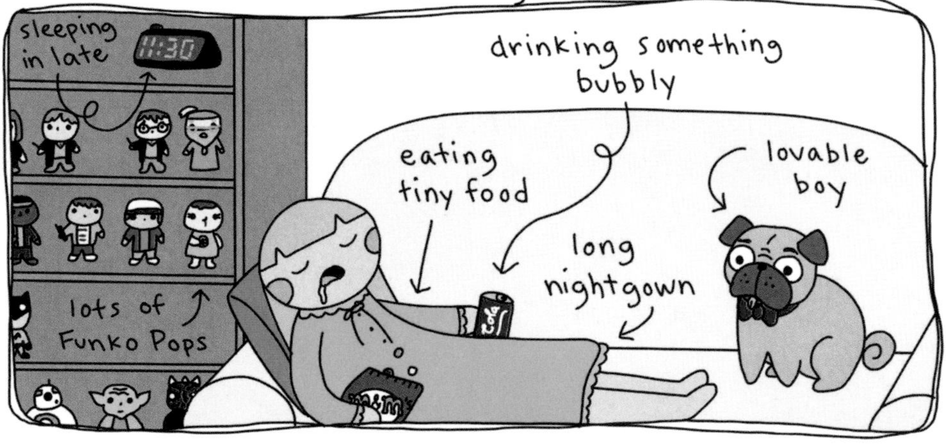
sleeping in late
11:30
drinking something bubbly
eating tiny food
lovable boy
long nightgown
lots of Funko Pops
Cola

ANTICIPATING SPRING

Watching the rain	Stopping to smell the tulips	Eating berries	Opening windows	Hiking
Dining on the patio	Soaking up the sun	Using an umbrella	Spotting a butterfly	Deep-cleaning the house
Mowing the lawn	Leaving my coat at home	Binging on Easter candy	Grilling	Admiring leaf buds
Riding a bike	Sipping a smoothie	Sneezing	Birds singing	Strolling through a garden center
Making dandelion crowns	Jumping in puddles	Reading outside	Wearing pastel clothes	Playing at the dog park

SOON

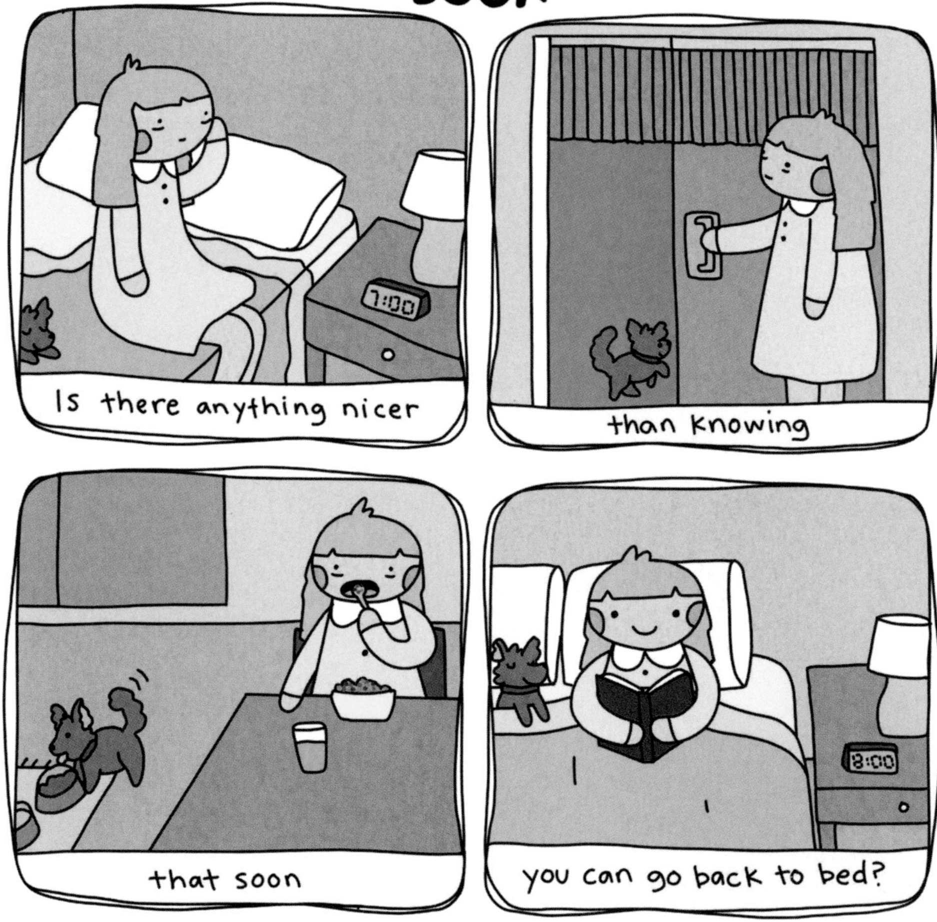
Is there anything nicer
7:00
than knowing
that soon
you can go back to bed?
8:00

STUFF I ANTICIPATE BUYING WHEN I'M RICH

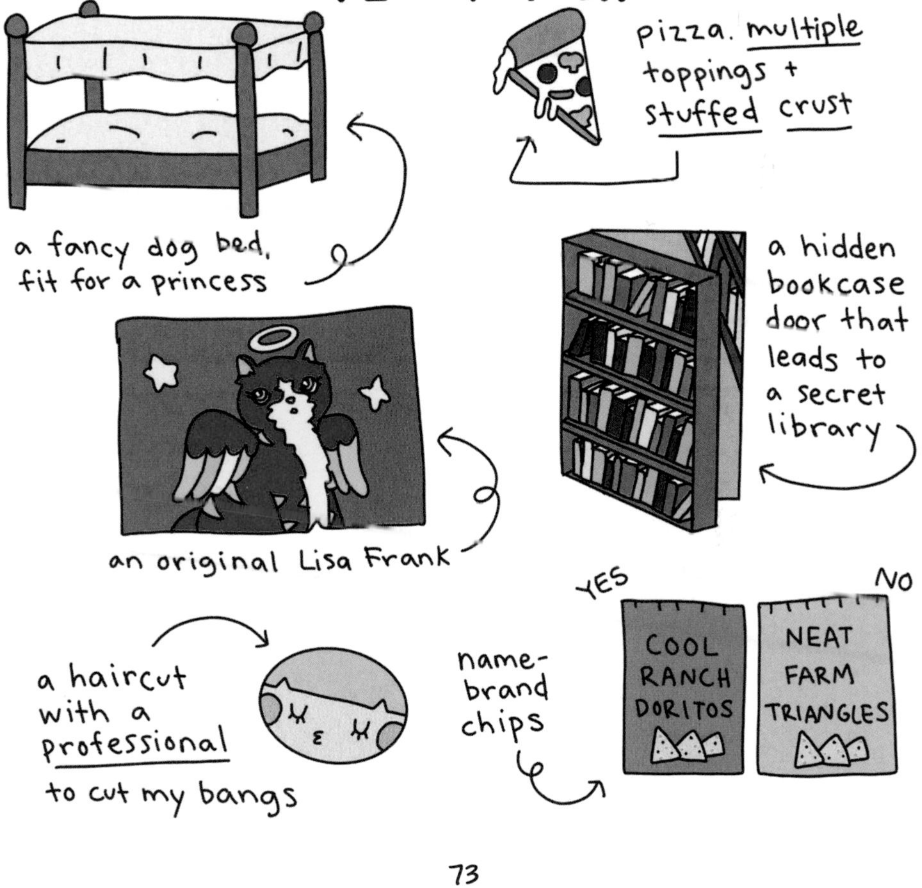
pizza. multiple toppings + stuffed crust
a fancy dog bed, fit for a princess
a hidden bookcase door that leads to a secret library
an original Lisa Frank
YES
NO
COOL RANCH DORITOS
NEAT FARM TRIANGLES
name-brand chips
a haircut with a professional to cut my bangs

SUMMER BUCKET LIST

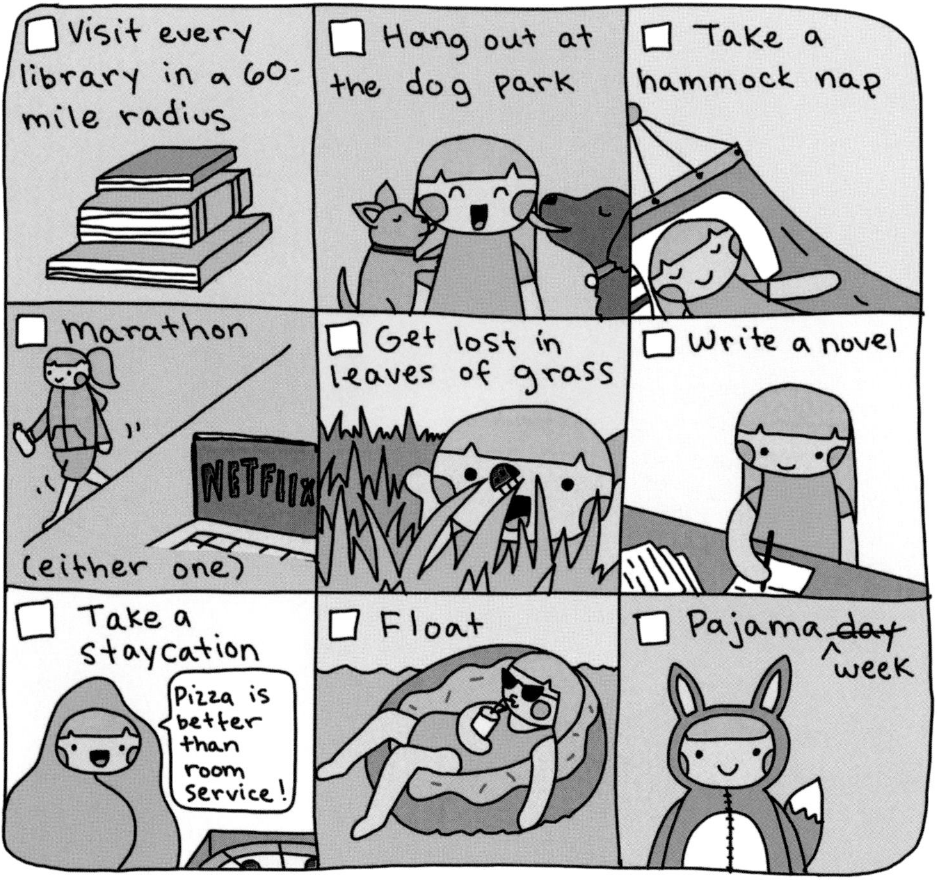

☐ Visit every library in a 60-mile radius
☐ Hang out at the dog park
☐ Take a hammock nap
☐ marathon
NETFLIX
(either one)
☐ Get lost in leaves of grass
☐ Write a novel
☐ Take a staycation
Pizza is better than room service!
☐ Float
☐ Pajama ~~day~~
^week

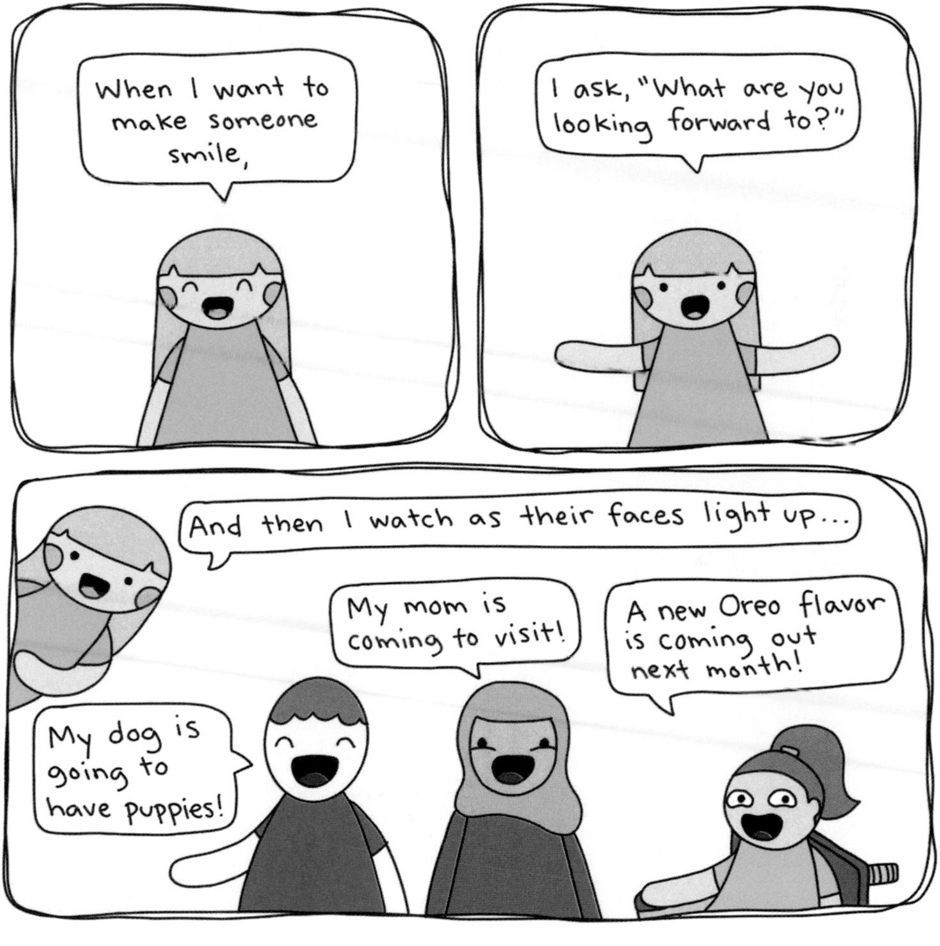
When I want to make someone smile,
I ask, "What are you looking forward to?"
And then I watch as their faces light up...
My dog is going to have puppies!
My mom is coming to visit!
A new Oreo flavor is coming out next month!

CHAPTER 7

TODAY I'M FEELING:

MISUNDERSTOOD

It's frustrating to feel misunderstood! For me, some of that feeling is rooted in my own awkwardness; I have a hard time with verbal communication, so connecting with others in conversation can be challenging. Sometimes the misunderstandings are due to my quirkiness. I seem to view the world a little differently than most people.

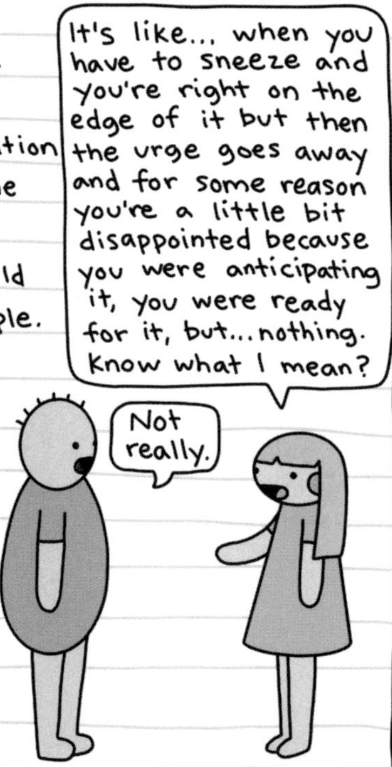
It's like... when you have to sneeze and you're right on the edge of it but then the urge goes away and for some reason you're a little bit disappointed because you were anticipating it, you were ready for it, but... nothing. Know what I mean?
Not really.

I've come to accept that some misunderstandings will happen. Not everyone is going to "get" me, and it won't always be easy for me to understand others. But there are a couple of questions I keep in mind to keep my relationships healthy...

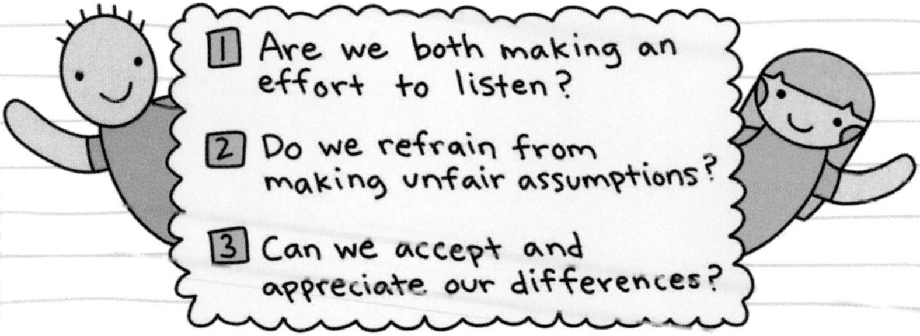
1 Are we both making an effort to listen?
2 Do we refrain from making unfair assumptions?
3 Can we accept and appreciate our differences?

There have been times when people have tried to convince me that I need to change. When that happens, I think over the criticism carefully, and hold it up to what I know to be true about myself. And I often come to the conclusion:

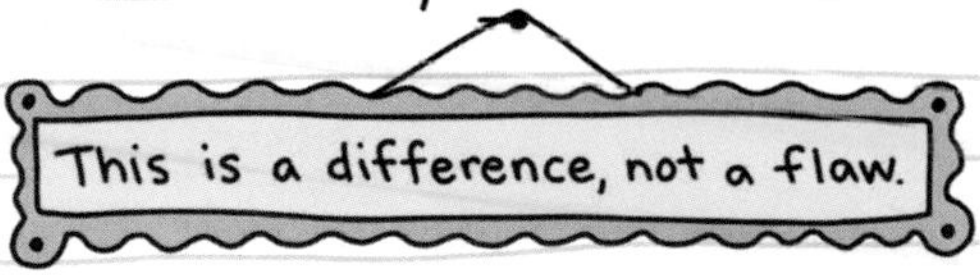
This is a difference, not a flaw.

I've discovered that the people who truly care about me will embrace my differences as part of what makes me special.

CHANGE

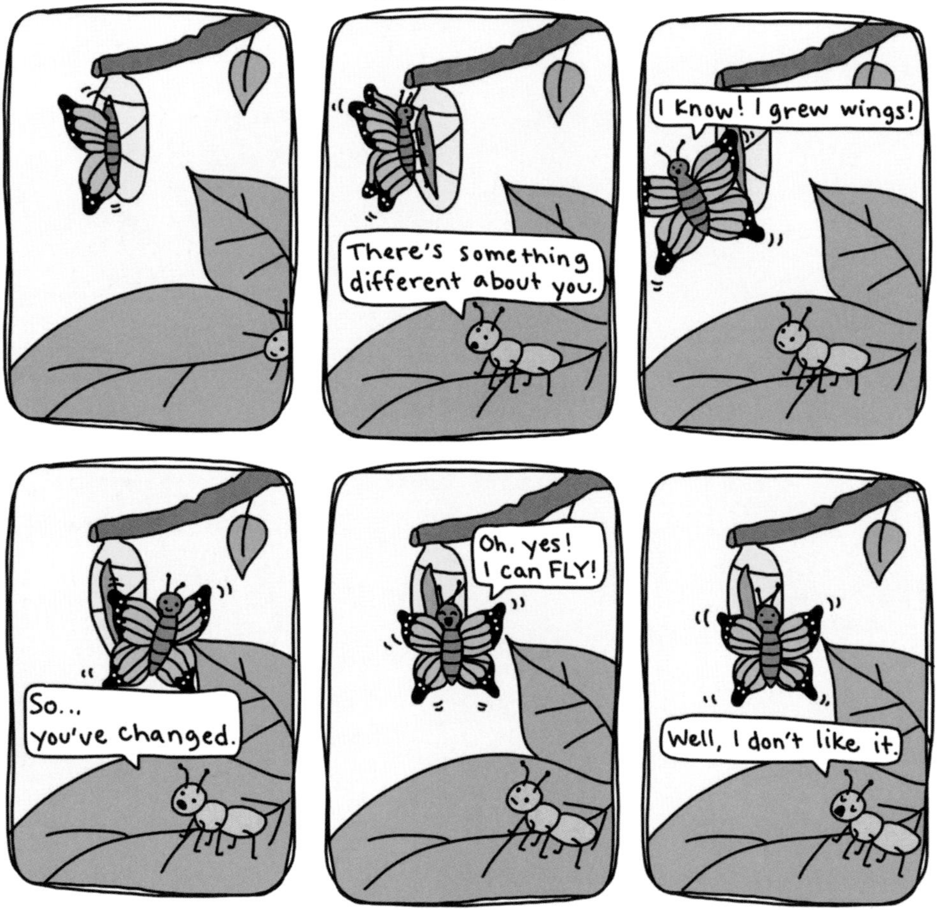
There's something different about you.
I know! I grew wings!
So...
you've changed.
Oh, yes!
I can FLY!
Well, I don't like it.

WHAT I THINK

Sometimes people say they want to know what I think...

So should I give him a second chance? What do you think?

Well...

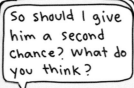

You've already given him a dozen chances. He's a narcissistic, mooching man-child, and you deserve better.

P.S.: His mustache looks like a deceased caterpillar.

Wow. How can you be so mean & unsupportive?

but I've realized that they actually don't.

I think you should follow your heart.

Thanks, Marzi!

LESS ISN'T MORE

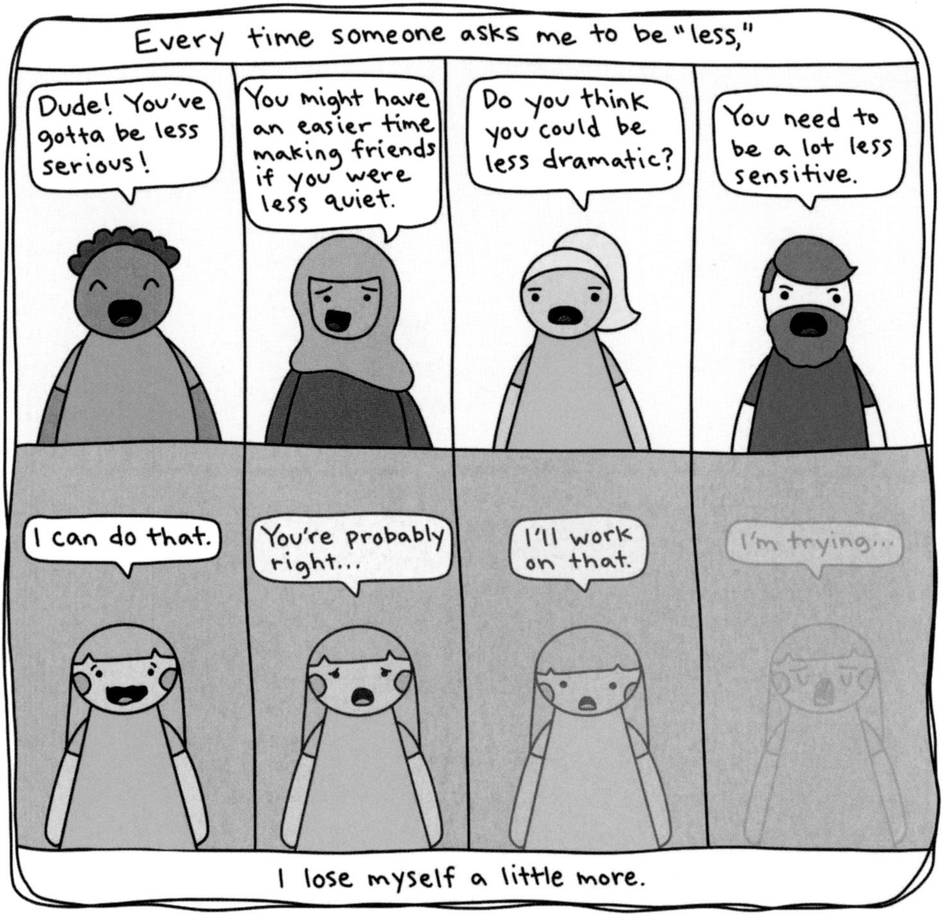
Every time someone asks me to be "less,"
Dude! You've gotta be less serious!
You might have an easier time making friends if you were less quiet.
Do you think you could be less dramatic?
You need to be a lot less sensitive.
I can do that.
You're probably right...
I'll work on that.
I'm trying...
I lose myself a little more.

What I Said	What He Heard	What I Meant
You remind me of Bill Nye the Science Guy!	She thinks I'm a nerd.	You're really smart and funny.
Wanna grab a coffee?	She's asking me out!	I NEED CAFFEINE.
I work from home.	Lucky! She has an awesome job!	I don't really have a job...
Thanks for the info.	She's impressed by my advanced knowledge and benevolent wisdom.	Did I ask for your opinion?
Why hello there, buddy!	She wants to be my friend!	I was talking to your dog. May I pet him?

WHEN THERE'S A MISUNDERSTANDING

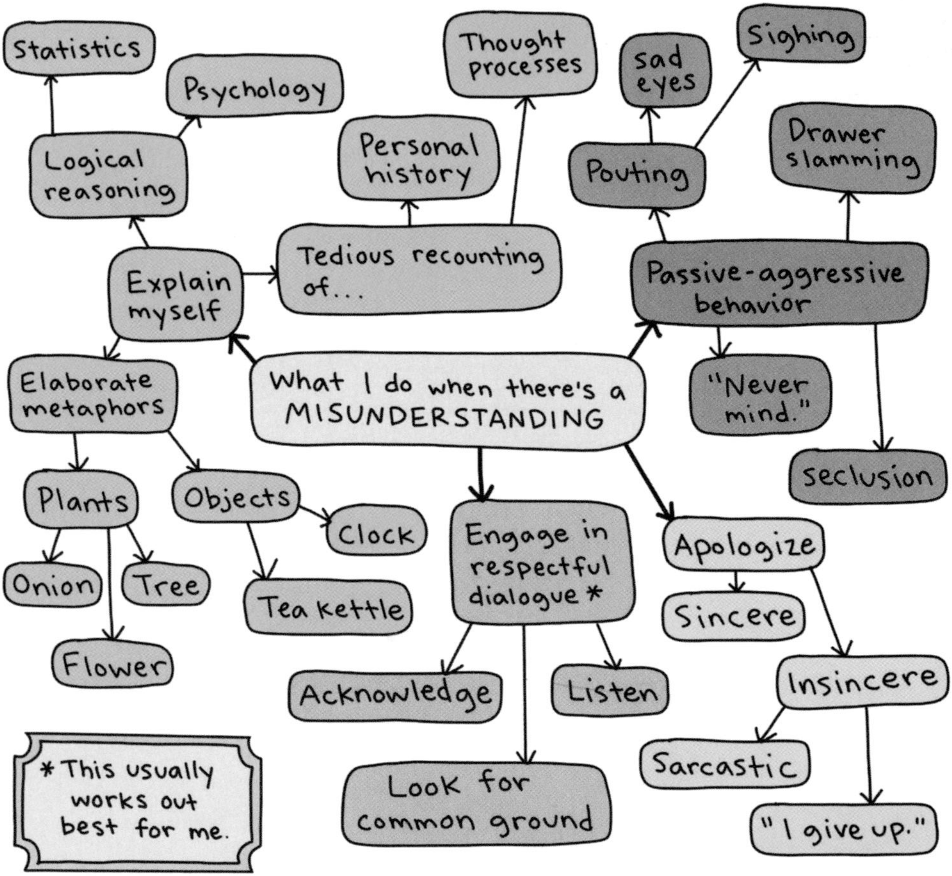

What I do when there's a MISUNDERSTANDING
Explain myself
Logical reasoning
Statistics
Psychology
Tedious recounting of...
Personal history
Thought processes
Elaborate metaphors
Plants
Onion
Tree
Flower
Objects
Clock
Tea kettle
Passive-aggressive behavior
Pouting
sad eyes
Sighing
Drawer slamming
"Never mind."
seclusion
Engage in respectful dialogue *
Acknowledge
Listen
Look for common ground
Apologize
Sincere
Insincere
Sarcastic
"I give up."
* This usually works out best for me.

CAN YOU HEAR* ME?

If you...

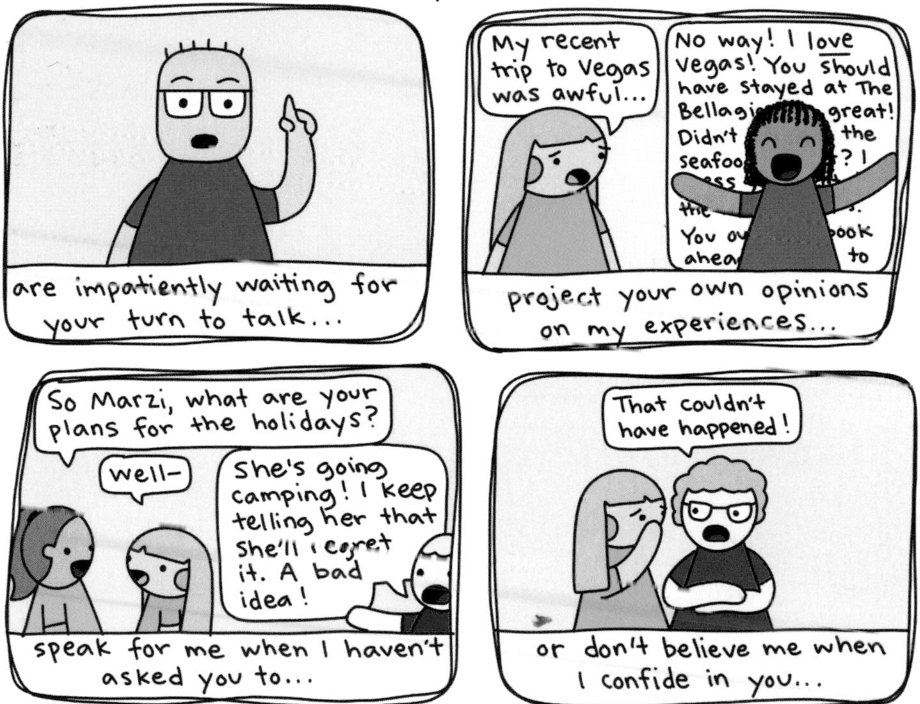
are impatiently waiting for your turn to talk...
My recent trip to Vegas was awful...
No way! I love Vegas! You should have stayed at The
project your own opinions on my experiences...
So Marzi, what are your plans for the holidays?
Well-
She's going camping! I keep telling her that
it. A bad idea!
speak for me when I haven't asked you to...
That couldn't have happened!
or don't believe me when I confide in you...

then you aren't hearing me.

*Being a "good listener" isn't dependent on auditory capabilities. It's about providing a safe space for others to share their ideas. There are many valid ways to communicate and offer understanding!

YOUR MISCONCEPTIONS OF ME

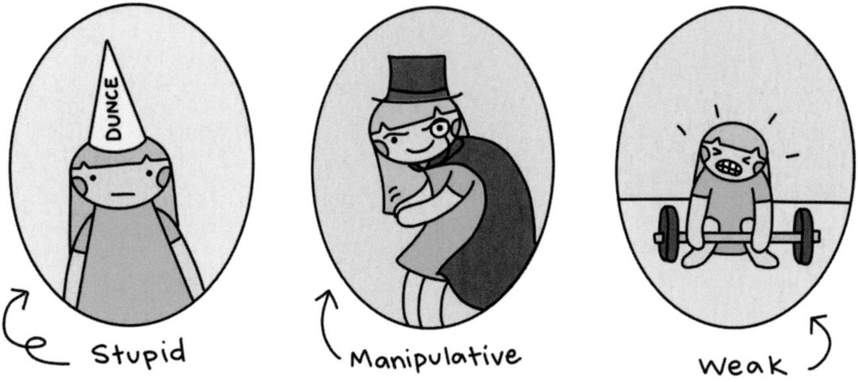
DUNCE
Stupid
Manipulative
Weak

ARE NOT A REFLECTION OF ME

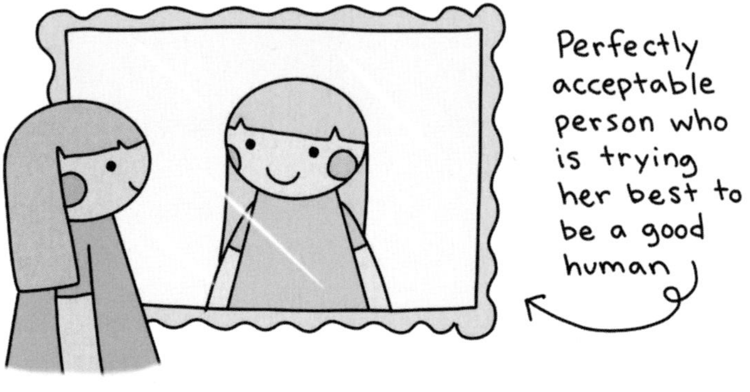
Perfectly acceptable person who is trying her best to be a good human

ME AT THE GROCERY STORE*

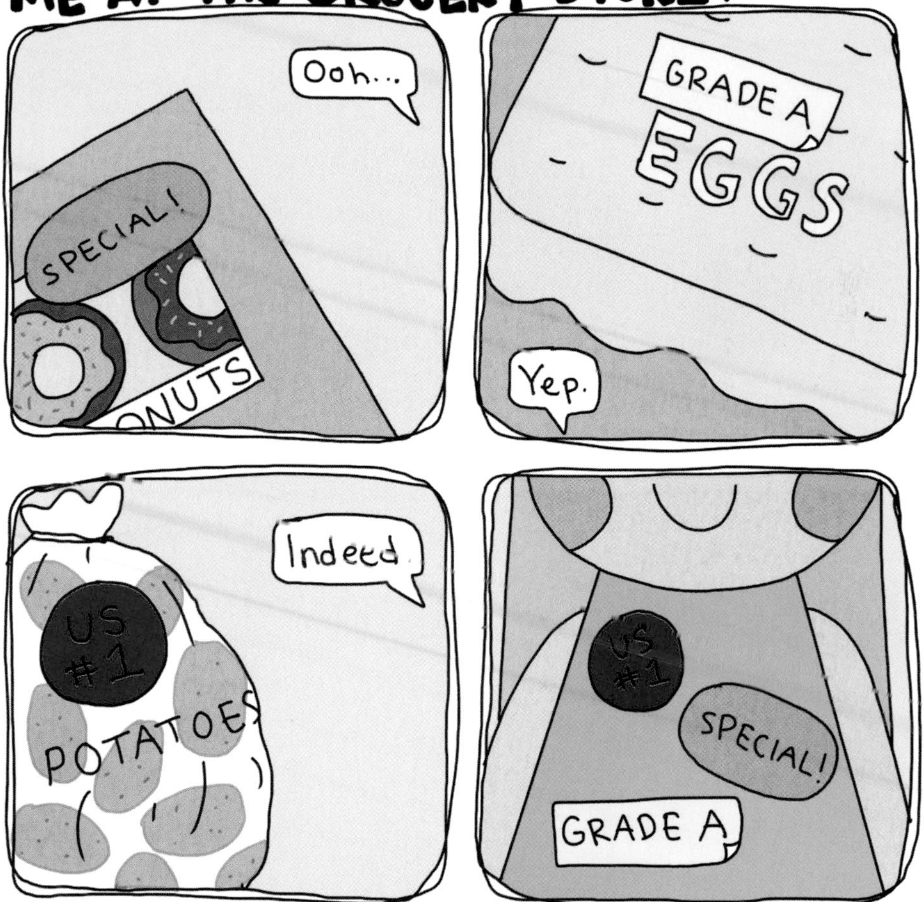
Ooh...
SPECIAL!
ONUTS
GRADE A
EGGS
Yep.
Indeed.
US #1
POTATOES
US #1
SPECIAL!
GRADE A

*I choose my own labels

TOO MUCH?

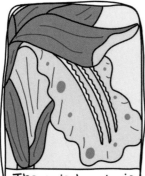

There is beauty in feeling deeply and existing fully.

You experience the world in vivid color, a rich spectrum most can't see.

That one looks like a lot of work... I'll pass.

Sometimes the world tells you that you're too much...

And it leaves you feeling like you aren't enough.

GASP! You're gorgeous!

But they're wrong. You aren't "too much," you're just "more."

You are more than enough. ♥

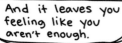

IDEAS FOR DEALING WITH FREQUENT MISUNDERSTANDINGS

Look for patterns: Why does this keep happening? What is the root cause?

Write it out: Explaining in writing helps to clarify the experience & how I feel about it.

I can't believe you'd say that to me!

That isn't what I meant!

What do I want? Is there a specific resolution I'm hoping for? Have I verbalized my desires?

Consider what I could give: Is there a compromise that we would both feel good about?

Take a time-out. If the situation is escalating, take a break to recenter & reflect. Address the problem when we both feel ready to engage thoughtfully.

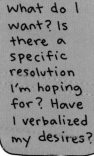

TODAY I'M FEELING:
JOYFUL

I prefer to use the word "joyful" instead of "happy," because "happy" always felt like pressure. As though happiness were a consistent state of being, a lifestyle to maintain.

Joy, though... joy seems more transitory. It's a brief, bright spark that lights my life for a moment, and then fades.

But isn't the feeling of joy made all the more precious because of its impermanence?

There's so much beauty in the contrast between the mundane and magical...

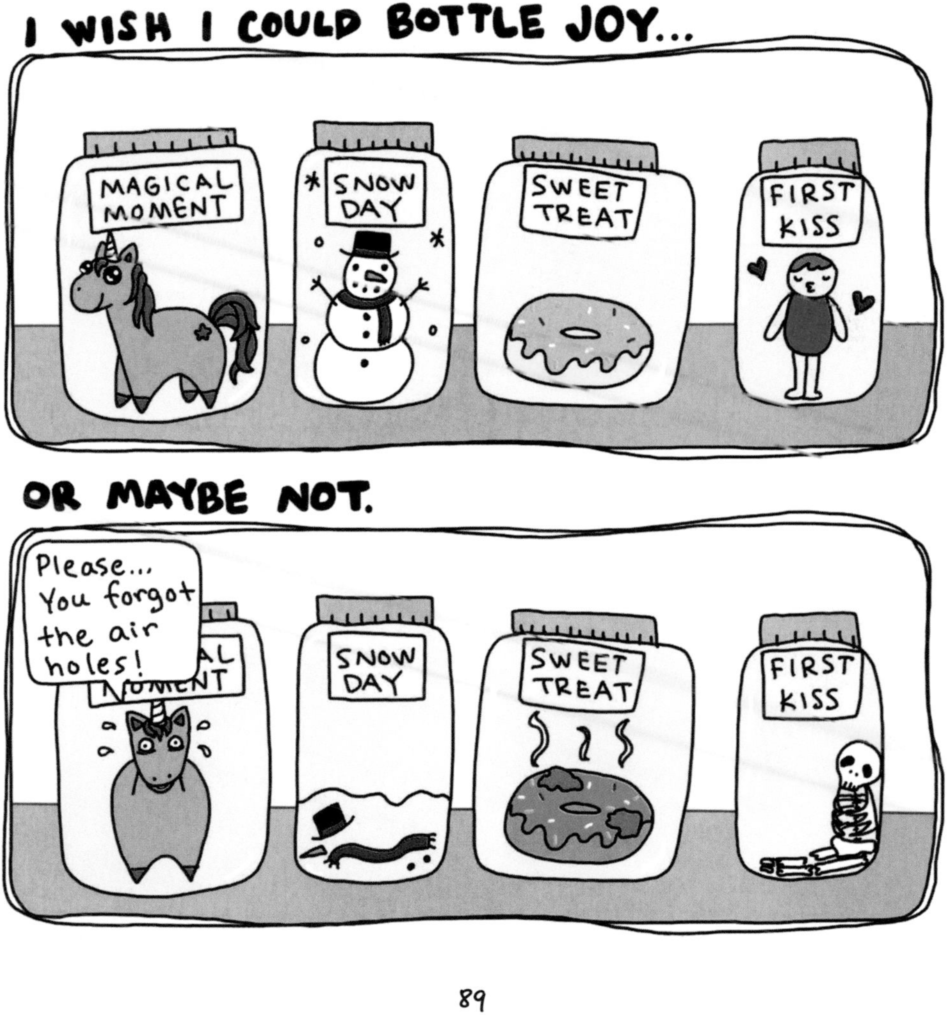
I WISH I COULD BOTTLE JOY...
MAGICAL MOMENT
SNOW DAY
SWEET TREAT
FIRST KISS
OR MAYBE NOT.
Please... You forgot the air holes!
SNOW DAY
SWEET TREAT
FIRST KISS

INVESTMENT

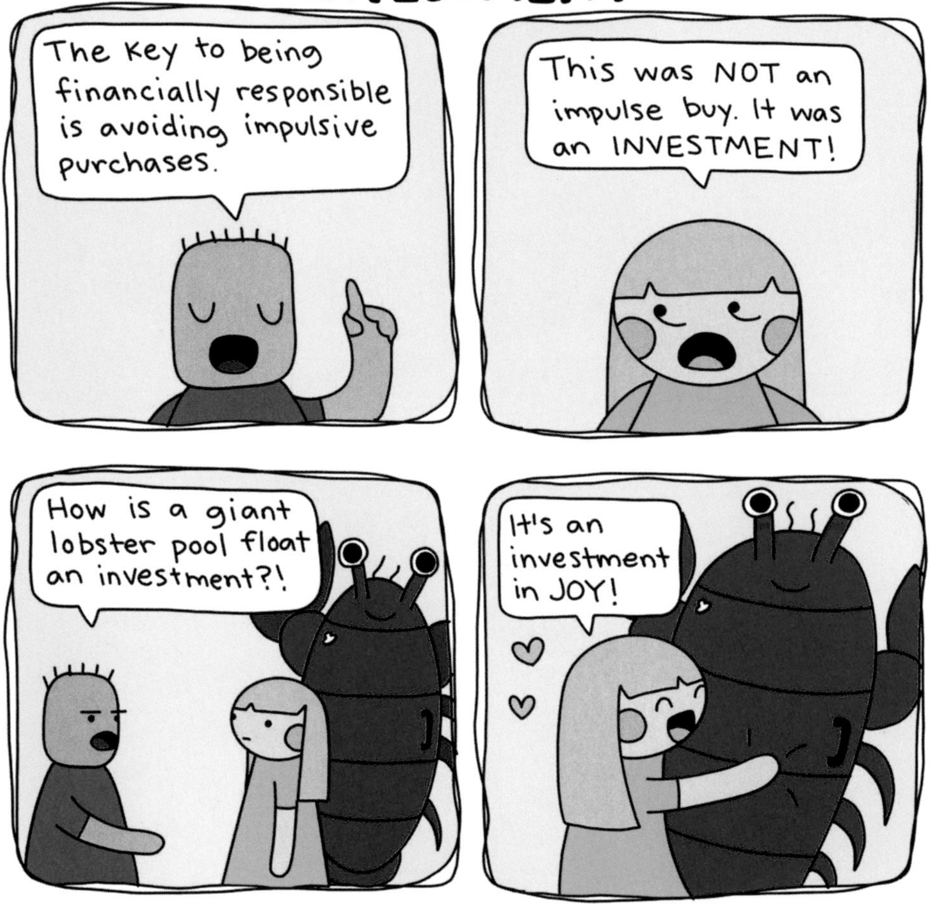
The key to being financially responsible is avoiding impulsive purchases.
This was NOT an impulse buy. It was an INVESTMENT!
How is a giant lobster pool float an investment?!
It's an investment in JOY!

~~ITEMS I OWN TOO MANY OF~~
ITEMS I WILL NEVER OWN ENOUGH OF

Surround yourself with whatever brings you joy.

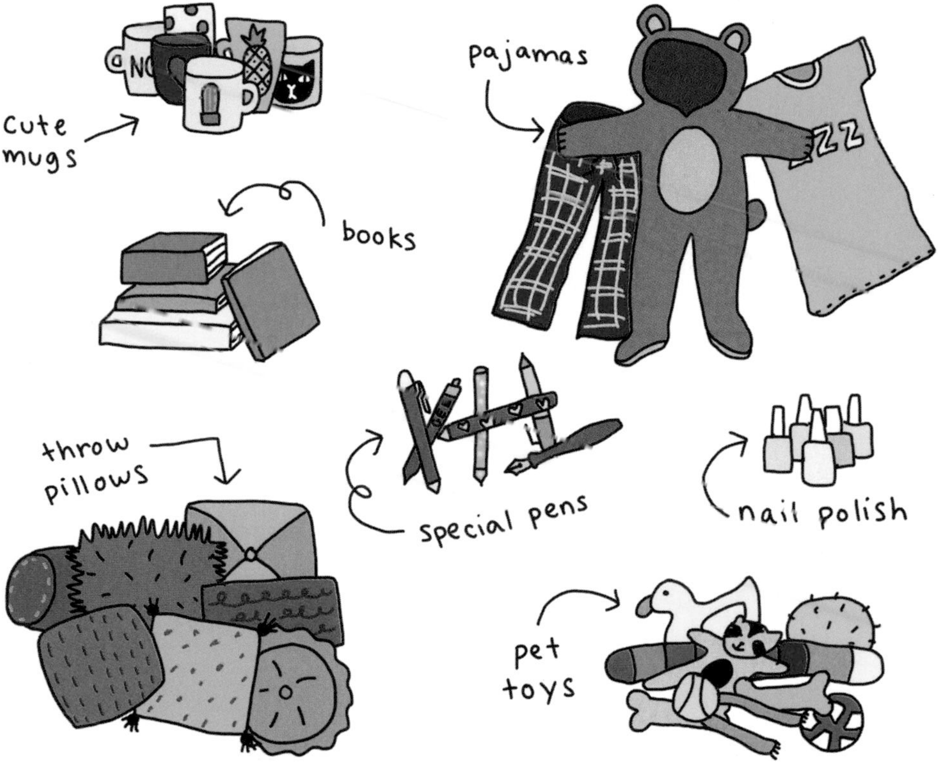
cute mugs
NO
pajamas
ZZZ
books
throw pillows
special pens
nail polish
pet toys

HOME

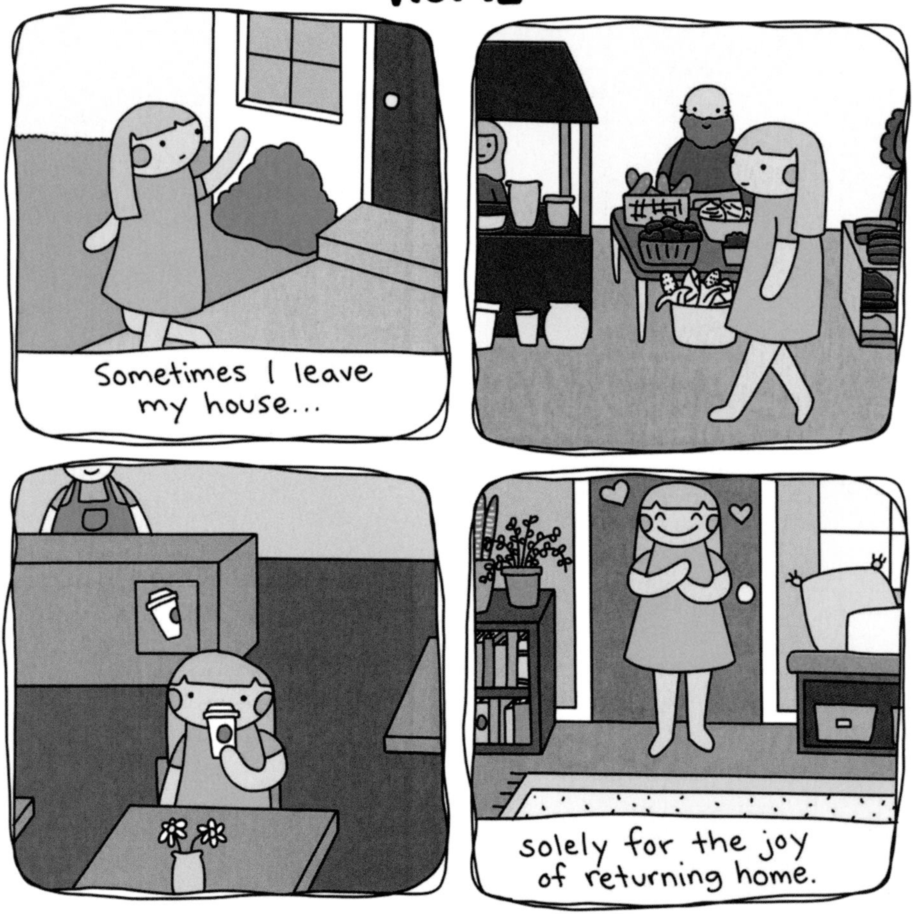
Sometimes I leave my house...
solely for the joy of returning home.

SMALL JOYS

Knowing there's leftover pizza in the fridge.

Laughing at an inside joke.

Binge-watching a new season on *Netflix*.

Falling in love with a book.

The fresh breeze through an open window.

Getting a card in the mail.

Watching my pet do something silly.

Putting on sweatpants.

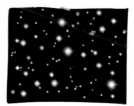

A starry night.

REASONS PEOPLE GO OUT ON WEEKENDS

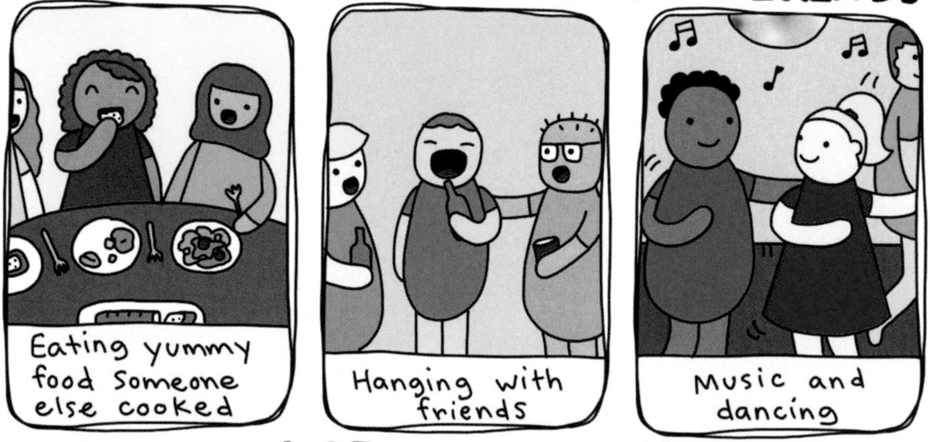
Eating yummy food someone else cooked
Hanging with friends
Music and dancing

REASONS I STAY IN ON WEEKENDS

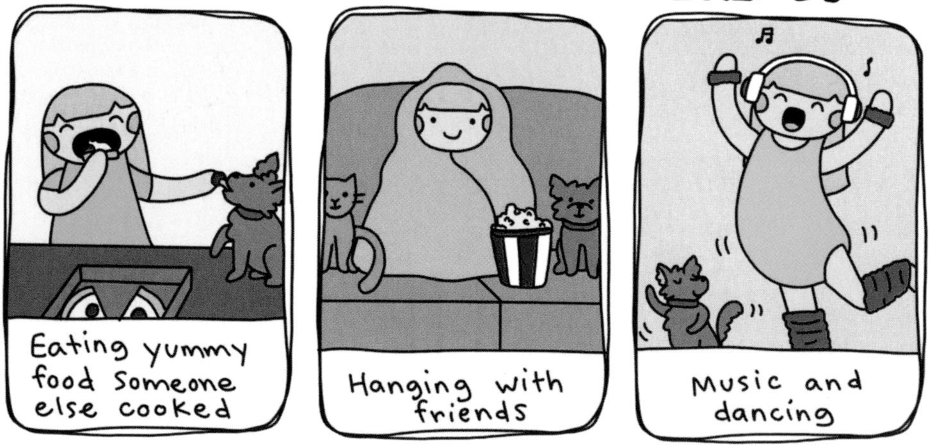
Eating yummy food someone else cooked
Hanging with friends
Music and dancing

THINGS THAT SPARK JOY

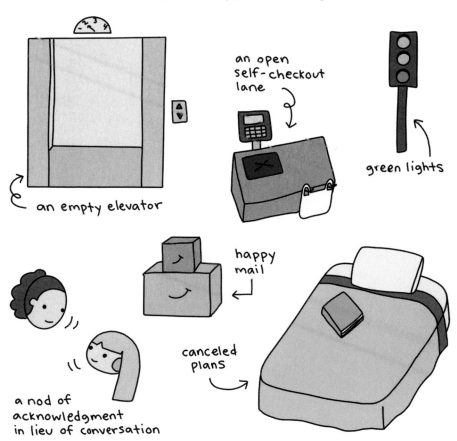

an empty elevator

an open self-checkout lane

green lights

happy mail

a nod of acknowledgment in lieu of conversation

canceled plans

MY PERFECT MORNING

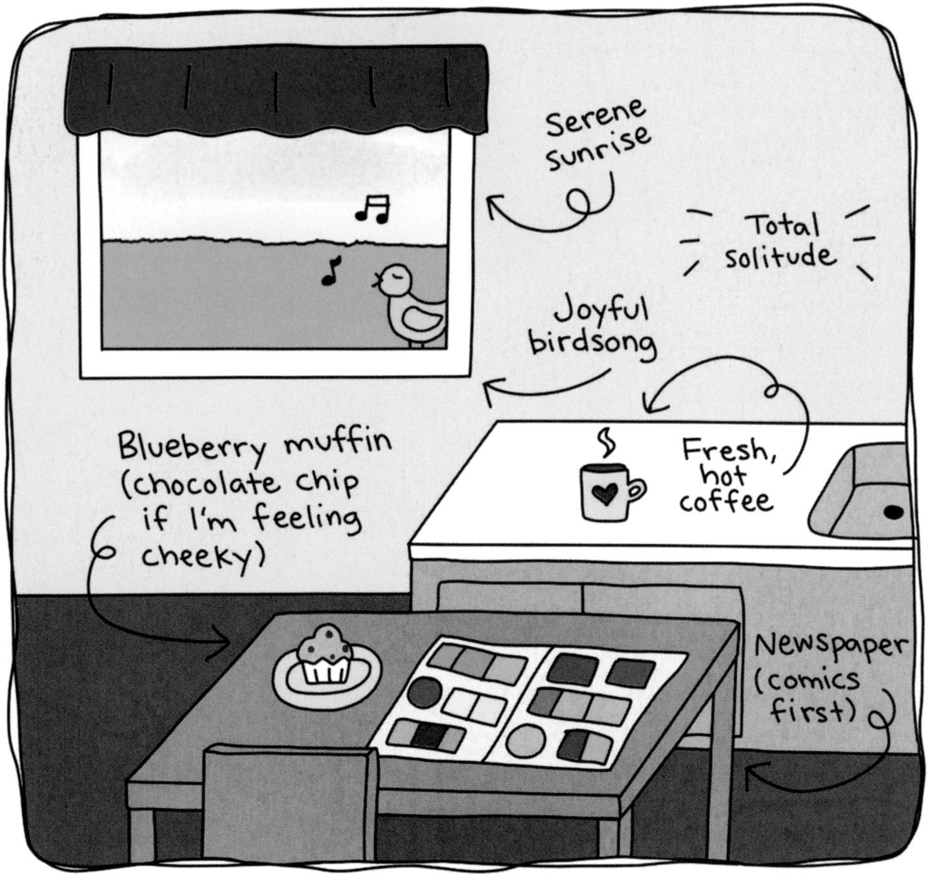
Serene sunrise
Total solitude
Joyful birdsong
Blueberry muffin (chocolate chip if I'm feeling cheeky)
Fresh, hot coffee
Newspaper (comics first)

WHY I LOVE THE NIGHT

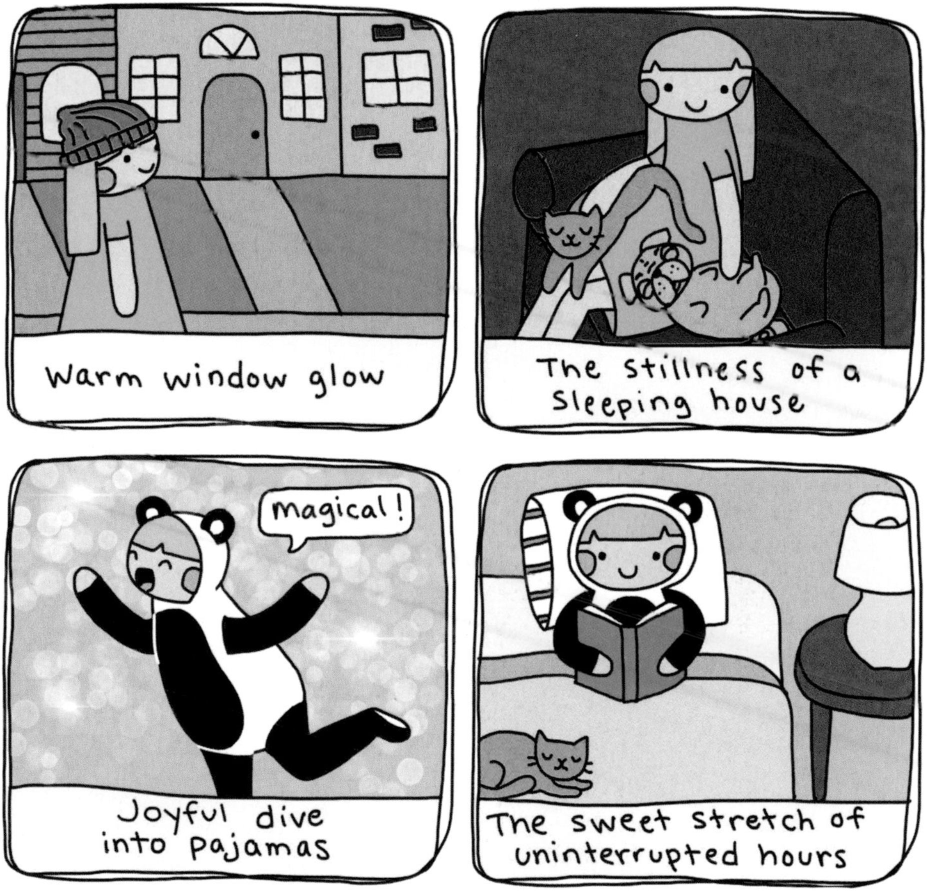
Warm window glow
The stillness of a sleeping house
magical!
Joyful dive into pajamas
The sweet stretch of uninterrupted hours

I love it when joy takes me by surprise...

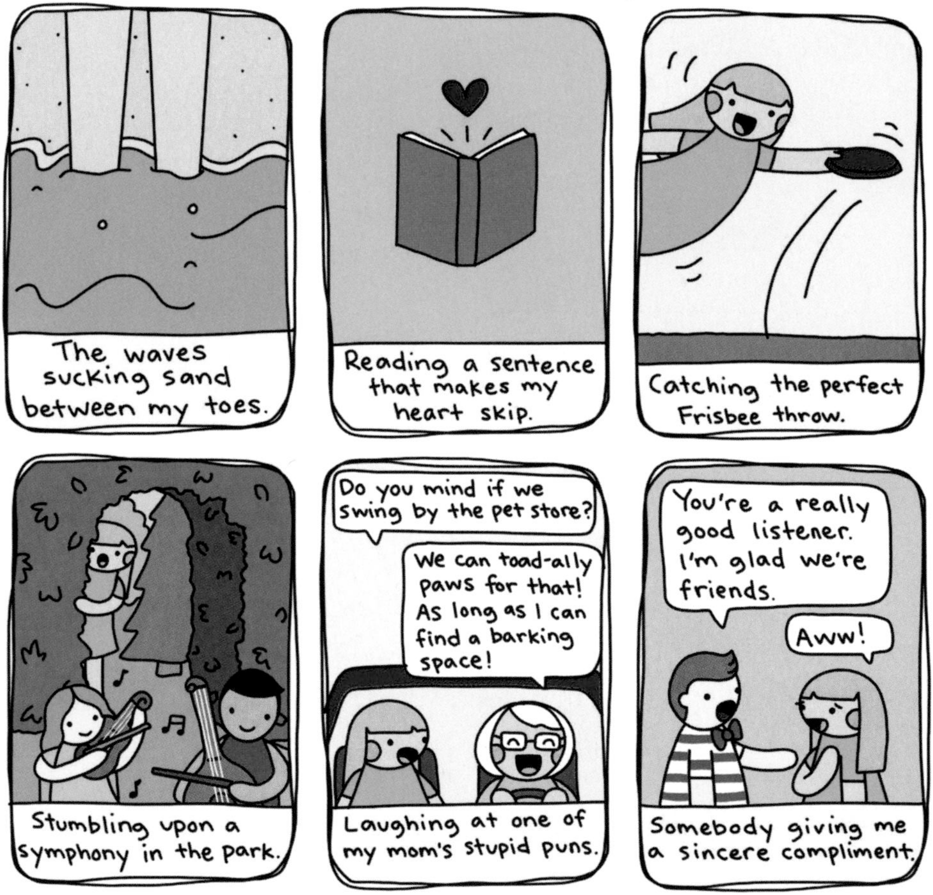
The waves sucking sand between my toes.
Reading a sentence that makes my heart skip.
Catching the perfect Frisbee throw.
Do you mind if we swing by the pet store?
We can toad-ally paws for that! As long as I can find a barking space!
You're a really good listener. I'm glad we're friends.
Aww!
Stumbling upon a symphony in the park.
Laughing at one of my mom's stupid puns.
Somebody giving me a sincere compliment.

CHAPTER 9

TODAY I'M FEELING:

SCARED

Fear is an evolutionary gift. It makes me wary and cautious, and that can keep me safe! When I feel scared, my body is alerting me to a perceived danger.

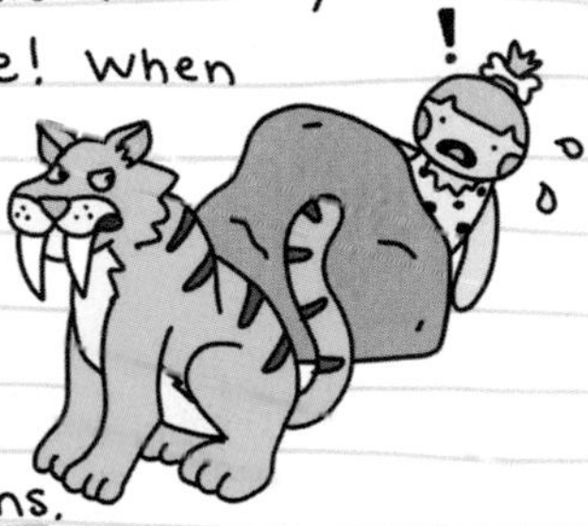

Of course, it's pretty unlikely that I'm going to get eaten. So I need to discern between dangerous scenarios and uncomfortable situations.

There are a lot of uncomfortable situations that make me nervous! Public speaking terrifies me. Travel induces feelings of panic. Introducing myself to a stranger is nerve-wracking! I often find myself wishing that I could be different. Braver.

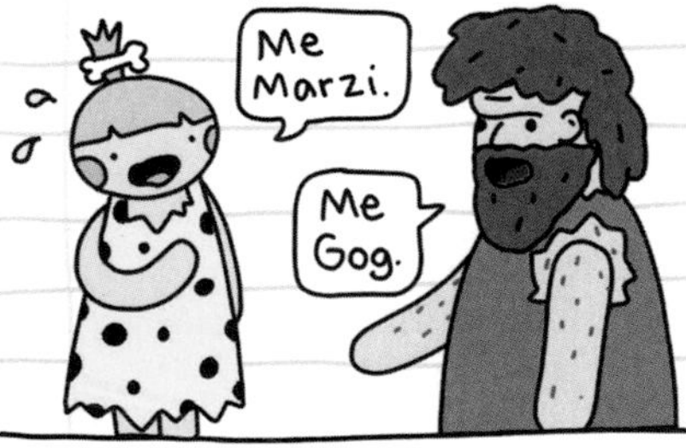
Me Marzi.
Me Gog.

But... if I still try, even though I'm afraid... isn't that incredibly brave? Isn't it courageous to keep going, in spite of being scared?

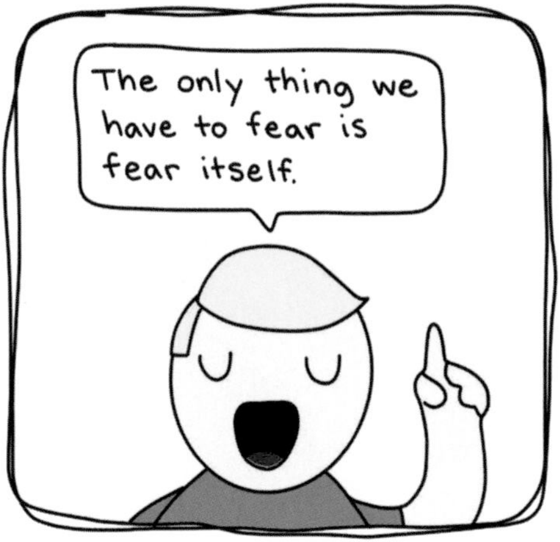
The only thing we have to fear is fear itself.

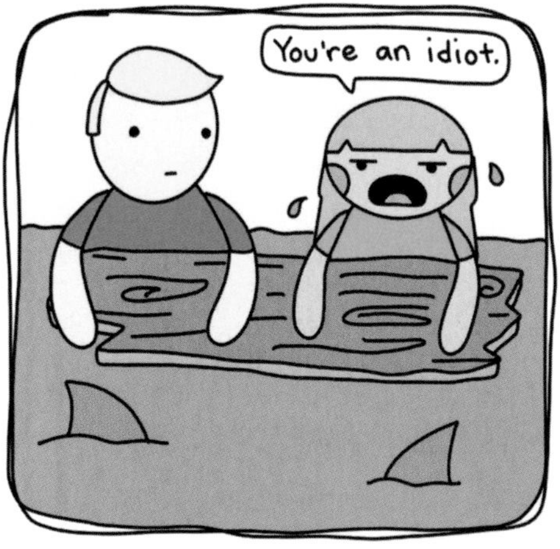
You're an idiot.

HOW SCARED ARE YOU?

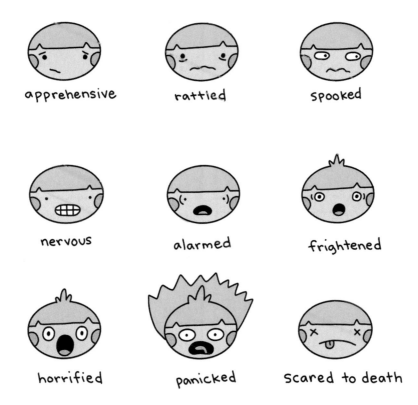

apprehensive

rattled

spooked

nervous

alarmed

frightened

horrified

panicked

scared to death

When I'm feeling nervous in a new location, it makes me feel better to scan the area for safe places.

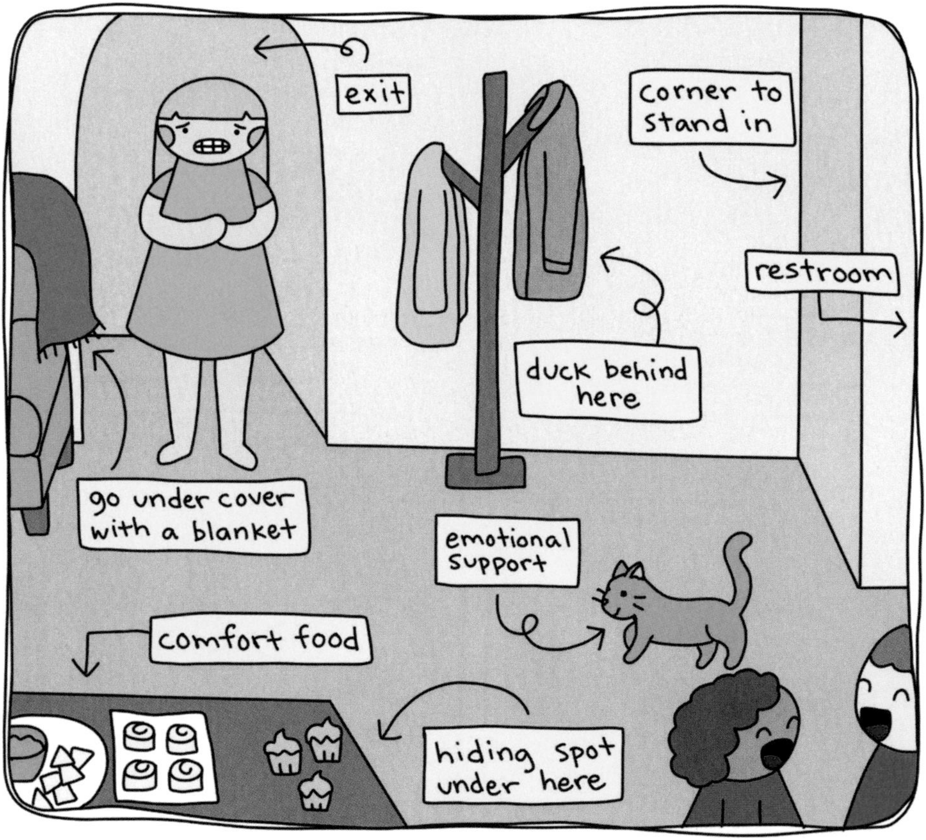
exit
corner to stand in
restroom
duck behind here
go under cover with a blanket
emotional support
comfort food
hiding spot under here

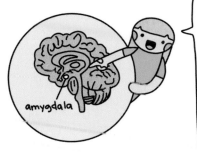

This is my amygdala. This cute little guy plays a big role in my response to fear, warning me of danger and preparing my body's fight-or-flight reaction. I'm glad my amygdala works so hard to keep me safe... but sometimes it can be a little overprotective.

Like, I appreciate your concern... but I'm gonna override this warning.

I think the odds of me being sucked into the escalator stairs are slim.

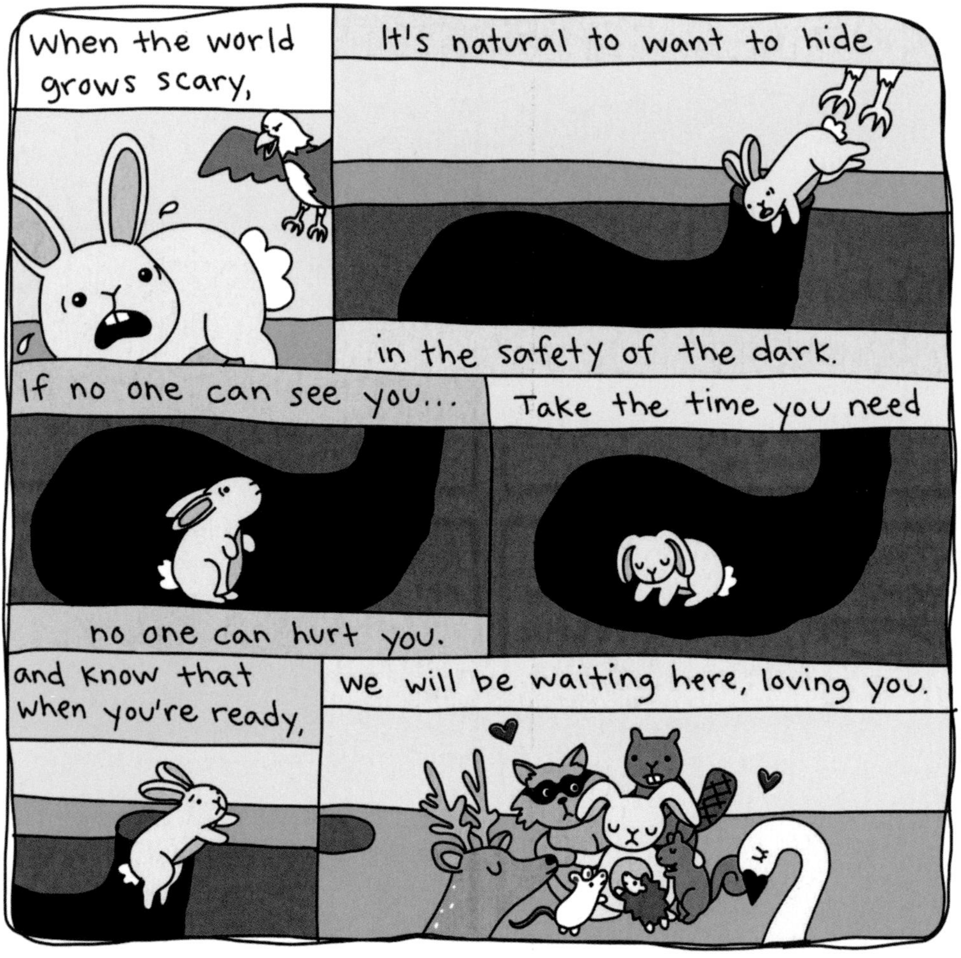
When the world grows scary,
It's natural to want to hide
in the safety of the dark.
If no one can see you...
no one can hurt you.
Take the time you need
and know that when you're ready,
we will be waiting here, loving you.

SMALL ACTS OF COURAGE

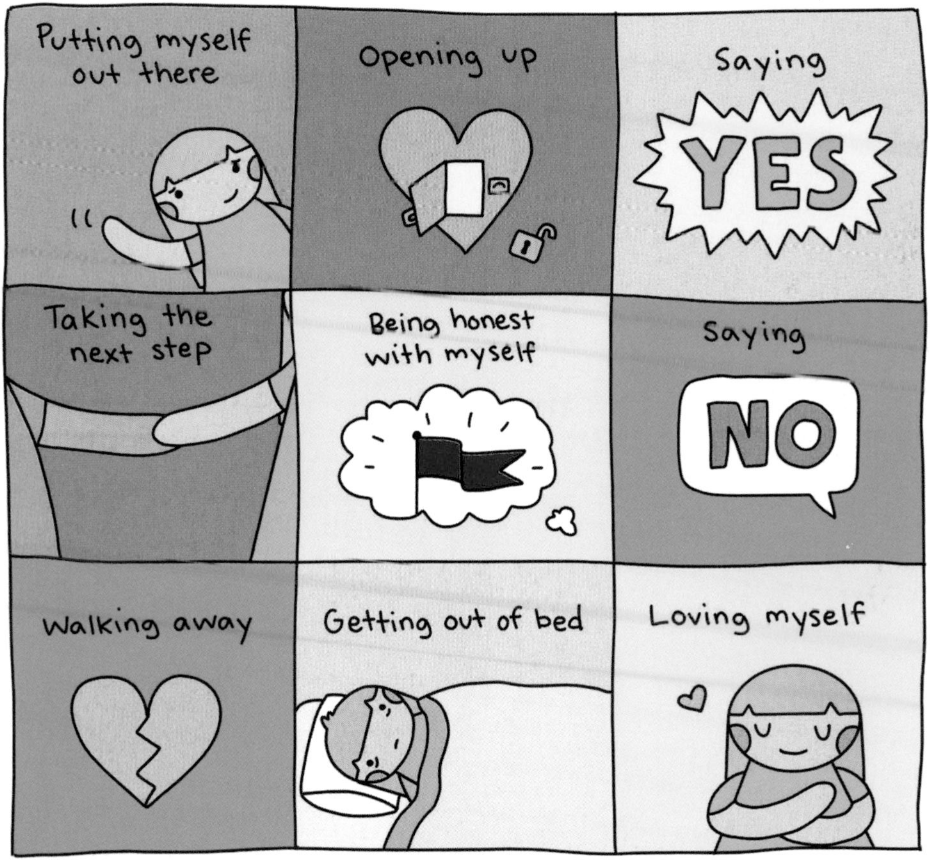
Putting myself out there
Opening up
Saying
YES
Taking the next step
Being honest with myself
Saying
NO
Walking away
Getting out of bed
Loving myself

WHAT IF?

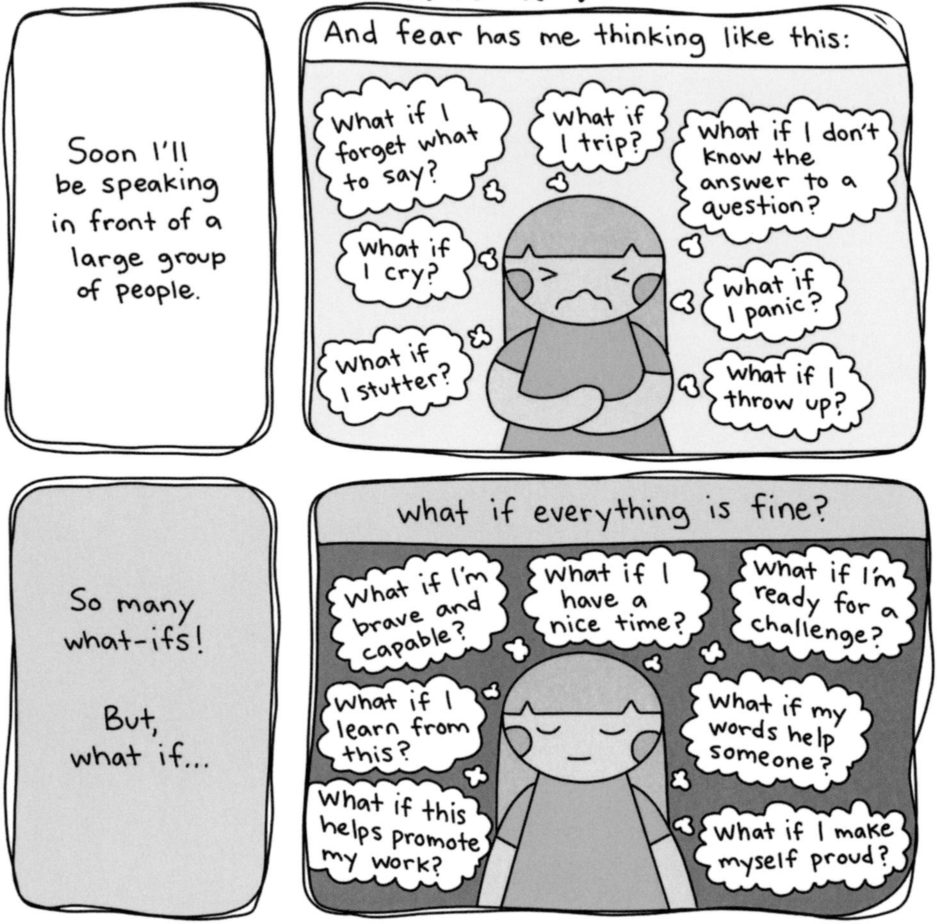
Soon I'll be speaking in front of a large group of people.
And fear has me thinking like this:
What if I forget what to say?
What if I trip?
What if I don't know the answer to a question?
What if I cry?
What if I panic?
What if I stutter?
What if I throw up?
So many what-ifs!
But, what if...
what if everything is fine?
What if I'm brave and capable?
What if I have a nice time?
What if I'm ready for a challenge?
What if I learn from this?
What if my words help someone?
What if this helps promote my work?
What if I make myself proud?

AWARDS FOR SCARY DAYS

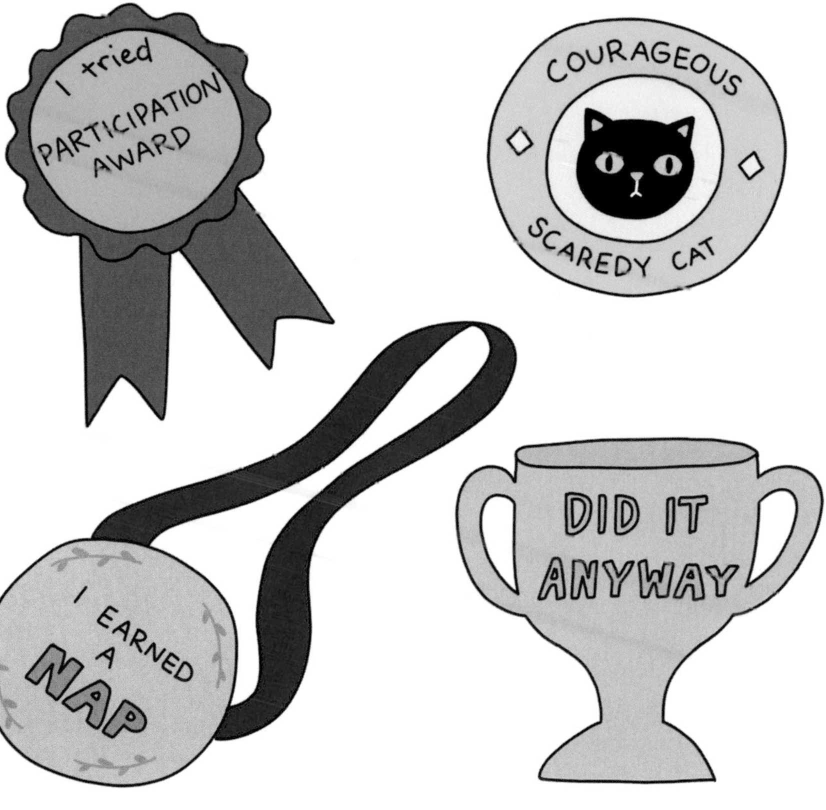
I tried
PARTICIPATION AWARD
COURAGEOUS
SCAREDY CAT
I EARNED A NAP
DID IT ANYWAY

FIRST IMPRESSION

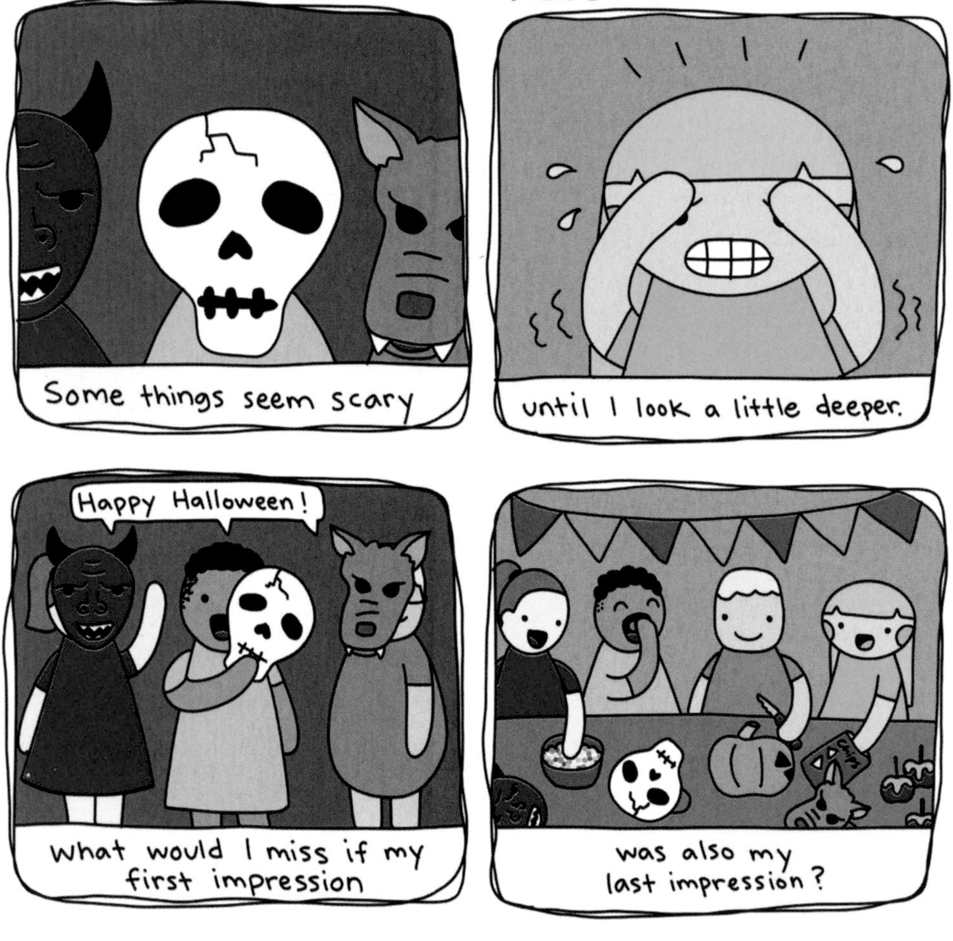
Some things seem scary
until I look a little deeper.
Happy Halloween!
What would I miss if my first impression
was also my last impression?
Chips

GUIDE TO TRYING SOMETHING NEW

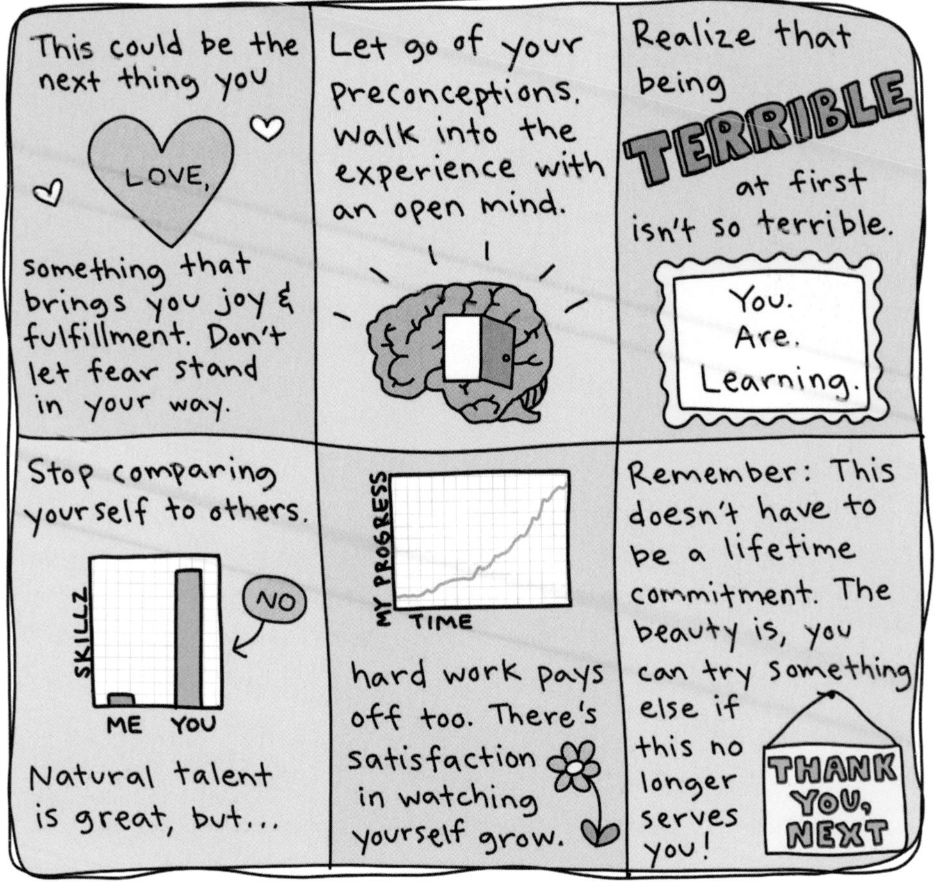
This could be the next thing you
LOVE,
something that brings you joy & fulfillment. Don't let fear stand in your way.
Let go of your preconceptions. Walk into the experience with an open mind.
Realize that being
TERRIBLE
at first isn't so terrible.
You. Are. Learning.
Stop comparing yourself to others.
SKILLZ
ME
YOU
NO
Natural talent is great, but...
MY PROGRESS
TIME
hard work pays off too. There's satisfaction in watching yourself grow.
Remember: This doesn't have to be a lifetime commitment. The beauty is, you can try something else if this no longer serves you!
THANK YOU, NEXT

CHAPTER 10

TODAY I'M FEELING:

EMPATHY

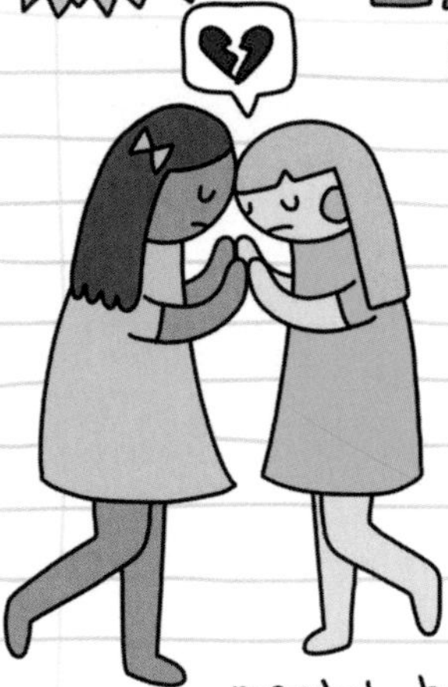

Empathy is a unique emotion because it entails understanding and feeling the emotions of another person. The ability to connect with, and feel compassion for, someone else is a beautiful gift. It can inspire selfless behavior and forge strong relationships.

When I see someone hurting, I desperately want to help. I get a lot of messages from folks facing serious mental health issues. My heart breaks every time I read one. I don't know how to help, so I carry their pain with me. My desire to save the world, one person at a time, leaves me vulnerable.

I decided to be proactive and take courses in mental health first aid and suicide prevention training. I was taught how to listen, what to say, and how to connect people with professional help and resources.

Most importantly, I learned:

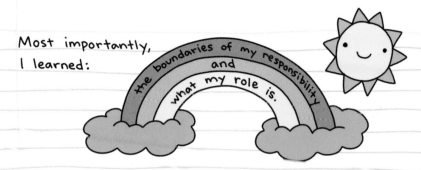

the boundaries of my responsibility and what my role is.

I can be compassionate, but I should ~~not~~—I must not—take personal ownership of everyone else's pain.

For my empathy to be beneficial, it needs to be properly channeled. That means giving—of my time, resources, and emotional support—in a sustainable way. I've found that there's great strength in distributing the weight of the burden more evenly. For example, when I created an online fundraiser for refugees, followers donated $4,000 in four days! That was an amazing display of empathy involving more than 100 people! I don't have to do it all on my own.

me alone

us together

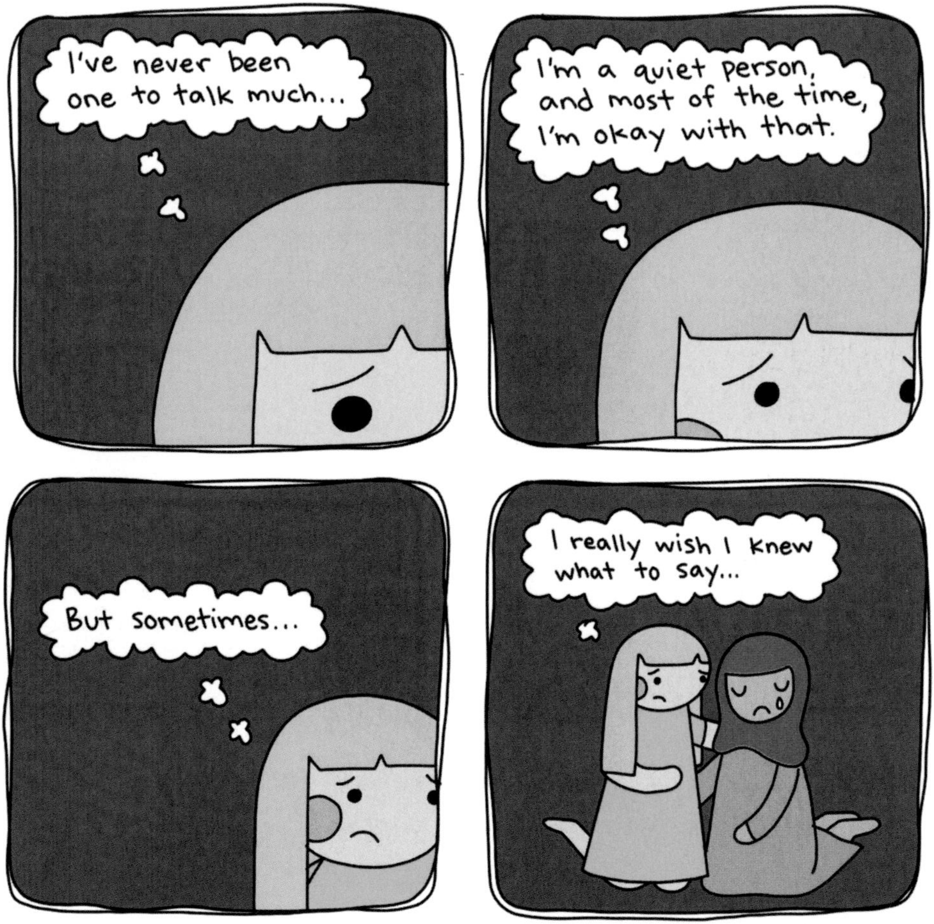
I've never been one to talk much...
I'm a quiet person, and most of the time, I'm okay with that.
But sometimes...
I really wish I knew what to say...

IS MY HEART IN THE RIGHT PLACE?

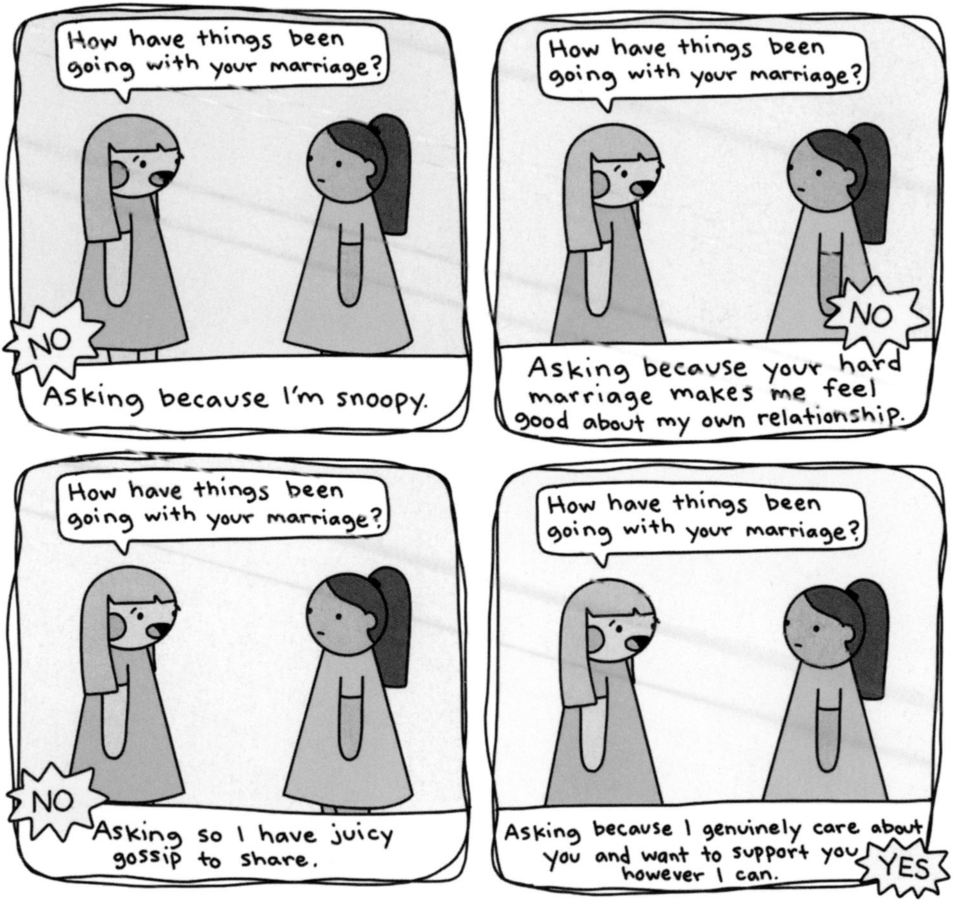

How have things been going with your marriage?
NO
Asking because I'm snoopy.
How have things been going with your marriage?
NO
Asking because your hard marriage makes me feel good about my own relationship.
How have things been going with your marriage?
NO
Asking so I have juicy gossip to share.
How have things been going with your marriage?
Asking because I genuinely care about you and want to support you however I can.
YES

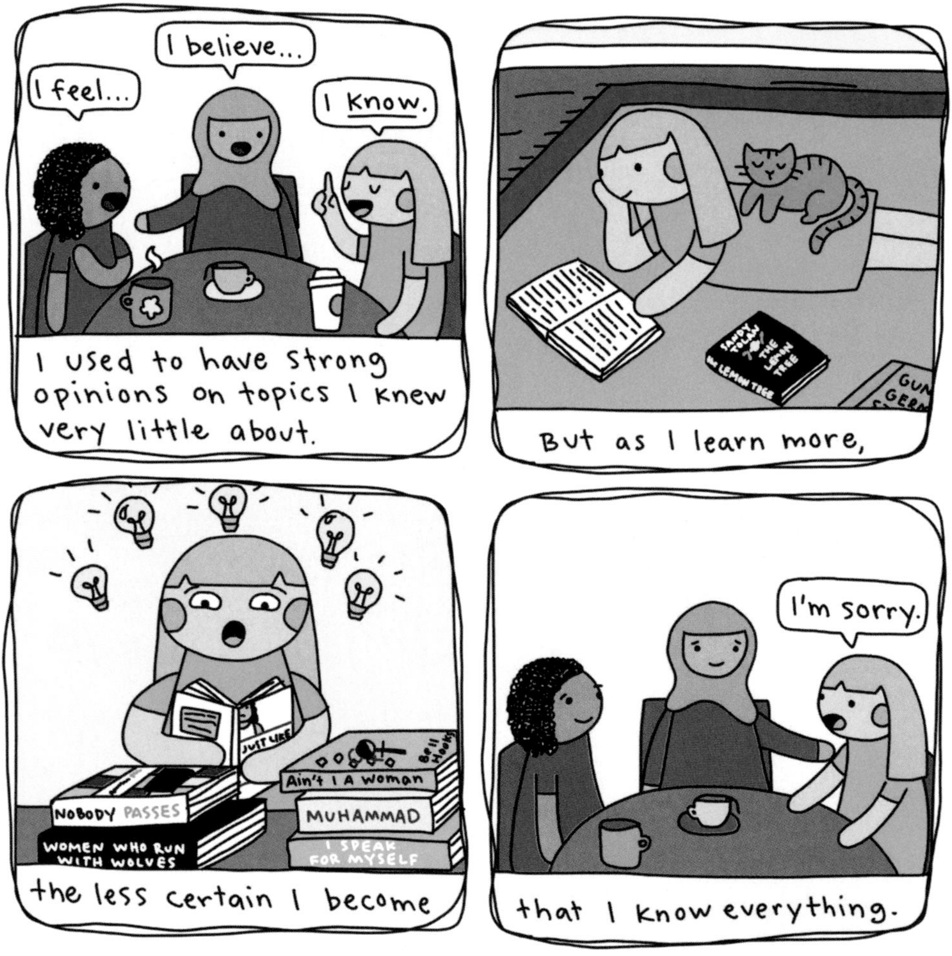
I feel...
I believe...
I know.
I used to have strong opinions on topics I knew very little about.
SANDY TOLAN
THE LEMON TREE
THE LEMON TREE
But as I learn more,
JUST LIKE
NOBODY PASSES
WOMEN WHO RUN WITH WOLVES
Bell Hooks
Ain't I A woman
MUHAMMAD
I SPEAK FOR MYSELF
the less certain I become
I'm sorry.
that I know everything.

DON'T GET BURNED

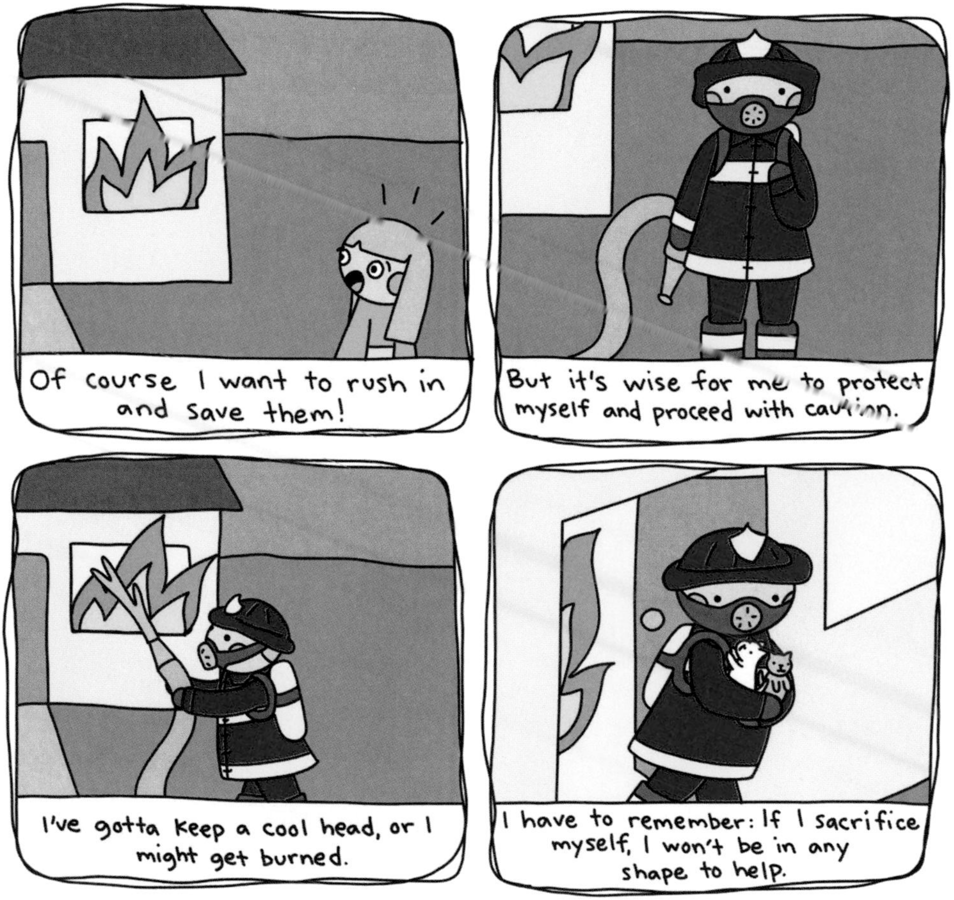
Of course I want to rush in and save them!
But it's wise for me to protect myself and proceed with caution.
I've gotta keep a cool head, or I might get burned.
I have to remember: If I sacrifice myself, I won't be in any shape to help.

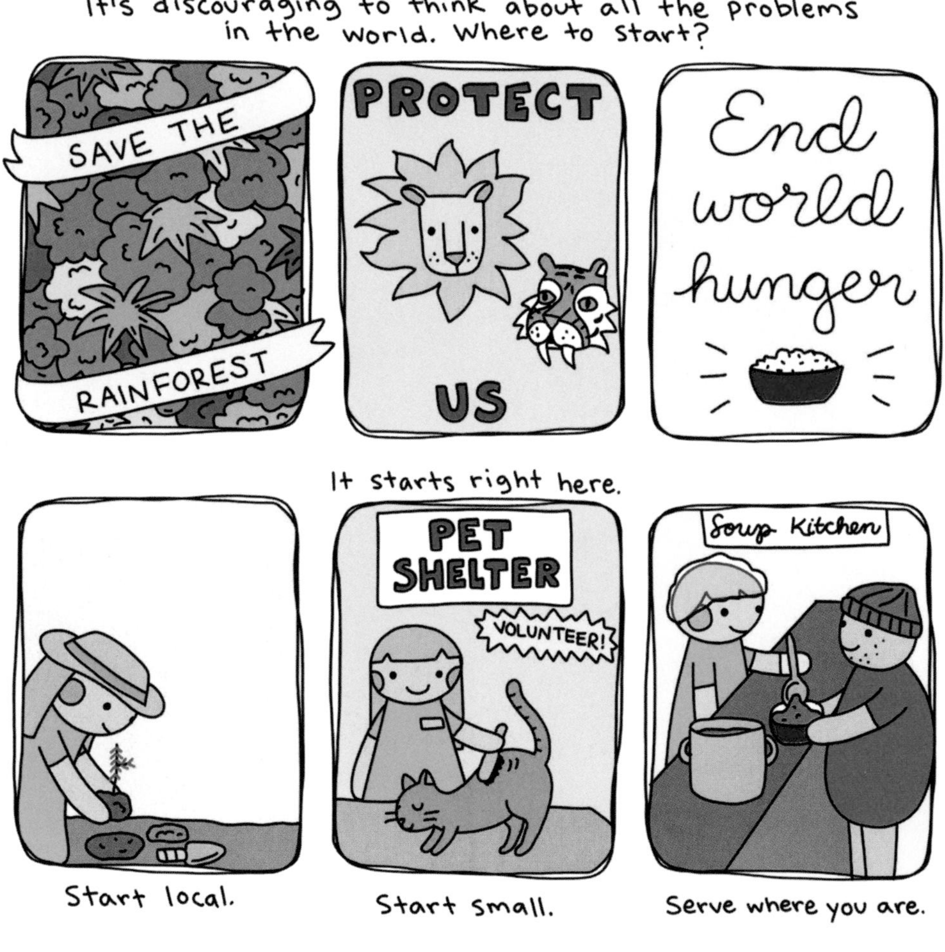
It's discouraging to think about all the problems in the world. Where to start?
SAVE THE
RAINFOREST
PROTECT
US
End world hunger
It starts right here.
PET SHELTER
VOLUNTEER!
Soup Kitchen
Start local.
Start small.
Serve where you are.

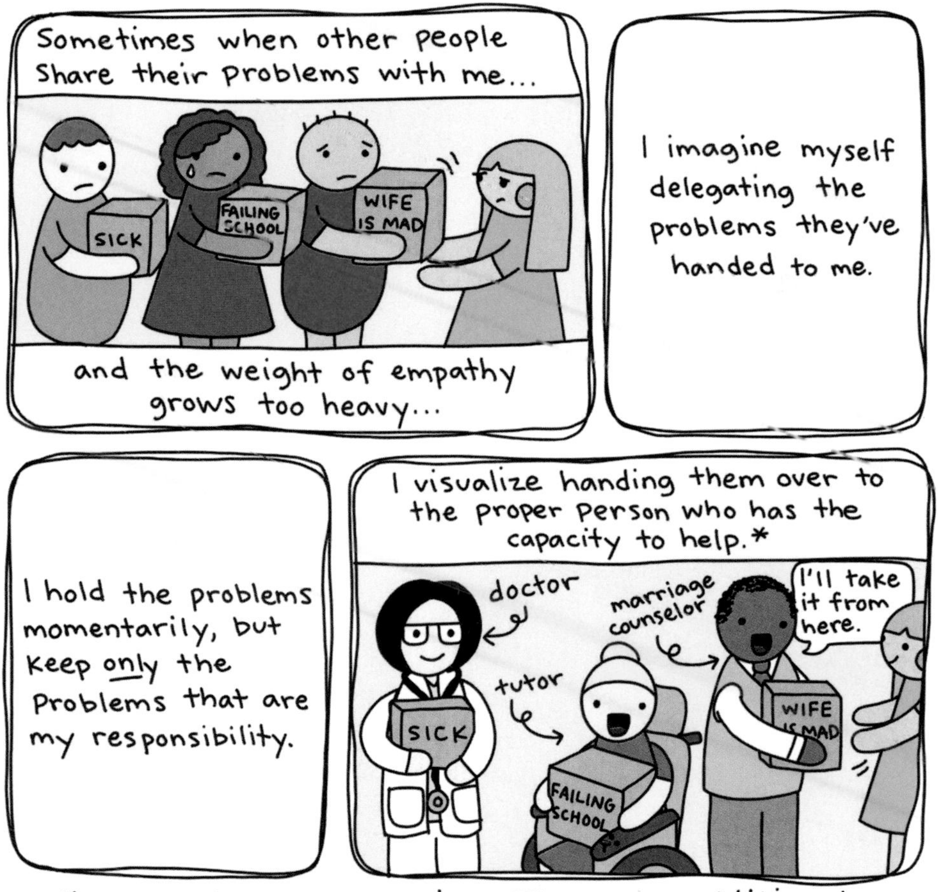
Sometimes when other people share their problems with me...
SICK
FAILING SCHOOL
WIFE IS MAD
and the weight of empathy grows too heavy...
I imagine myself delegating the problems they've handed to me.
I hold the problems momentarily, but keep only the problems that are my responsibility.
I visualize handing them over to the proper person who has the capacity to help.*
doctor
tutor
marriage counselor
I'll take it from here.
SICK
FAILING SCHOOL
WIFE IS MAD

*Caring doesn't = carrying. There are additional sources of support.

WHAT MY DOG HAS TAUGHT ME ABOUT EMPATHY

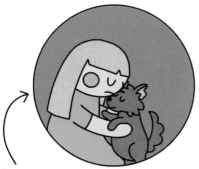

Don't worry if you can't speak what's in your heart. Your presence is more important than words can say.

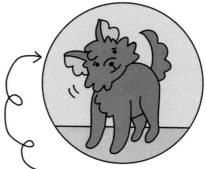

You don't need to offer advice or fix the problem. Just listen.

BLAH BLAH BLA
BLAH KIKO BLA
BLAH BLAH BLAH BLA
STAY BLAH

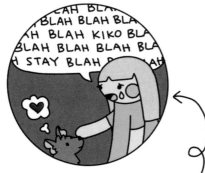

It's okay if you don't fully understand what they're going through. You can still offer support.

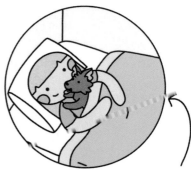

Sometimes a good cuddle can do wonders. (Face licks are optional.)

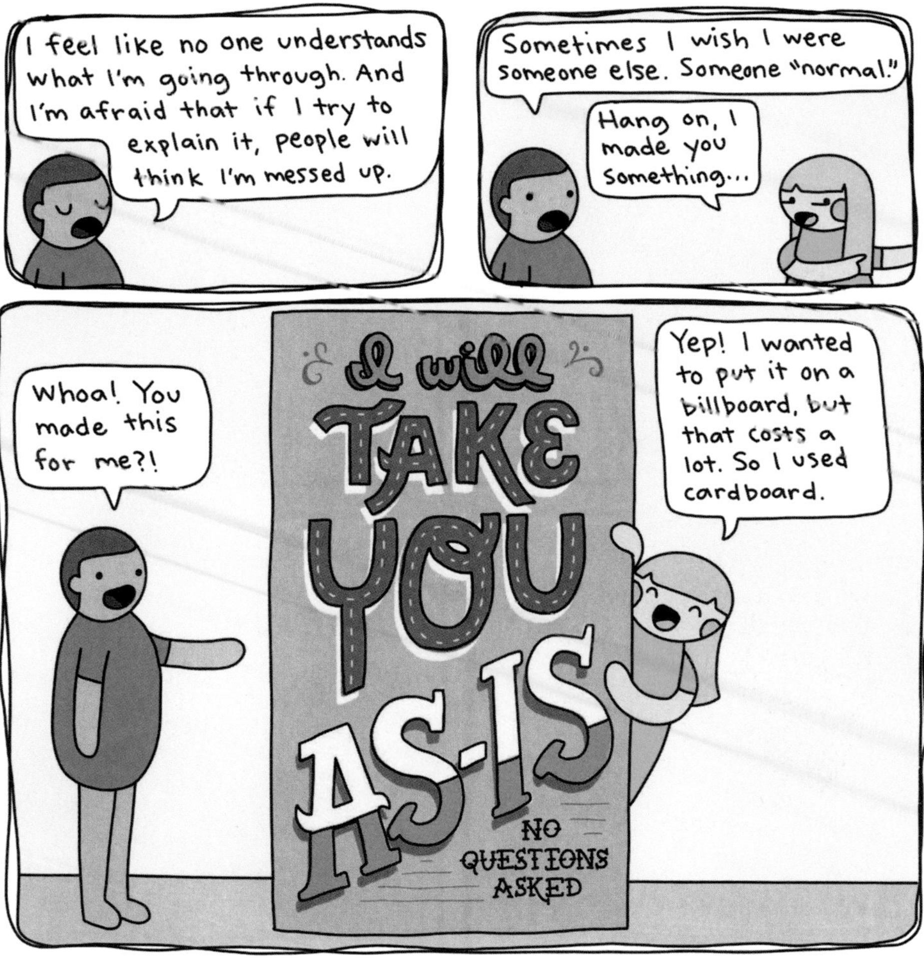
I feel like no one understands what I'm going through. And I'm afraid that if I try to explain it, people will think I'm messed up.
Sometimes I wish I were someone else. Someone "normal."
Hang on, I made you something...
Whoa! You made this for me?!
I will TAKE YOU AS-IS
NO QUESTIONS ASKED
Yep! I wanted to put it on a billboard, but that costs a lot. So I used cardboard.

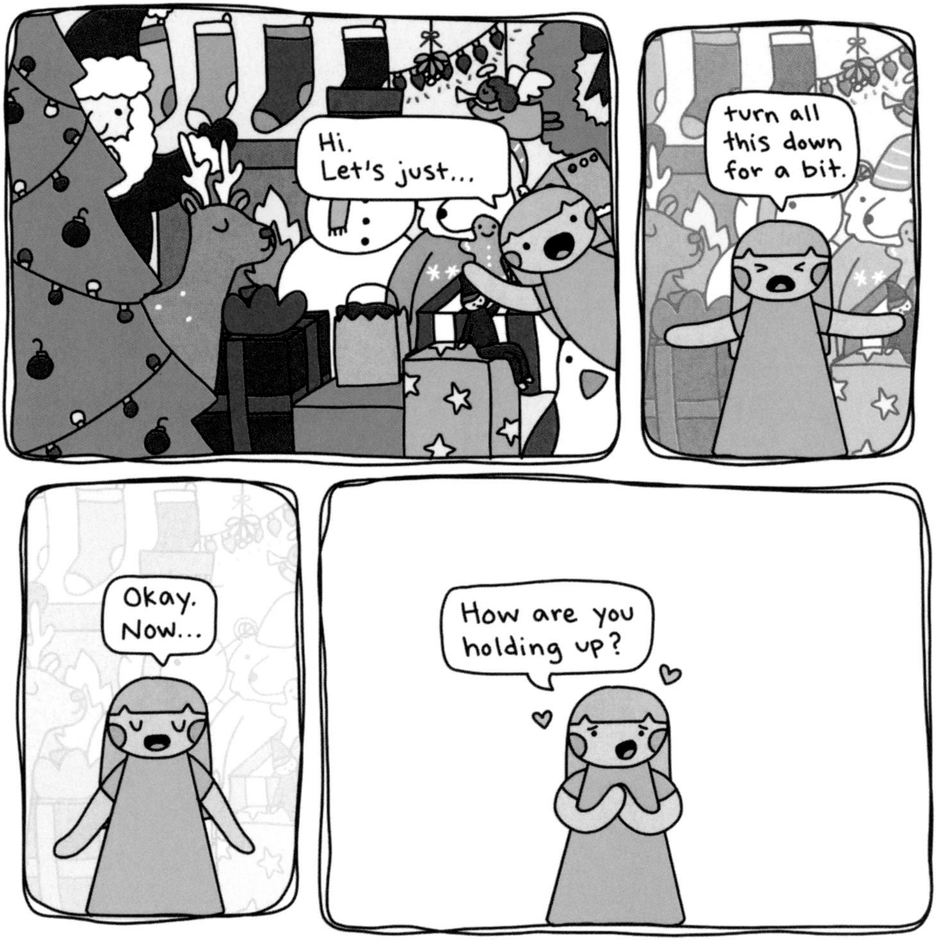
Hi.
Let's just...
turn all this down for a bit.
Okay. Now...
How are you holding up?

HEAL

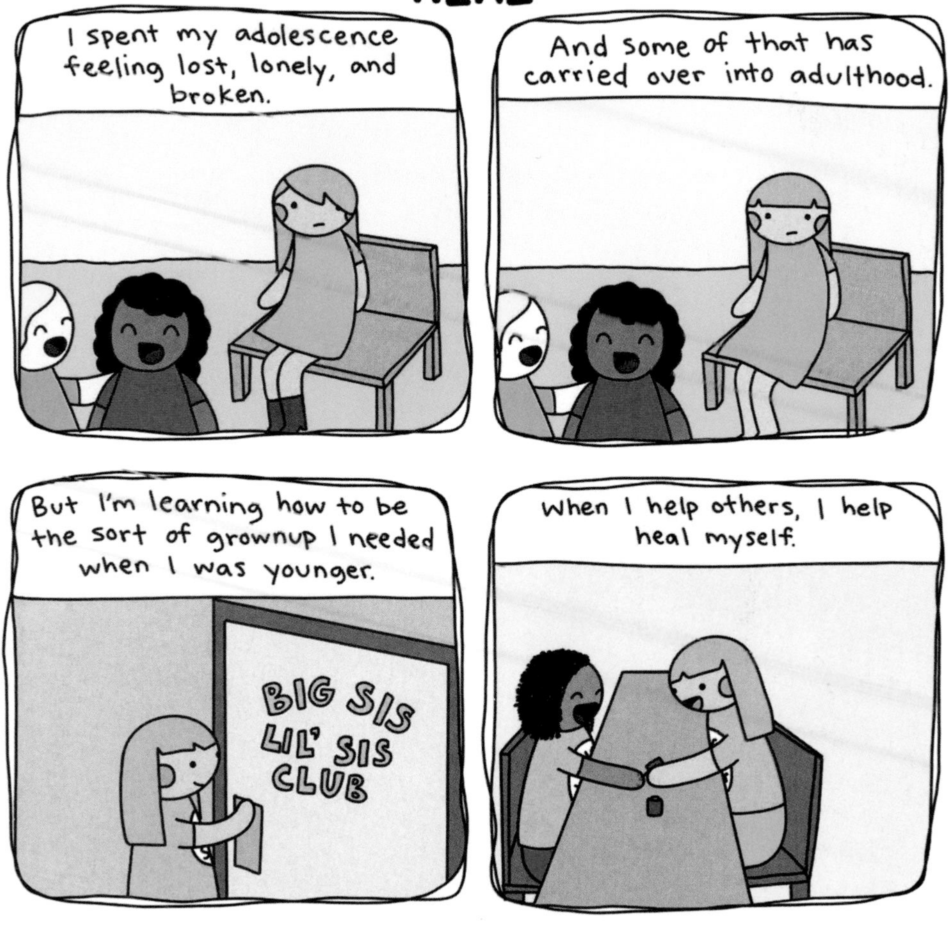
I spent my adolescence feeling lost, lonely, and broken.
And some of that has carried over into adulthood.
But I'm learning how to be the sort of grownup I needed when I was younger.
BIG SIS LIL' SIS CLUB
When I help others, I help heal myself.

CHAPTER 11

TODAY I'M FEELING: ANGRY

I was raised to believe that anger is a terrible emotion that needs immediate correction. Luckily, anger wasn't a feeling I experienced often.

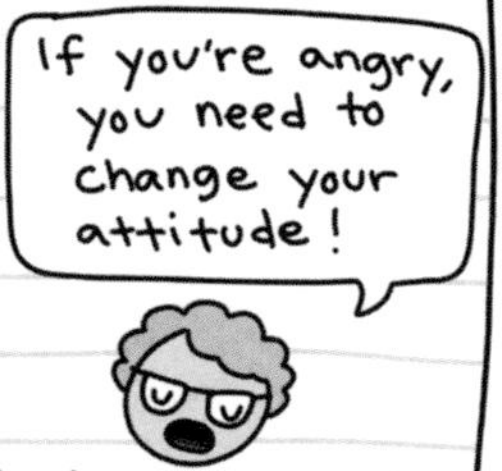
If you're angry, you need to change your attitude!

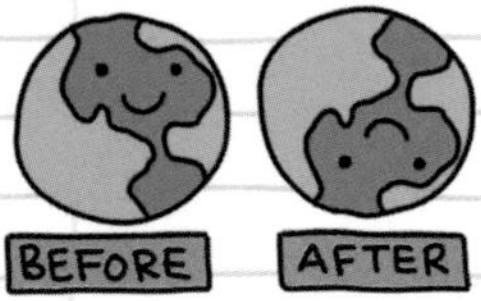
BEFORE
AFTER

At least it used to be that way, until I faced a life transition that turned my world upside down. At that stage, anger became a constant, unwanted companion. So I begged my therapist to show me how to get rid of it.

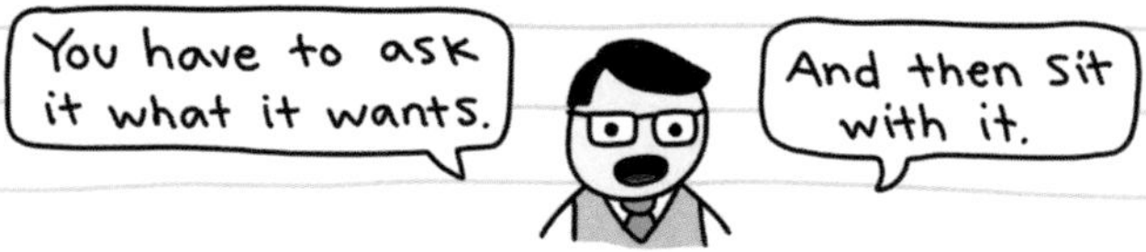
You have to ask it what it wants.
And then sit with it.

What a strange and uncomfortable concept: To acknowledge my anger, to give it a voice, to allow myself to feel it fully... that wasn't something I'd ever dared to do.

I had to figure out how to listen to my anger, to learn what it was trying to teach me. It told me:

1. I had been treated poorly.
2. My boundaries were violated.
3. I was taken advantage of.
4. NONE OF THAT WAS OKAY.

My anger taught me that I needed to stand up for myself and disengage from a negative situation. When I could finally acknowledge the anger and its source, it gradually began to lessen.

Of course, I still feel angry sometimes. But now I realize that anger is not simply a flaw to be fixed; it is a waving red flag. It's a sign that

boundaries were crossed and something needs to be addressed...

123

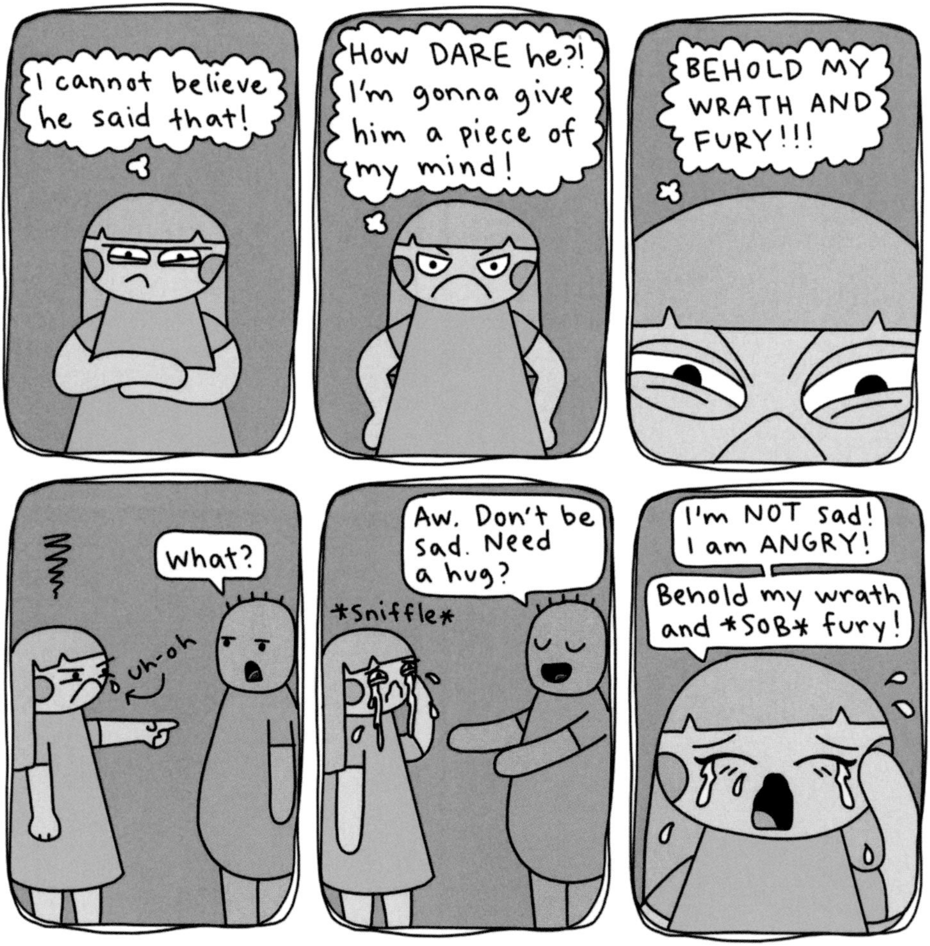
I cannot believe he said that!
HOW DARE he?! I'm gonna give him a piece of my mind!
BEHOLD MY WRATH AND FURY!!!
What?
uh-oh
Sniffle
Aw. Don't be sad. Need a hug?
I'm NOT sad! I am ANGRY!
Behold my wrath and *SOB* fury!

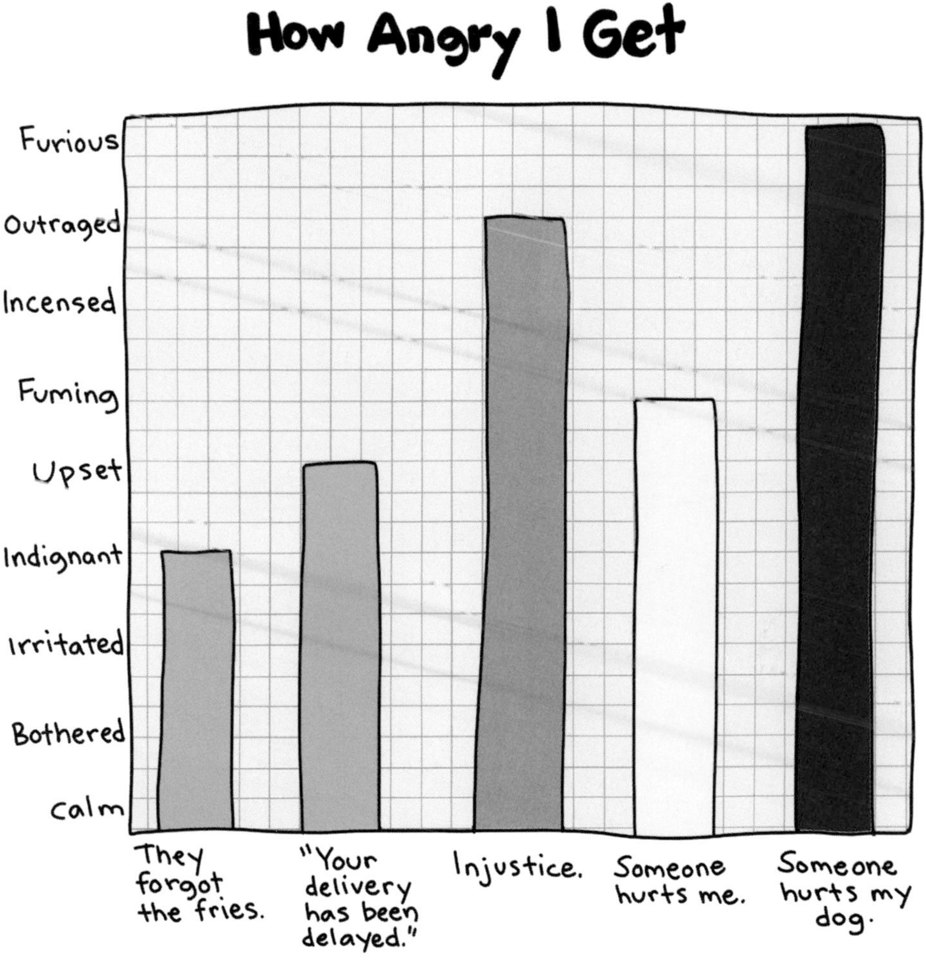
How Angry I Get
Furious
Outraged
Incensed
Fuming
Upset
Indignant
Irritated
Bothered
Calm
They forgot the fries.
"Your delivery has been delayed."
Injustice.
Someone hurts me.
Someone hurts my dog.

BEING MYSELF

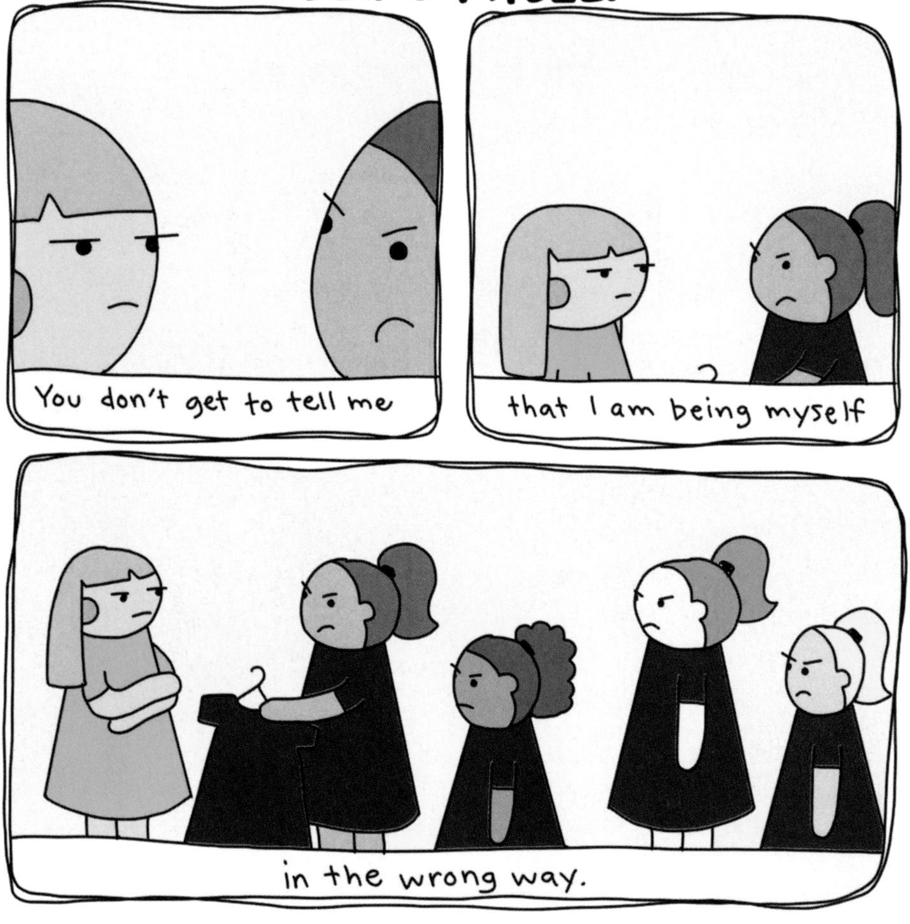
You don't get to tell me
that I am being myself
in the wrong way.

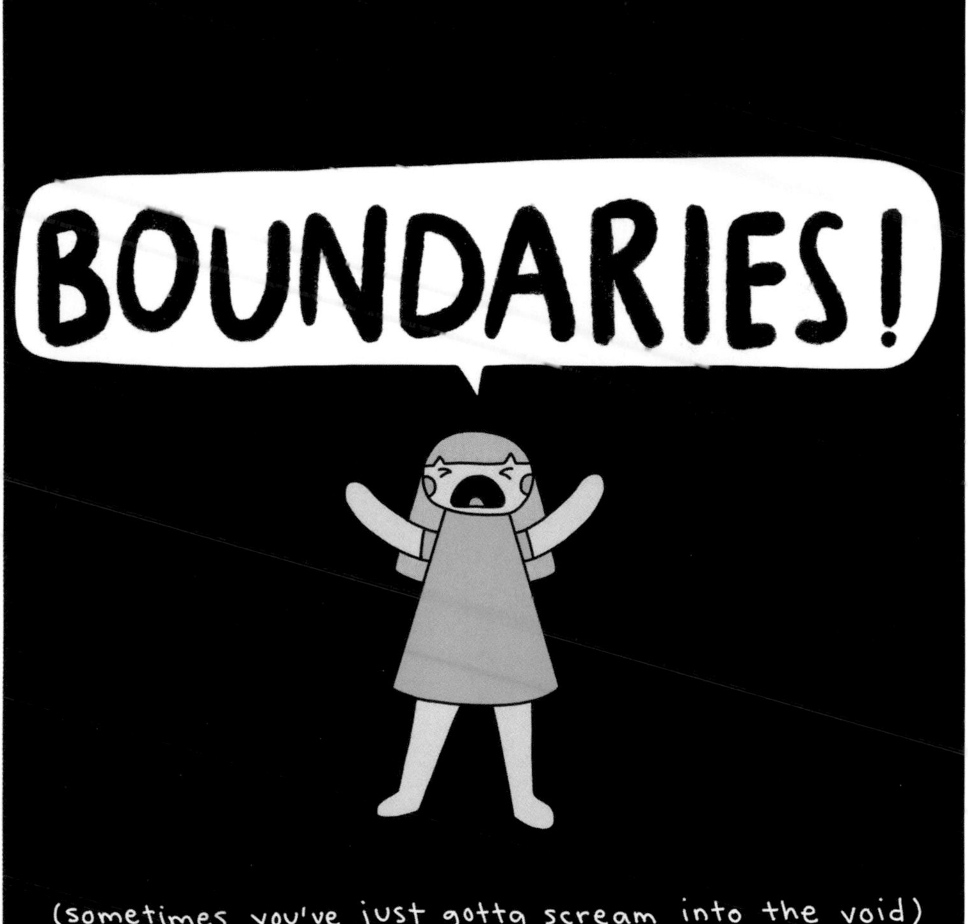
BOUNDARIES!
(sometimes you've just gotta scream into the void)

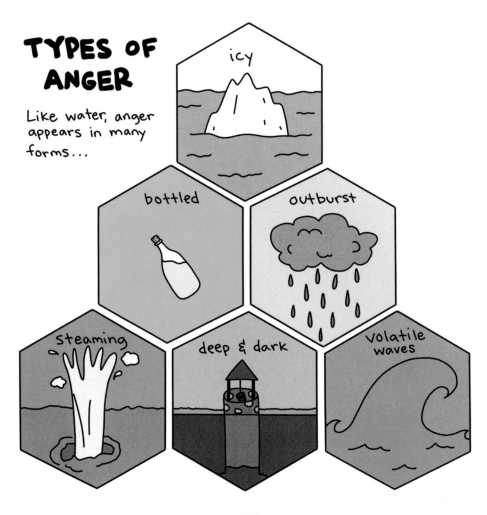

TYPES OF ANGER

Like water, anger appears in many forms...

icy

bottled

outburst

Steaming

deep & dark

Volatile waves

WAYS TO VENT MY ANGER

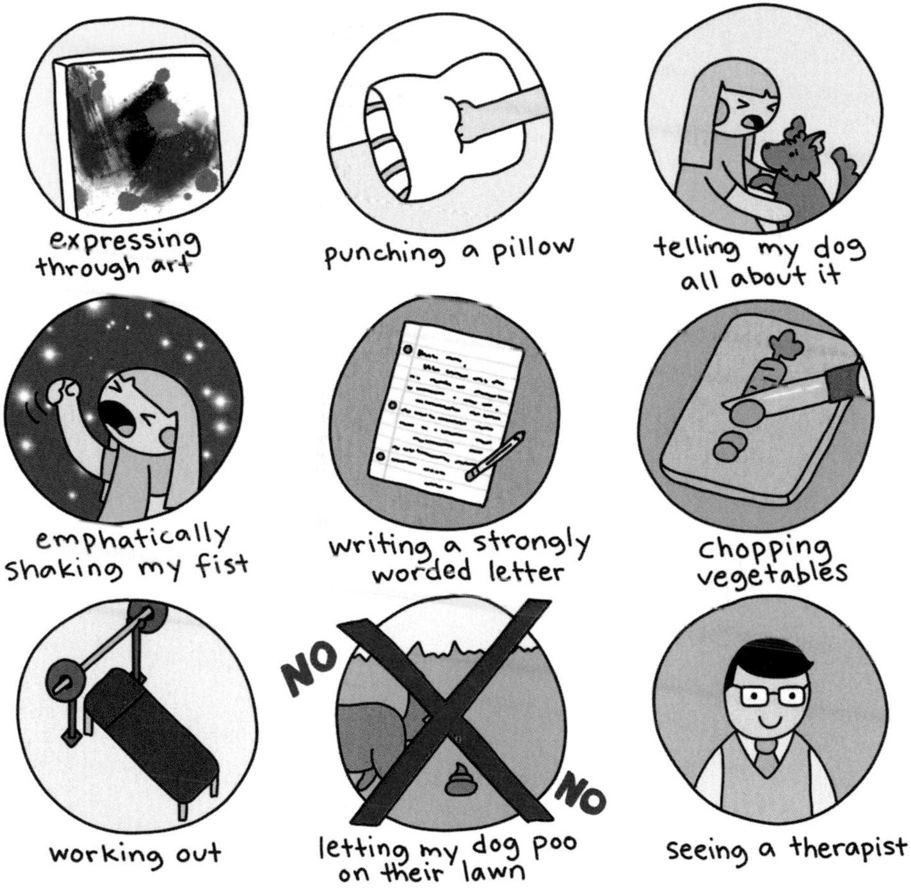
expressing through art
punching a pillow
telling my dog all about it
emphatically shaking my fist
writing a strongly worded letter
chopping vegetables
working out
NO
NO
letting my dog poo on their lawn
seeing a therapist

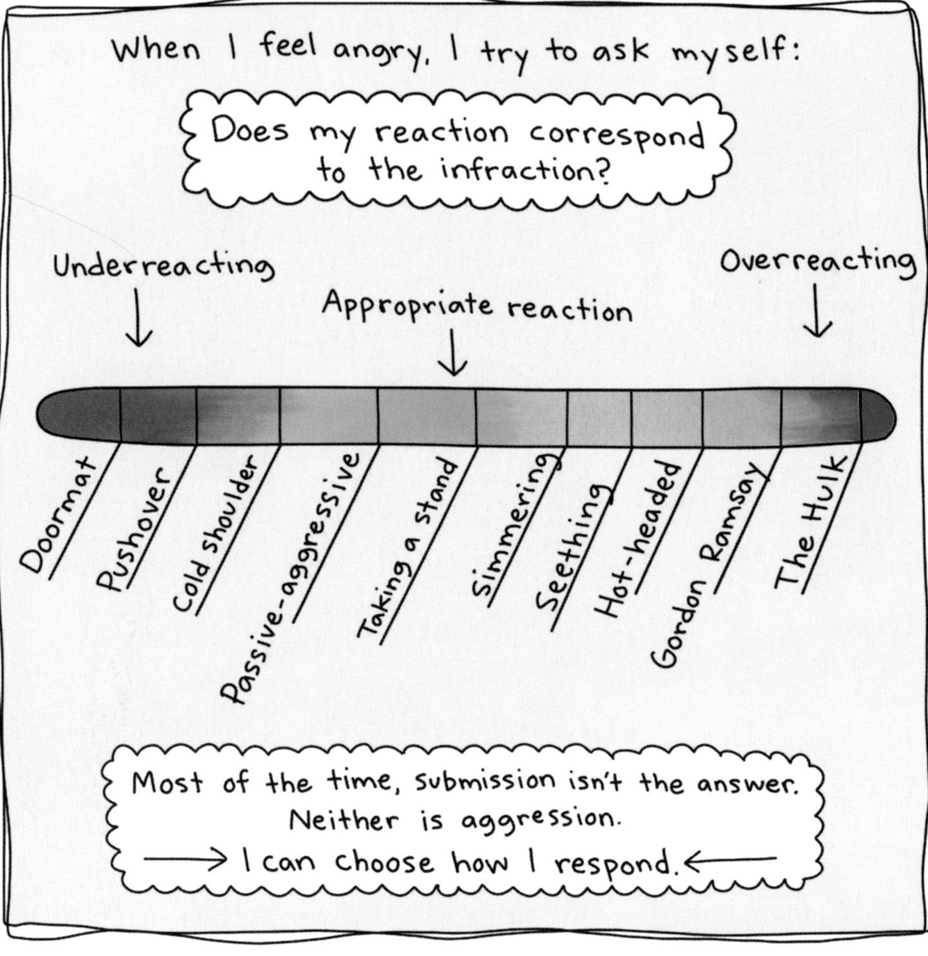
When I feel angry, I try to ask myself:
Does my reaction correspond to the infraction?
Underreacting
Appropriate reaction
Overreacting
Doormat
Pushover
Cold shoulder
Passive-aggressive
Taking a stand
Simmering
Seething
Hot-headed
Gordon Ramsay
The Hulk
Most of the time, submission isn't the answer.
Neither is aggression.
→ I can choose how I respond. ←

UNPACK

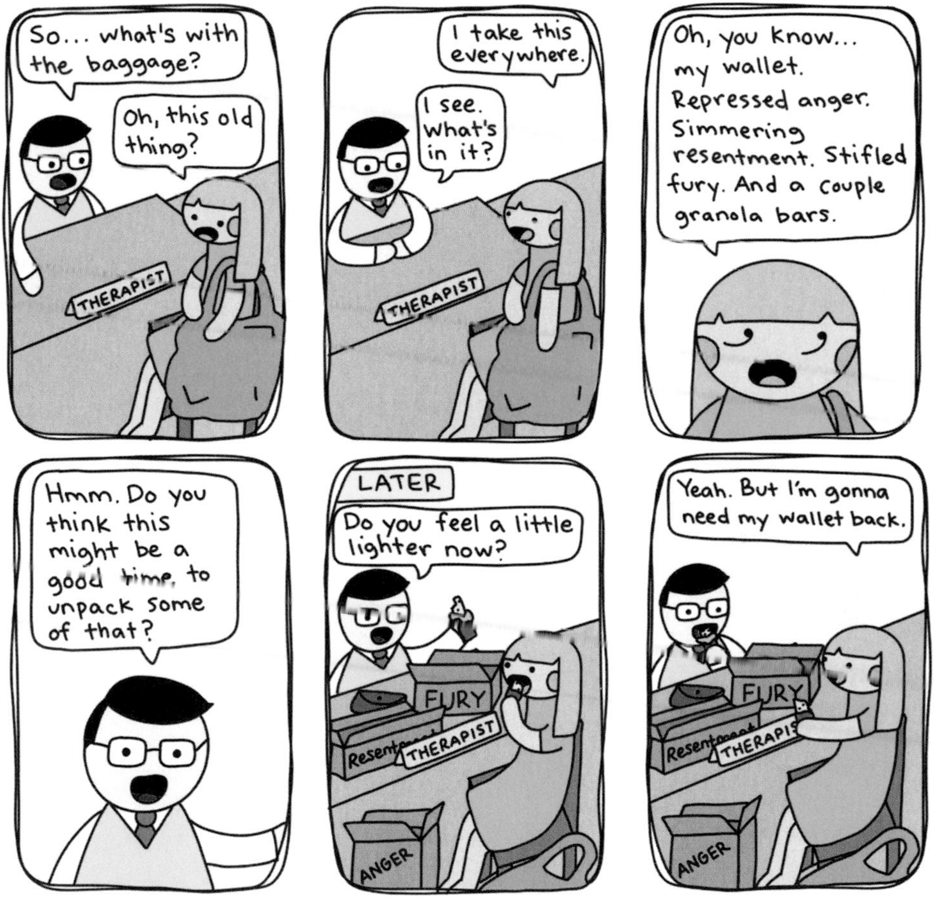

So... what's with the baggage?
Oh, this old thing?
THERAPIST
I take this everywhere.
I see. What's in it?
THERAPIST
Oh, you know... my wallet. Repressed anger. Simmering resentment. Stifled fury. And a couple granola bars.
Hmm. Do you think this might be a good time, to unpack some of that?
LATER
Do you feel a little lighter now?
FURY
THERAPIST
ANGER
Yeah. But I'm gonna need my wallet back.
FURY
ANGER

When someone says something ignorant...

Birds aren't intelligent. That's why "birdbrain" is synonymous with "stupid."

it doesn't take long for the angry horde to descend.

I've found it helpful to consider these questions before weighing in:

☐ What was their intention?

☐ Is this a pattern of behavior or a thoughtless mistake?

☐ What steps have they taken to make amends?

☐ What do I hope to accomplish by joining in?

Whatever I decide, I will choose to be humane & civil. I don't have to resort to personal attacks to communicate my feelings.

ANGER THAT'S CHANGED THE WORLD

Some things are worth getting angry about.

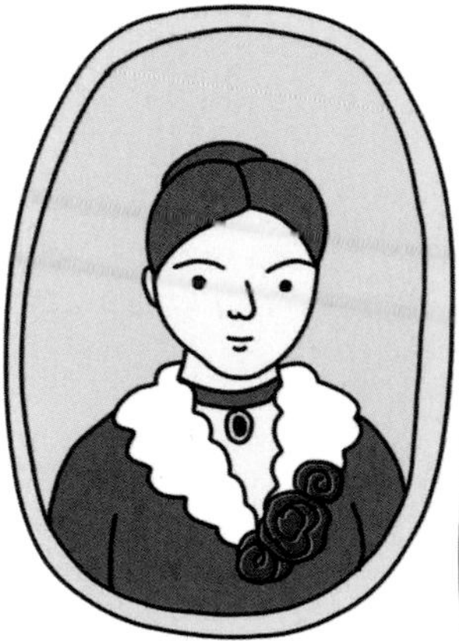

Lydia Becker

Suffragist, women's rights

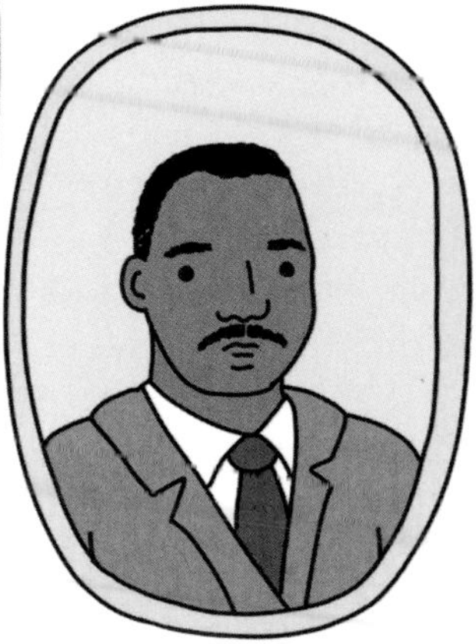

Martin Luther King Jr.

Civil rights activist

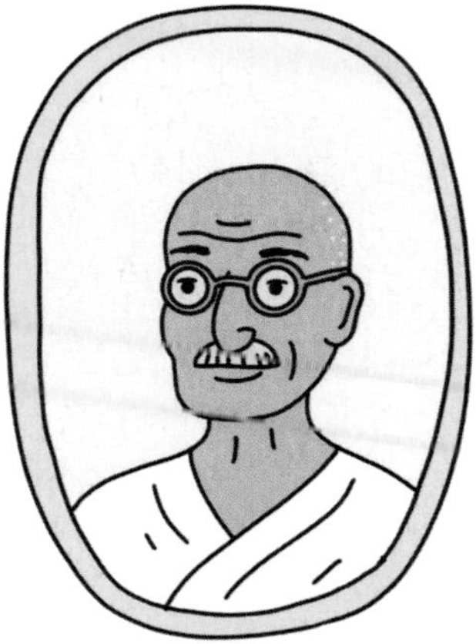

Mahatma Gandhi

Leader of nonviolent independence movement

Constructive anger can fuel positive change.

CHAPTER 12

TODAY I'M FEELING:

GRATEFUL

Most of my therapy sessions go something like this:

Beginning of Session

Everything is awful!
My friend is mad at me.
I'm in a creative slump!
I did something stupid.
I'm worried about money.
My meds have weird side effects!
The news makes me cry.

First, I vent about everything that's going wrong. I let all my emotions spill out: anger, sadness, confusion, fear. My therapist listens, and he helps me work through things for awhile. Then, he always says something like this:

Now that we've discussed the more challenging aspects of your life...

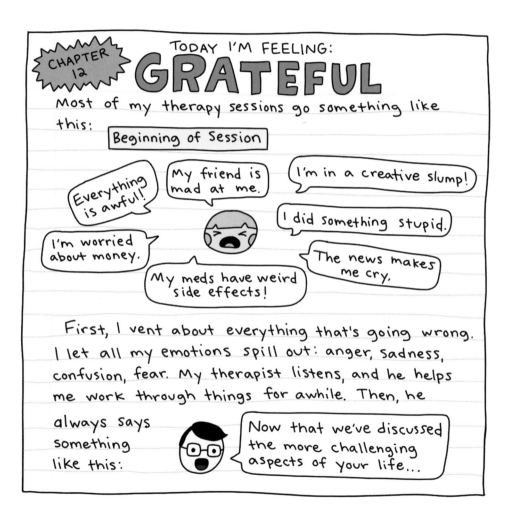

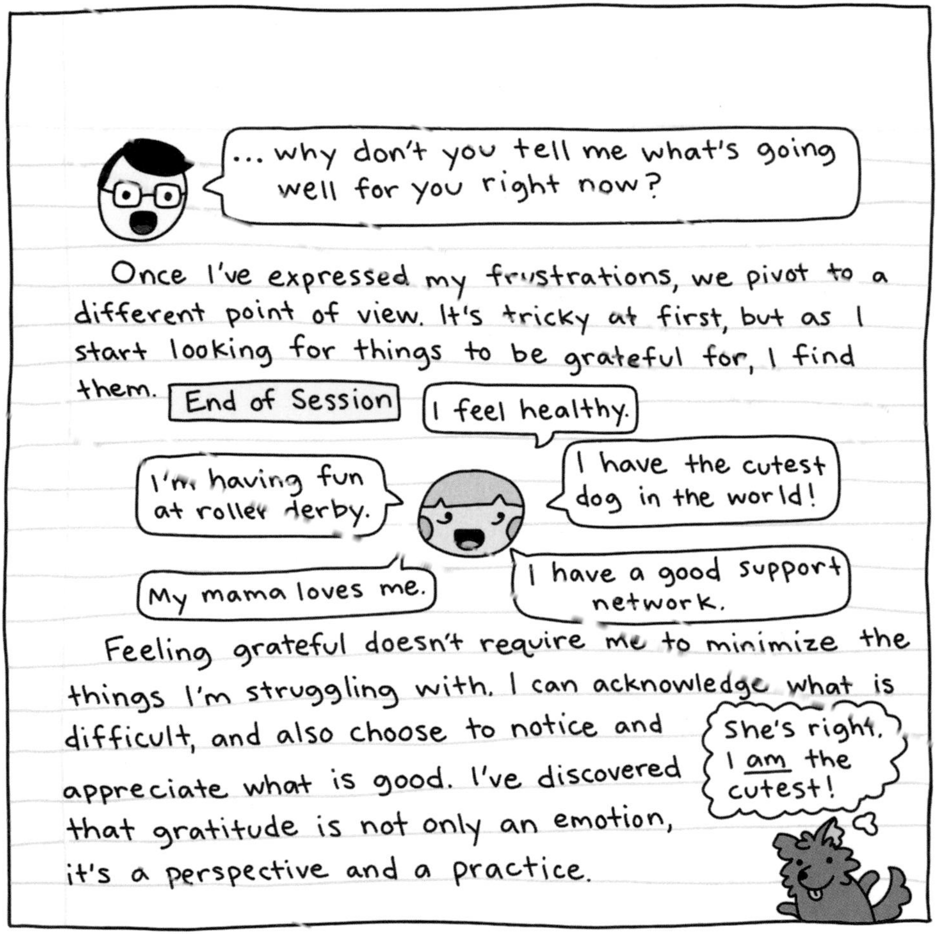
...why don't you tell me what's going well for you right now?
Once I've expressed my frustrations, we pivot to a different point of view. It's tricky at first, but as I start looking for things to be grateful for, I find them.
End of Session
I feel healthy.
I'm having fun at roller derby.
I have the cutest dog in the world!
My mama loves me.
I have a good support network.
Feeling grateful doesn't require me to minimize the things I'm struggling with. I can acknowledge what is difficult, and also choose to notice and appreciate what is good. I've discovered that gratitude is not only an emotion, it's a perspective and a practice.
She's right. I am the cutest!

I hate it when people tell me I'm supposed to feel grateful.

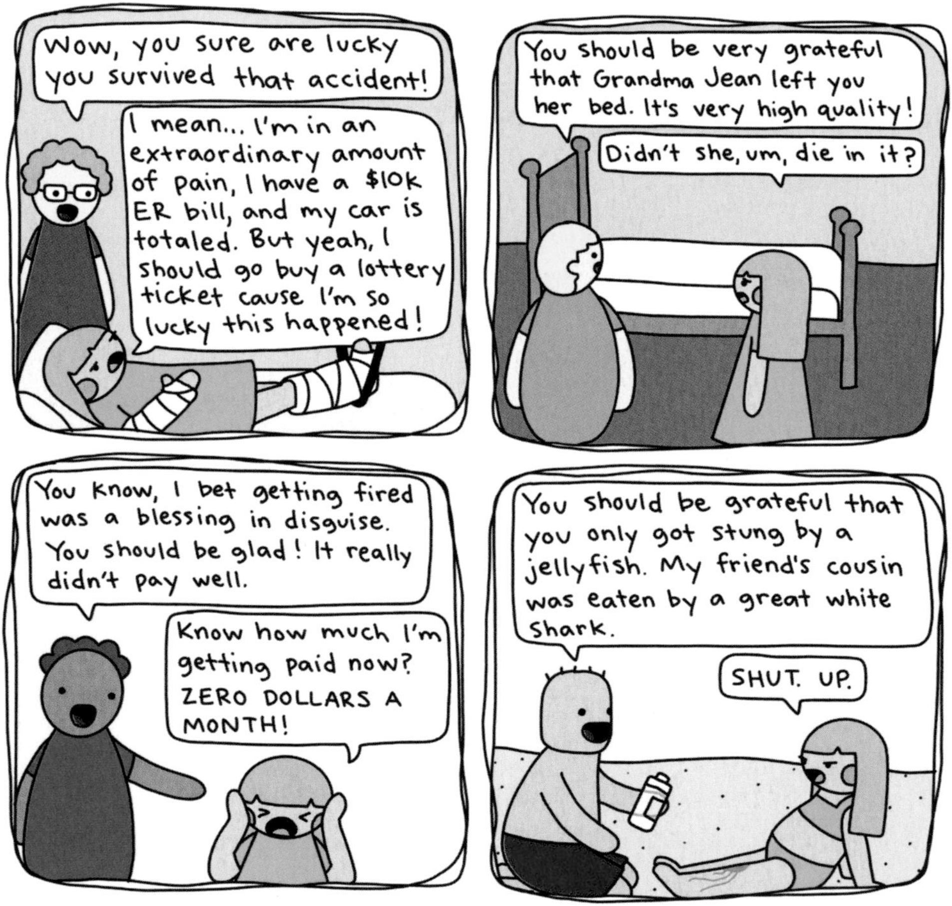
Wow, you sure are lucky you survived that accident!
I mean... I'm in an extraordinary amount of pain, I have a $10k ER bill, and my car is totaled. But yeah, I should go buy a lottery ticket cause I'm so lucky this happened!
You should be very grateful that Grandma Jean left you her bed. It's very high quality!
Didn't she, um, die in it?
You know, I bet getting fired was a blessing in disguise. You should be glad! It really didn't pay well.
Know how much I'm getting paid now? ZERO DOLLARS A MONTH!
You should be grateful that you only got stung by a jellyfish. My friend's cousin was eaten by a great white shark.
SHUT. UP.

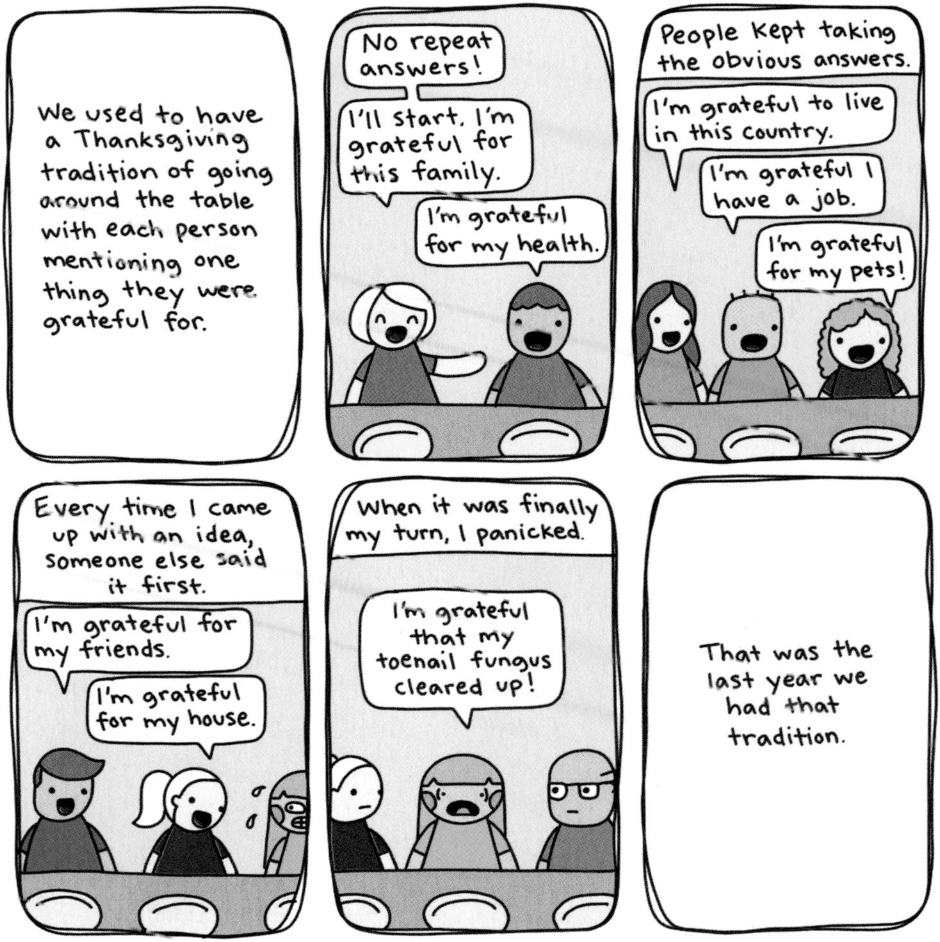
We used to have a Thanksgiving tradition of going around the table with each person mentioning one thing they were grateful for.
No repeat answers!
I'll start. I'm grateful for this family.
I'm grateful for my health.
People kept taking the obvious answers.
I'm grateful to live in this country.
I'm grateful I have a job.
I'm grateful for my pets!
Every time I came up with an idea, someone else said it first.
I'm grateful for my friends.
I'm grateful for my house.
When it was finally my turn, I panicked.
I'm grateful that my toenail fungus cleared up!
That was the last year we had that tradition.

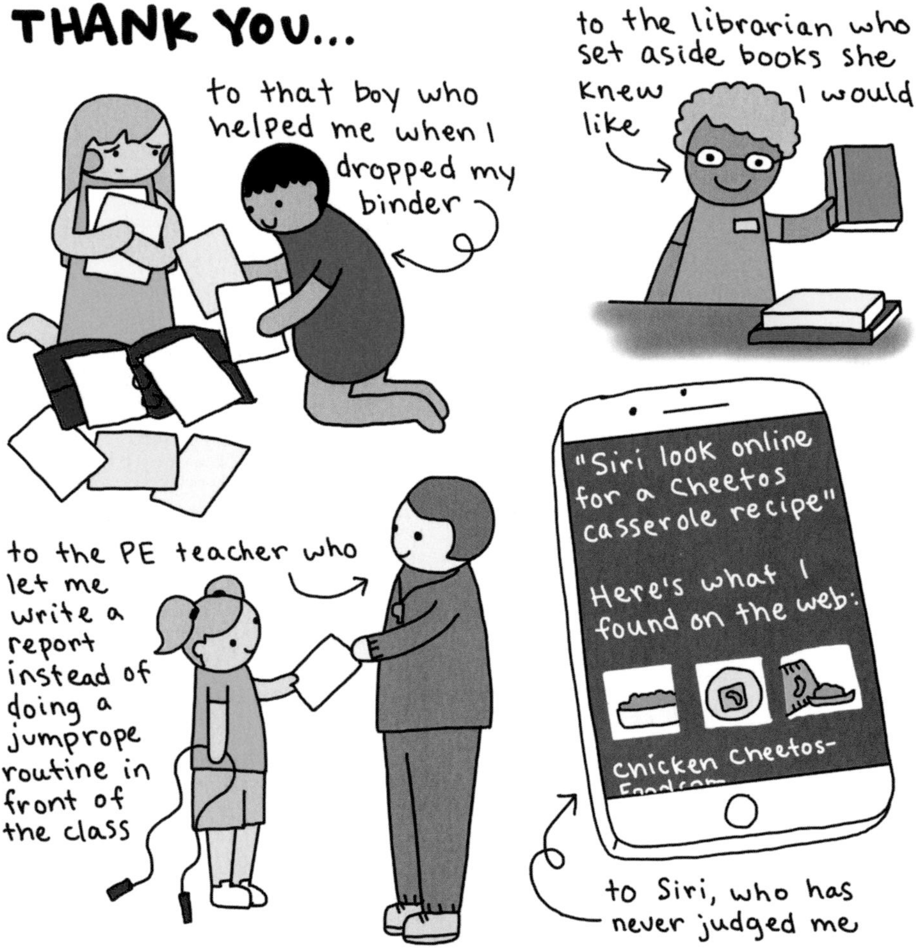
THANK YOU...
to that boy who helped me when I dropped my binder
to the librarian who set aside books she knew I would like
to the PE teacher who let me write a report instead of doing a jumprope routine in front of the class
"Siri look online for a Cheetos casserole recipe"
Here's what I found on the web:
Chicken Cheetos-
to Siri, who has never judged me

WHY I'M GRATEFUL FOR MY DOG

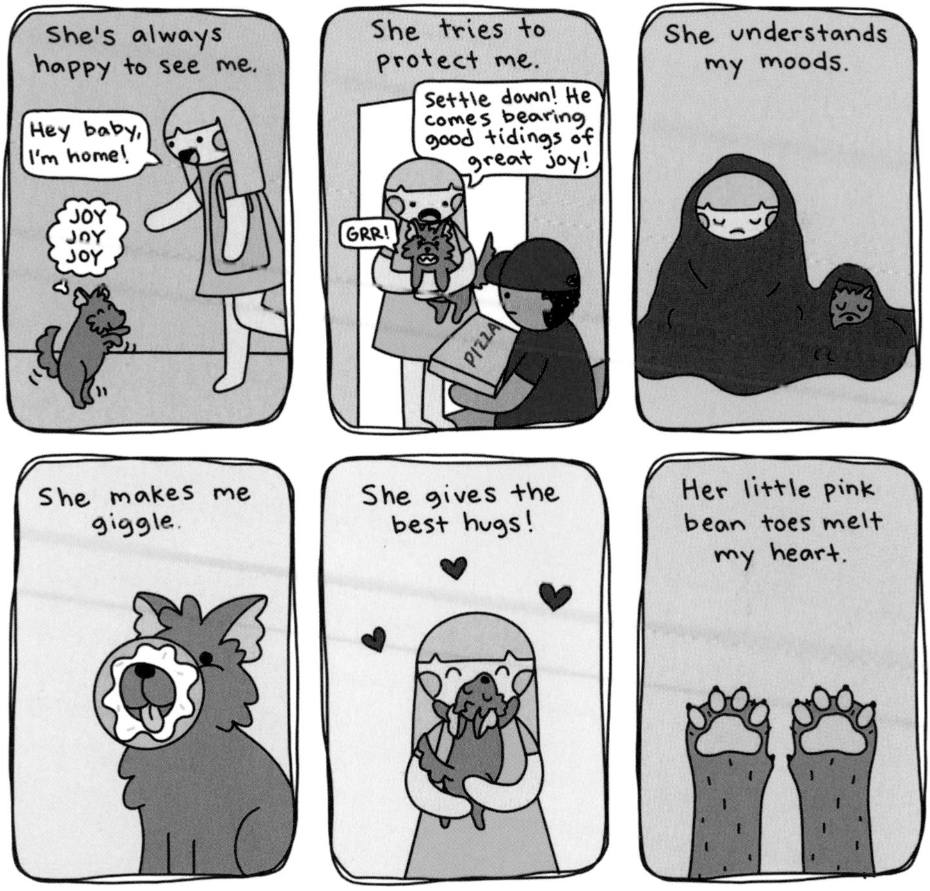
She's always happy to see me.
Hey baby, I'm home!
JOY JOY JOY
She tries to protect me.
Settle down! He comes bearing good tidings of great joy!
GRR!
PIZZA
She understands my moods.
She makes me giggle.
She gives the best hugs!
Her little pink bean toes melt my heart.

PLACES I'M GRATEFUL FOR

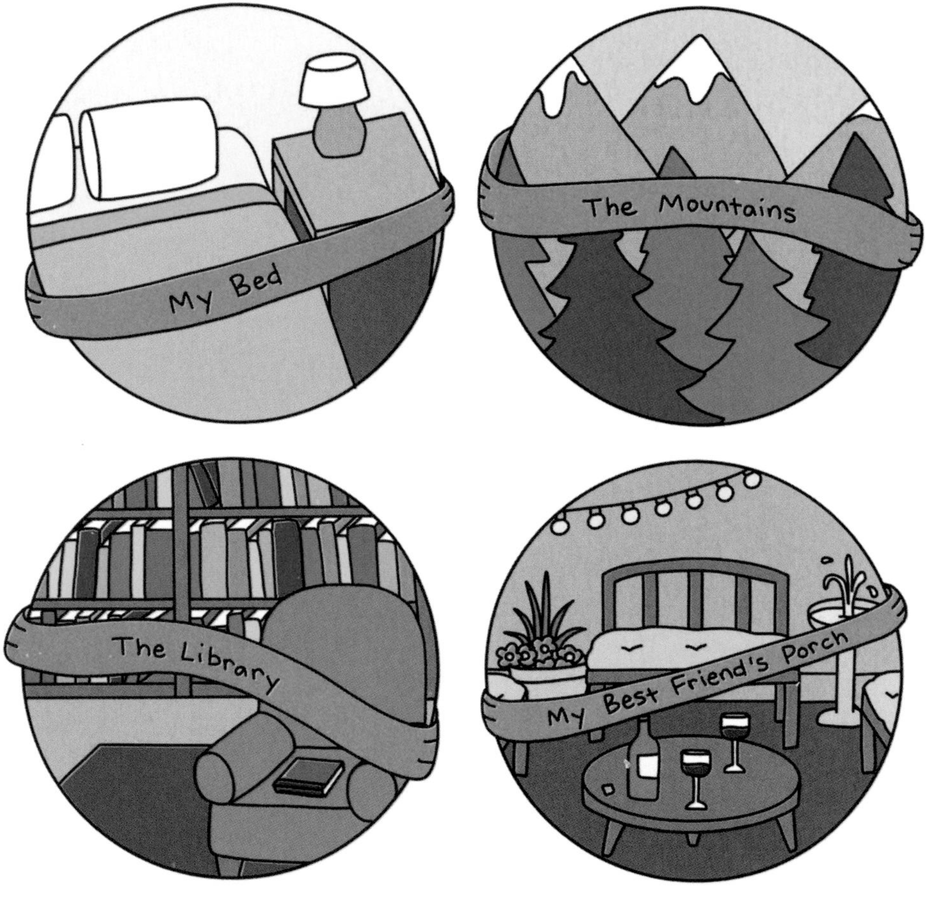
My Bed
The Mountains
The Library
My Best Friend's Porch

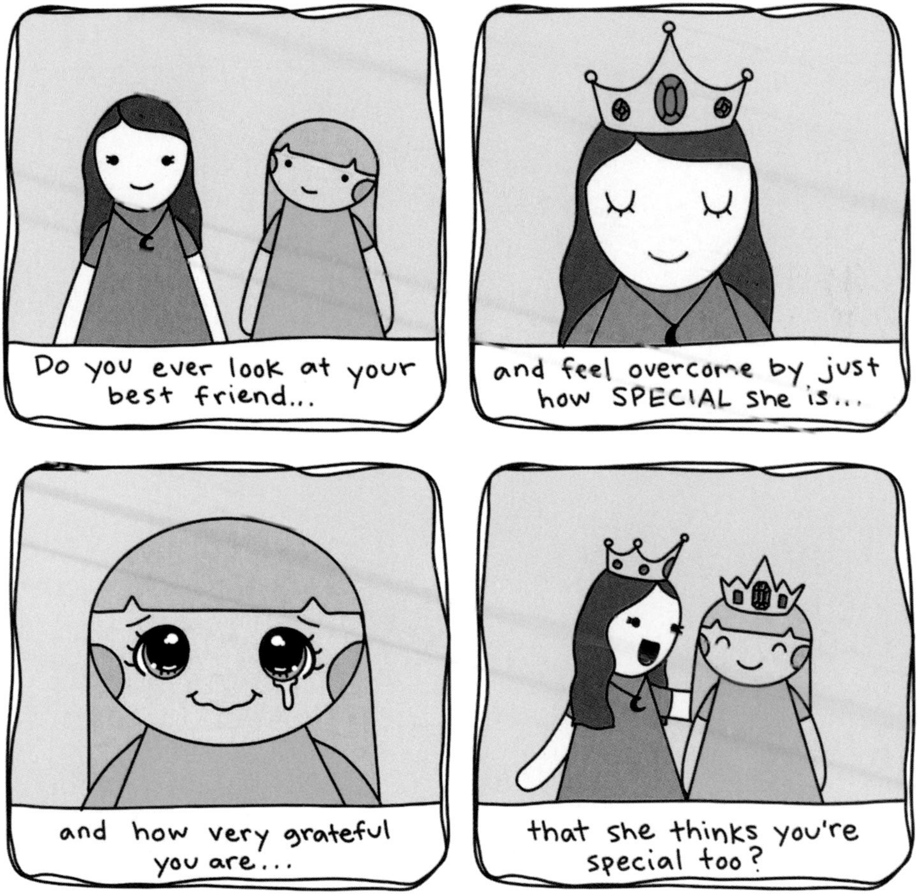
Do you ever look at your best friend...
and feel overcome by just how SPECIAL she is...
and how very grateful you are...
that she thinks you're special too?

WHAT ARE YOU GRATEFUL FOR?

*mark all that apply

☐ stretchy pants
☐ music
☐ rainy days
☐ memes
☐ porch swings
☐ deodorant
☐ art supplies
☐ chocolate
☐ good conversation
☐ silence
☐ freshly mowed grass
☐ Instagram
☐ kittens
☐ toilet paper
☐ chicken nuggets
☐ garage sales
☐ teachers
☐ pine trees

☐ family
☐ glitter
☐ air conditioning
☐ baby animal videos
☐ naps
☐ the ocean
☐ medication
☐ Wi-Fi
☐ moonlight
☐ hot running water
☐ dogs
☐ holidays
☐ texting
☐ house plants
☐ cheese
☐ video games
☐ colors
☐ forgiveness

Sometimes when stuff goes wrong... it helps me appreciate the things I usually take for granted.

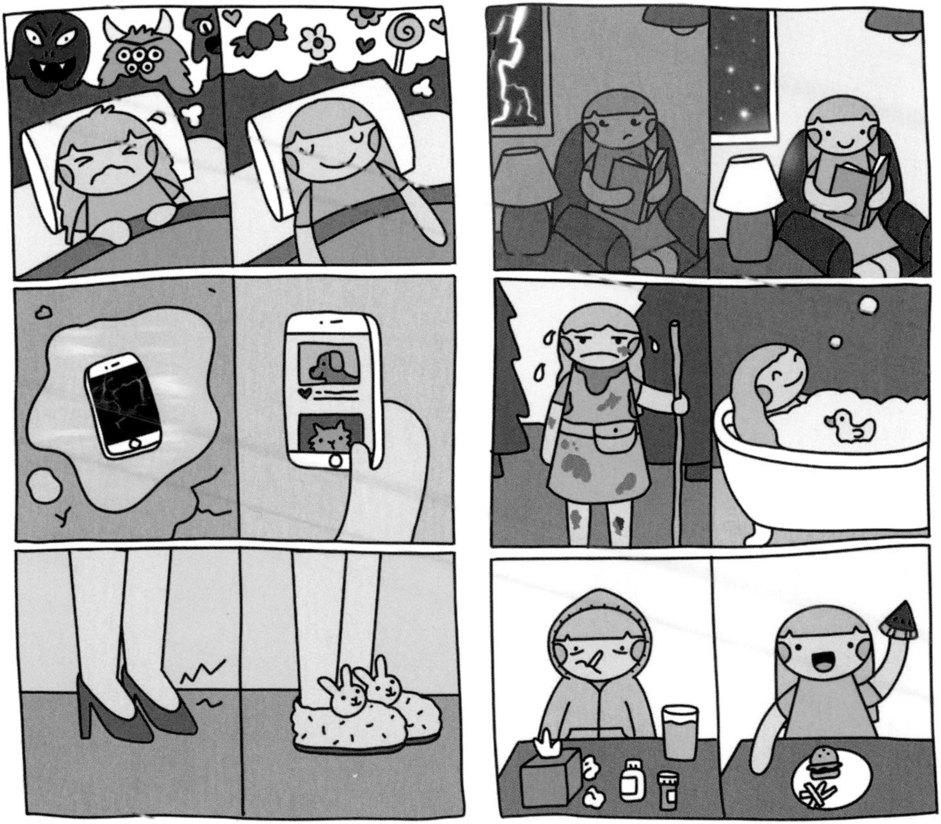

THINGS I CAN BE GRATEFUL FOR (EVEN ON HARD DAYS)

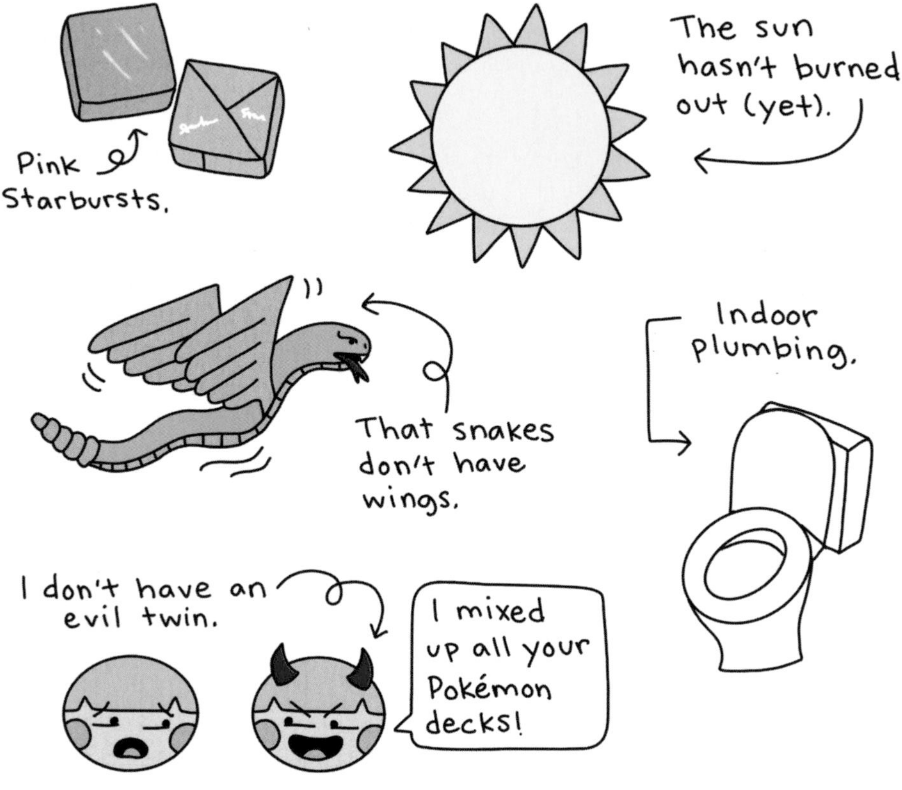
Pink Starbursts.
The sun hasn't burned out (yet).
That snakes don't have wings.
Indoor plumbing.
I don't have an evil twin.
I mixed up all your Pokémon decks!

SMALL MOMENTS

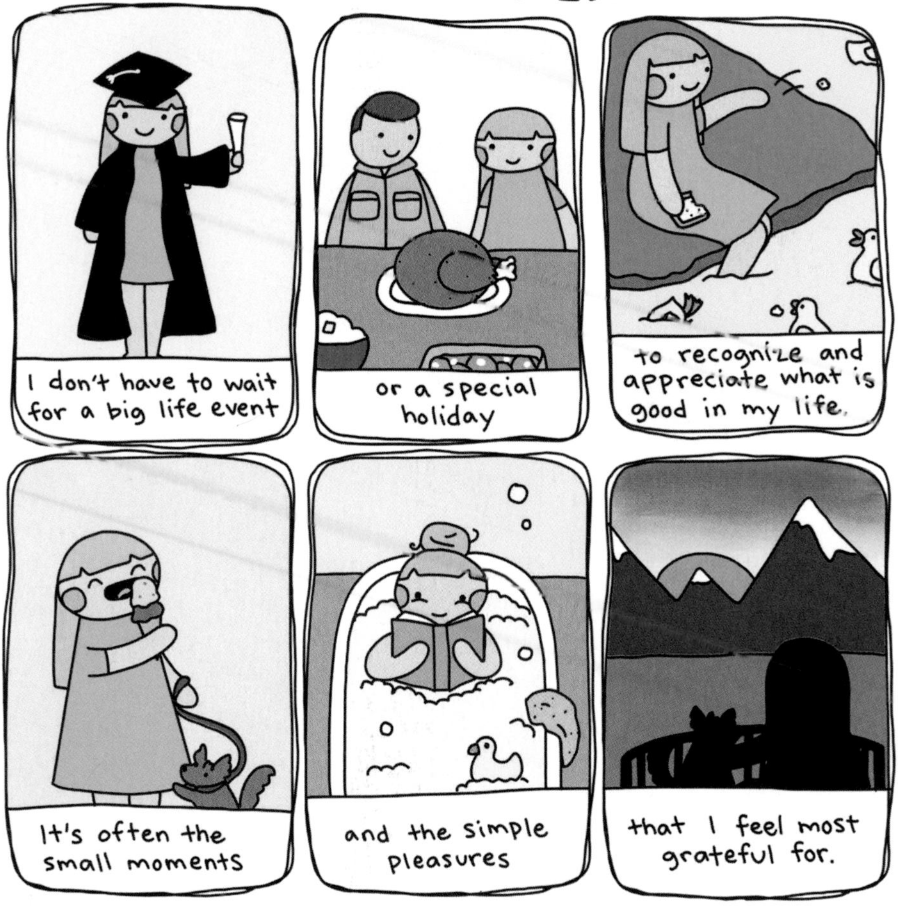
I don't have to wait for a big life event
or a special holiday
to recognize and appreciate what is good in my life.
It's often the small moments
and the simple pleasures
that I feel most grateful for.

CHAPTER 13

TODAY I'M FEELING:

PEACEFUL

For several years I had a recurring thought:

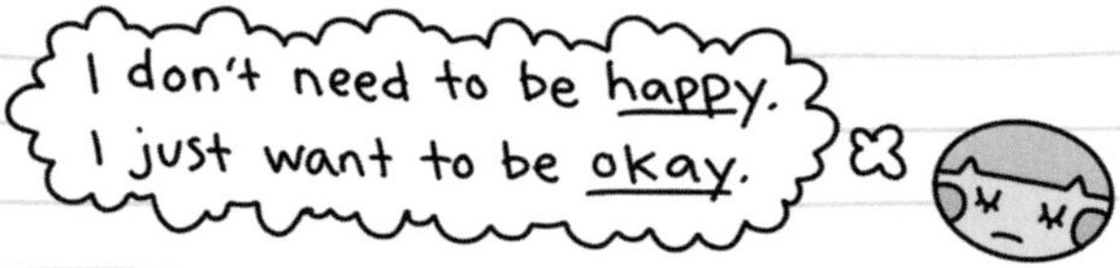
I don't need to be happy.
I just want to be okay.

I was longing for PEACE, but it proved elusive. I searched for answers in books, churches, and apps. I found good things there, but I didn't find peace. I tried the activities I'd been told would work: yoga, meditation, and getting back to nature. I found value in each, but I didn't find peace.

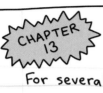

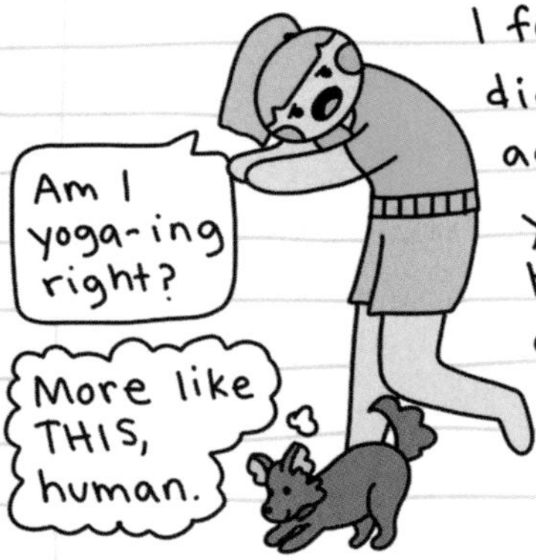
Am I yoga-ing right?
More like THIS, human.

I began to feel frustrated; the harder I tried to induce more peaceful feelings, the more stressed out I felt! Why didn't I feel the way I was "supposed" to?

I gradually began to realize that for me, peace is about BALANCE.

Peace comes when my inner beliefs are in harmony with my actions. I am at peace when:

- [x] I honor myself.
- [x] I enforce healthy boundaries.
- [x] I speak my truth.
- [x] I am trying to be a good human.

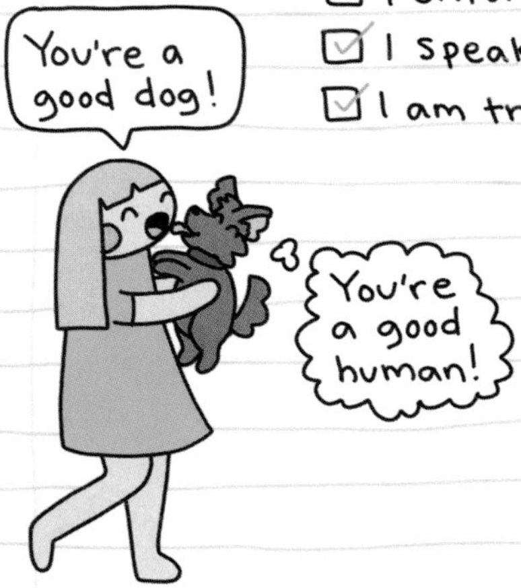
You're a good dog!
You're a good human!

Now when peace eludes me, I take a look at my life and ask myself:

What's out of balance, and how can I regain equilibrium?

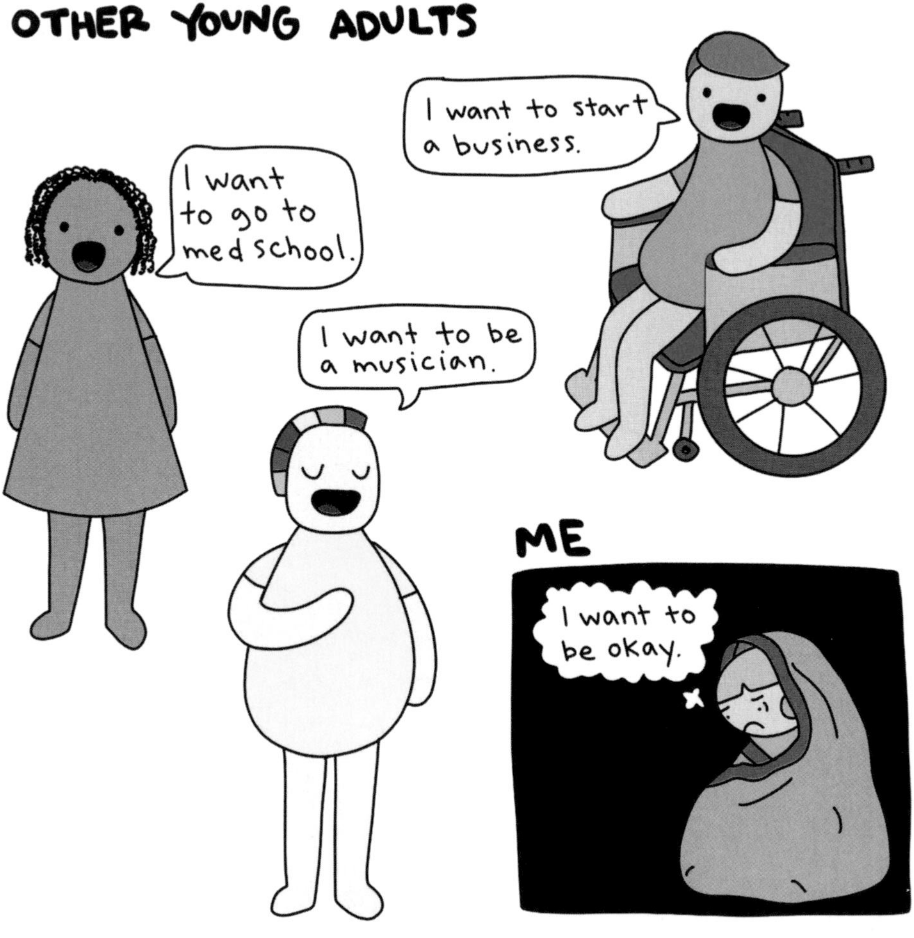
OTHER YOUNG ADULTS
I want to go to med school.
I want to start a business.
I want to be a musician.
ME
I want to be okay.

MEDITATION

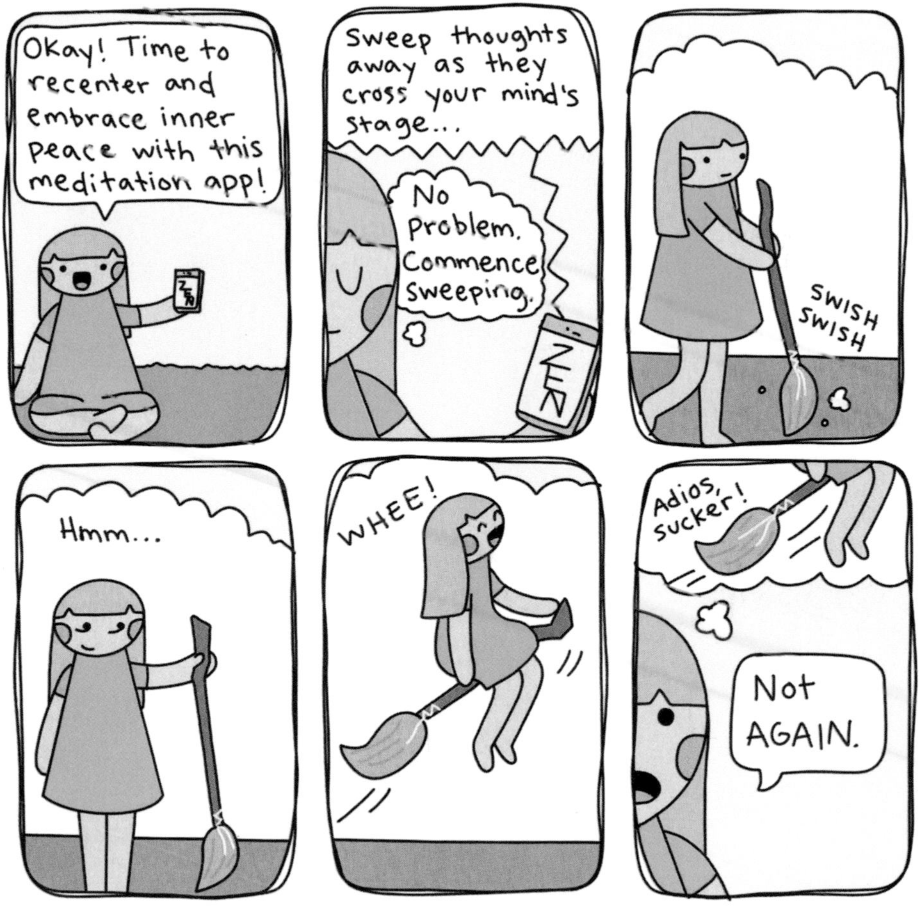

Okay! Time to recenter and embrace inner peace with this meditation app!
ZEN
Sweep thoughts away as they cross your mind's stage...
No Problem. Commence sweeping.
ZEN
SWISH SWISH
Hmm...
WHEE!
Adios, sucker!
Not AGAIN.

LAZY

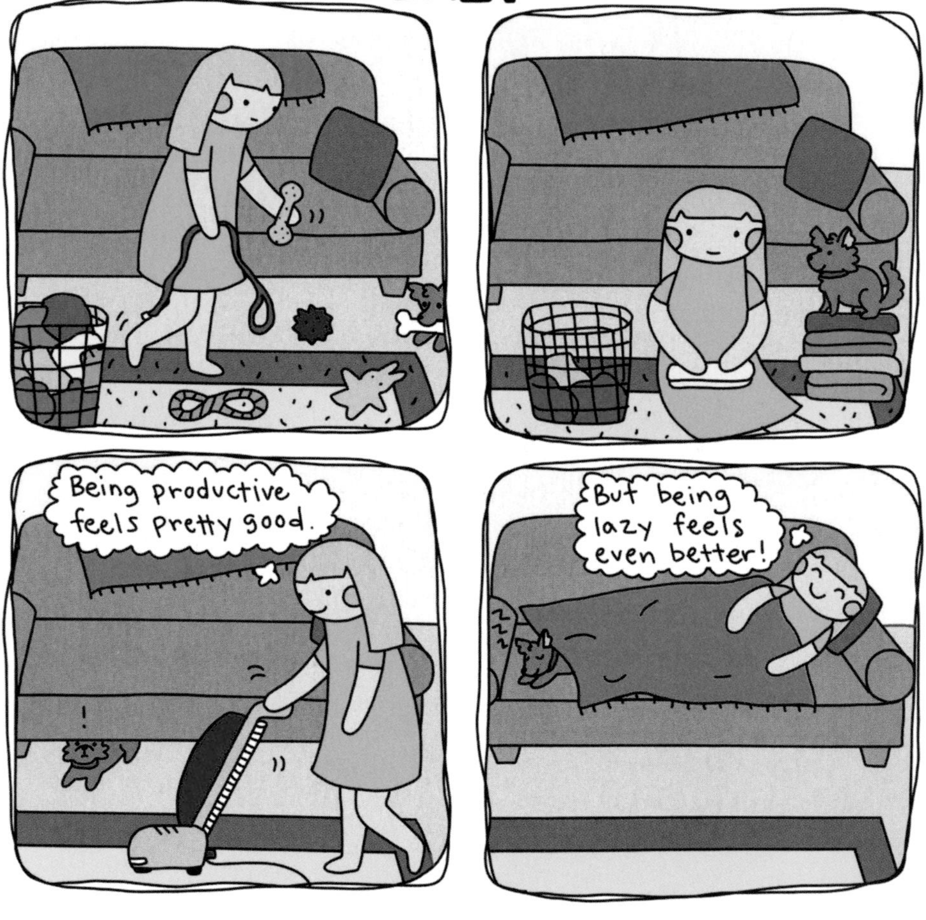
Being productive feels pretty good.
But being lazy feels even better!
Z
Z
Z

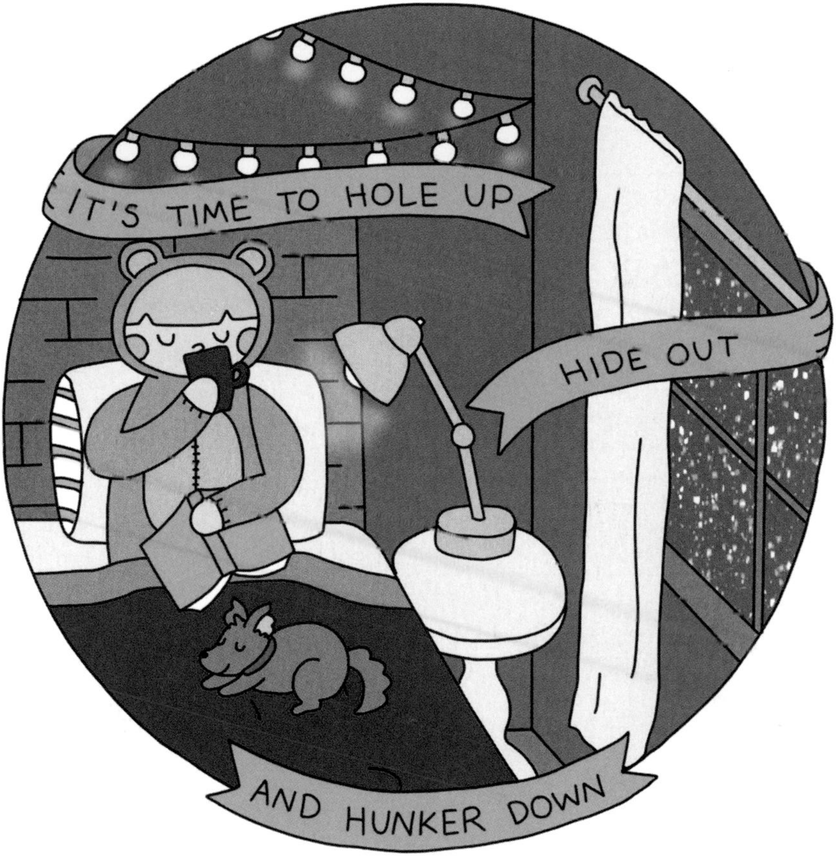
IT'S TIME TO HOLE UP
HIDE OUT
AND HUNKER DOWN

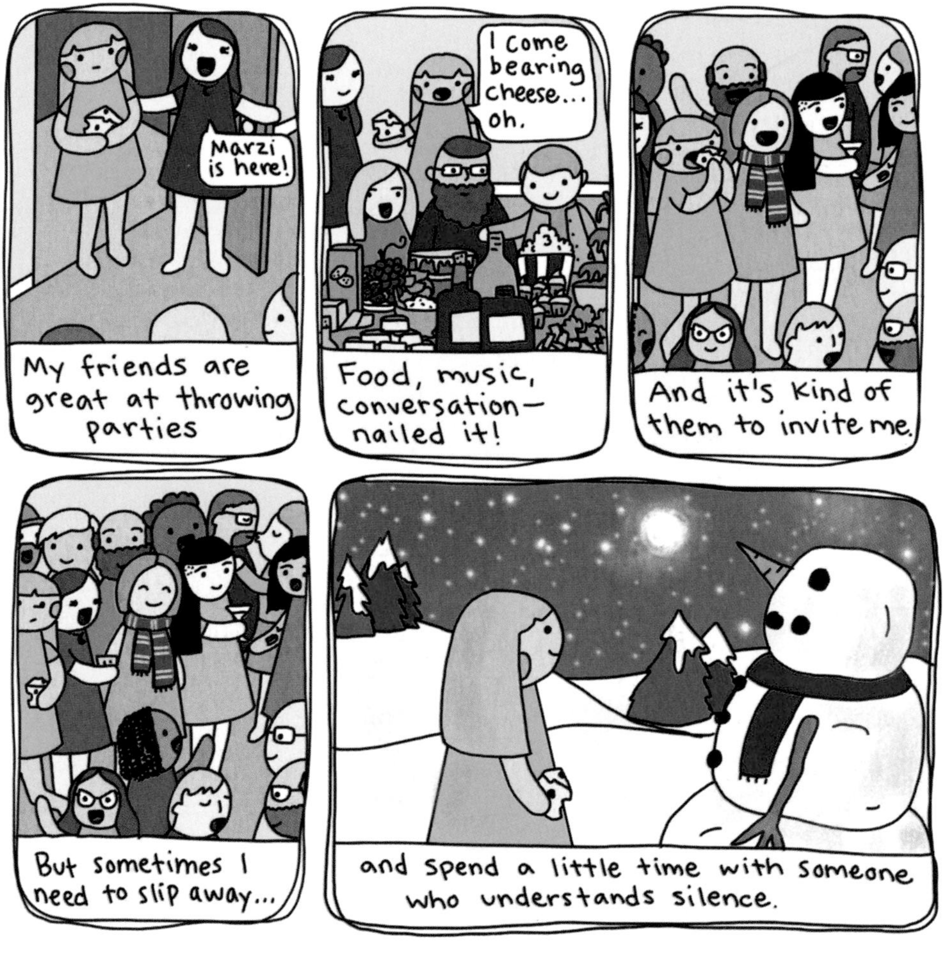
Marzi is here!
My friends are great at throwing parties
I come bearing cheese... oh.
Food, music, conversation—nailed it!
And it's kind of them to invite me.
But sometimes I need to slip away...
and spend a little time with someone who understands silence.

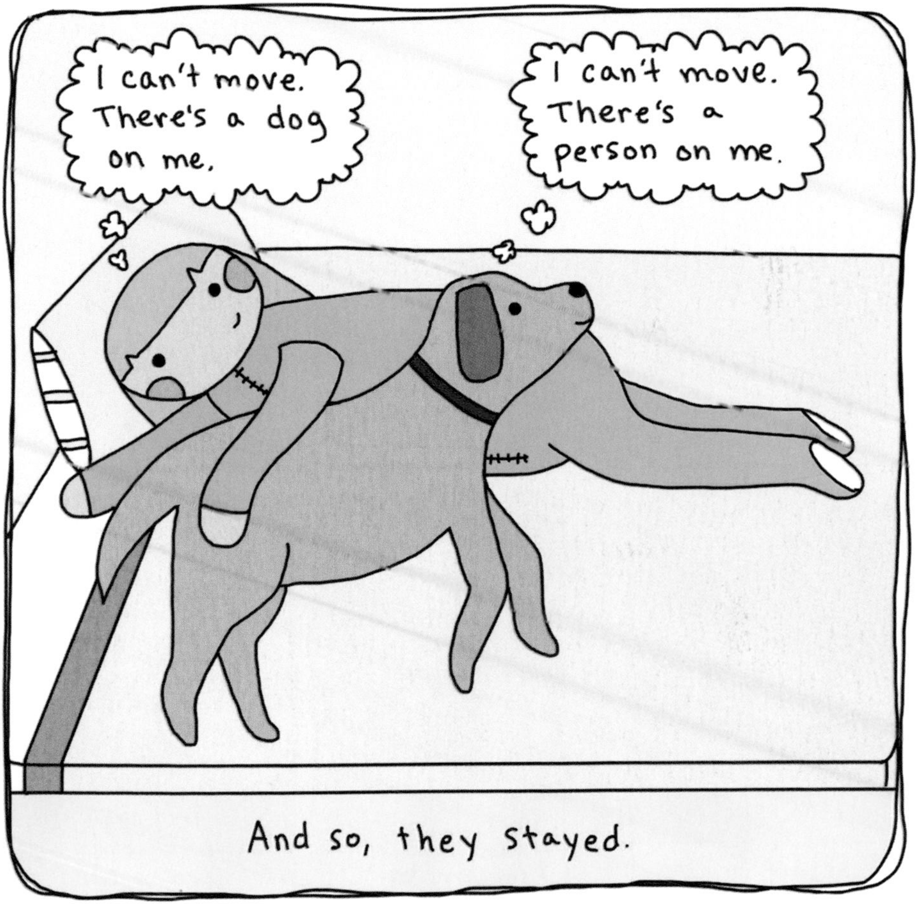
I can't move. There's a dog on me.
I can't move. There's a person on me.
And so, they stayed.

SUNDAY

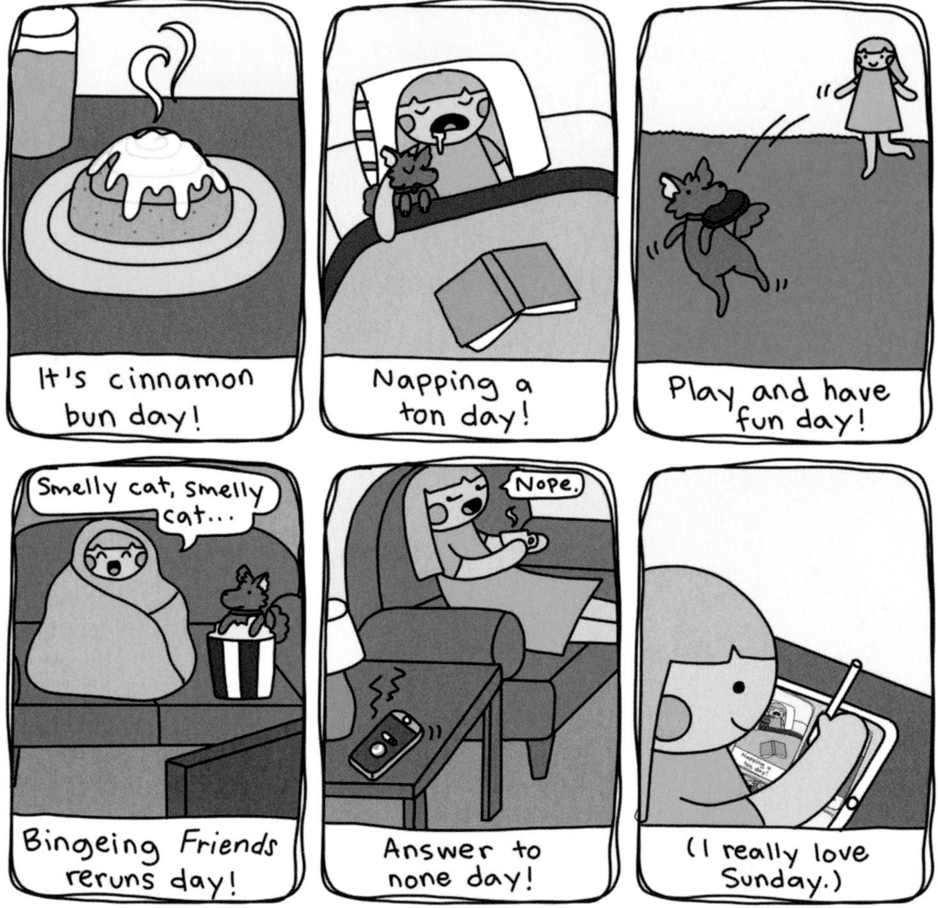
It's cinnamon bun day!
Napping a ton day!
Play and have fun day!
Smelly cat, smelly cat...
Bingeing Friends reruns day!
Nope.
Answer to none day!
(I really love Sunday.)

If I'm feeling "messy," I check to see whether I'm neglecting one of these four areas. How can I regain balance?

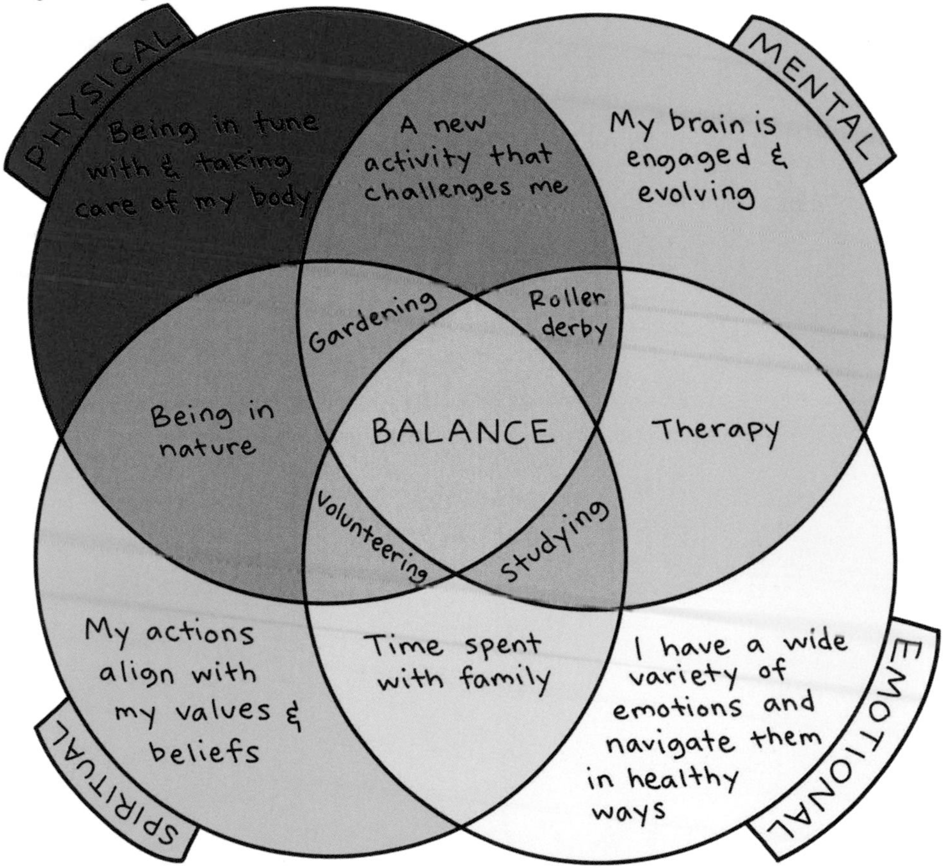

PHYSICAL
MENTAL
EMOTIONAL
SPIRITUAL
Being in tune with & taking care of my body
A new activity that challenges me
My brain is engaged & evolving
Gardening
Roller derby
Being in nature
BALANCE
Therapy
Volunteering
Studying
My actions align with my values & beliefs
Time spent with family
I have a wide variety of emotions and navigate them in healthy ways

NIGHT

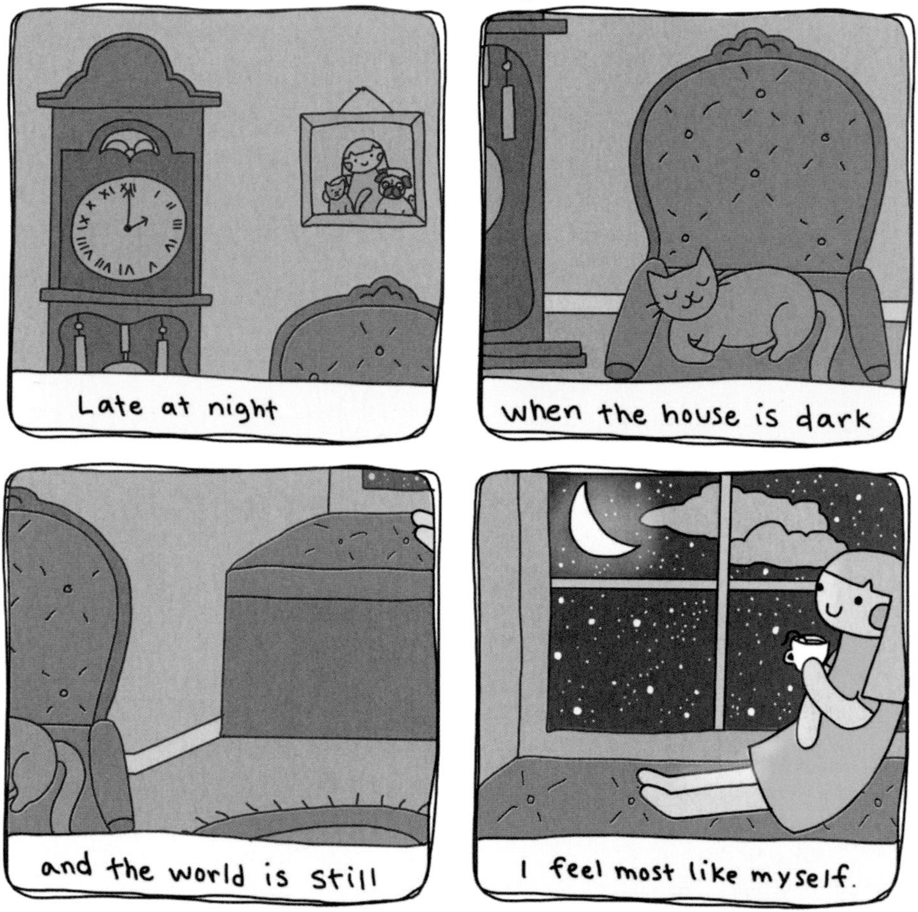
Late at night
when the house is dark
and the world is still
I feel most like myself.

MY LIST OF SERENE THINGS*

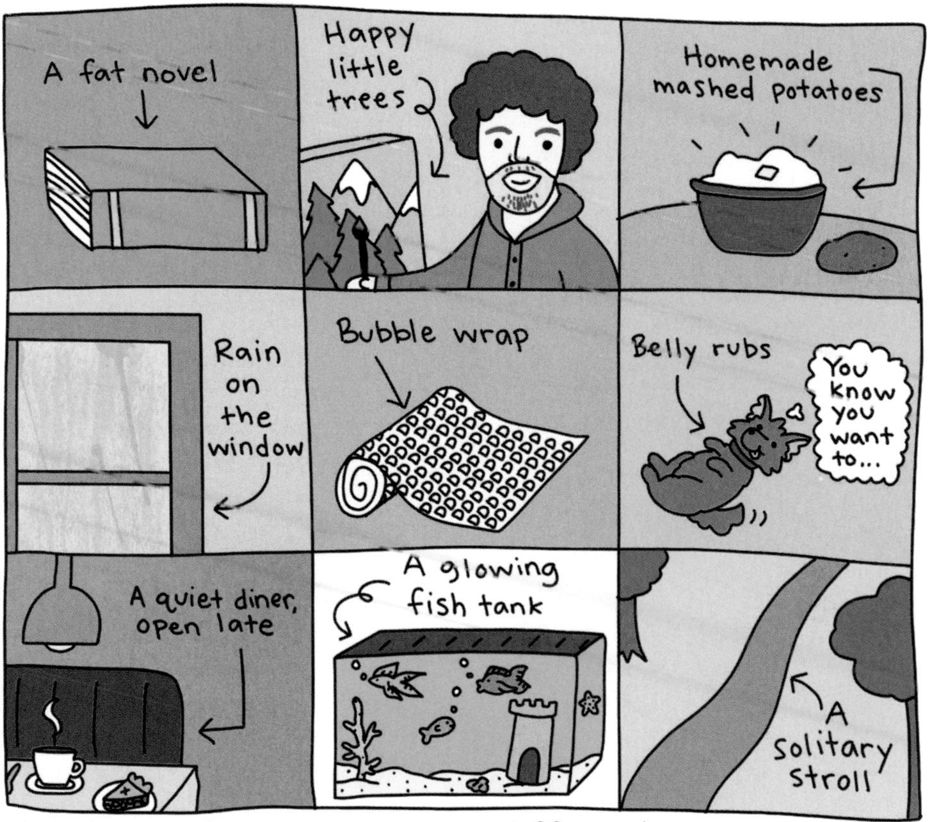

A fat novel
Happy little trees
Homemade mashed potatoes
Rain on the window
Bubble wrap
Belly rubs
You know you want to...
A quiet diner, open late
A glowing fish tank
A solitary stroll

*It's okay for your list to be different! Give yourself permission to embrace whatever brings you peace.

CHAPTER 14

TODAY I'M FEELING:

SAD

Let's just be real: I don't like to be sad. No matter how I look at it, sadness doesn't seem like an emotion worth celebrating. But it is an emotion that needs to be honored. I've thought a lot about what that means, and I believe it includes:

- ☑ Being honest with myself and acknowledging my sadness.
- ☑ Withholding self-judgment for my feelings.
- ☑ Allowing myself to talk about my sadness.
- ☑ Not giving myself a set timeline for healing.

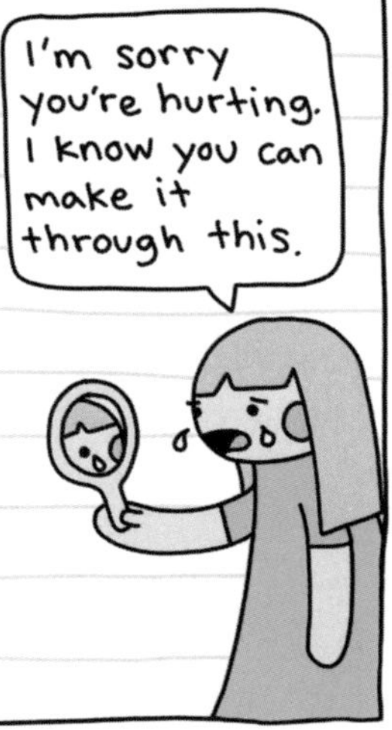
I'm sorry you're hurting. I know you can make it through this.

Sadness felt more manageable once I recognized that it's a normal reaction to emotional pain or loss.

Heart of Stone:
Strong, but cold and hard. Pretty useless.

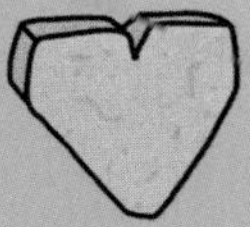

Healthy Heart:
Prone to pain, but also capable of empathy & love.

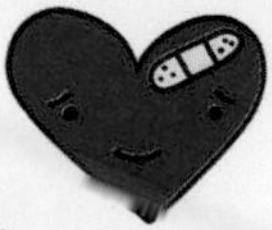

It means that, even if it feels like my heart is broken, it's actually working exactly the way it's supposed to. It means I'm still capable of caring.

There's no need to be ashamed of feeling sad; it simply means I'm processing difficult events. Just like every other emotion, the sadness, too, will pass. Meanwhile, it's okay for me to feel this way.

(Note: Persistent, ongoing sadness that interferes with daily life might be a symptom of depression. Doctors and therapists can help. Please reach out.)

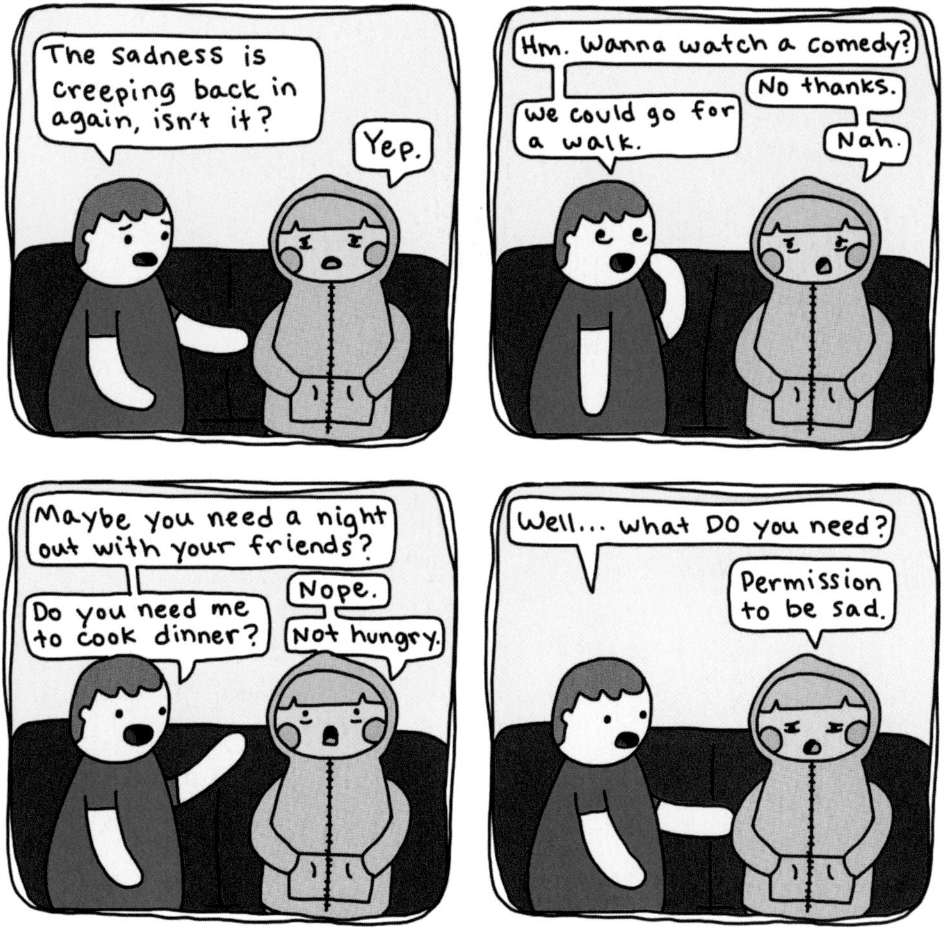
The sadness is creeping back in again, isn't it?
Yep.
Hm. Wanna watch a comedy?
No thanks.
We could go for a walk.
Nah.
Maybe you need a night out with your friends?
Nope.
Do you need me to cook dinner?
Not hungry.
Well... what DO you need?
Permission to be sad.

DIFFERENT SORTS OF SADNESS

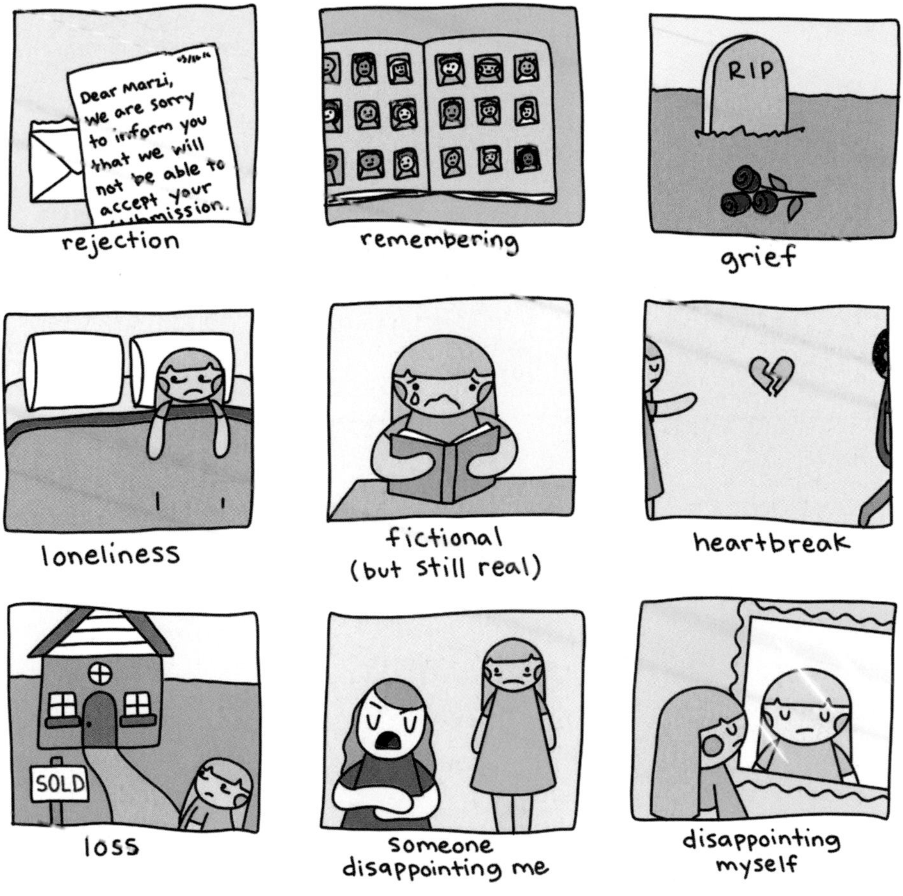
Dear Marzi,
we are sorry
to inform you
that we will
not be able to
accept your
submission.
rejection
remembering
RIP
grief
loneliness
fictional
(but still real)
heartbreak
SOLD
loss
someone
disappointing me
disappointing
myself

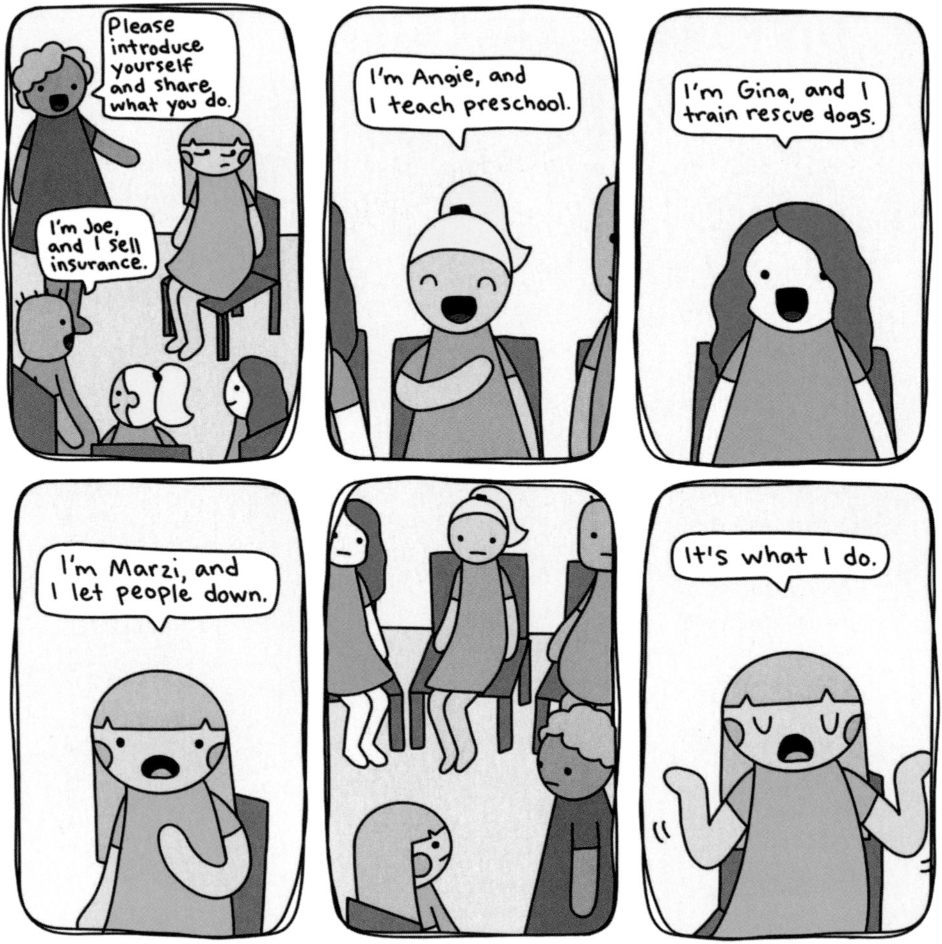
Please introduce yourself and share what you do.
I'm Joe, and I sell insurance.
I'm Angie, and I teach preschool.
I'm Gina, and I train rescue dogs.
I'm Marzi, and I let people down.
It's what I do.

BLUE DAY VIBES

driving with no
destination

reading
poetry

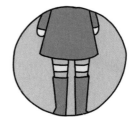

monochromatic
clothes

classic movies

corner table in a
coffeehouse

photo albums

journal writing

staring at the
ceiling

violin music

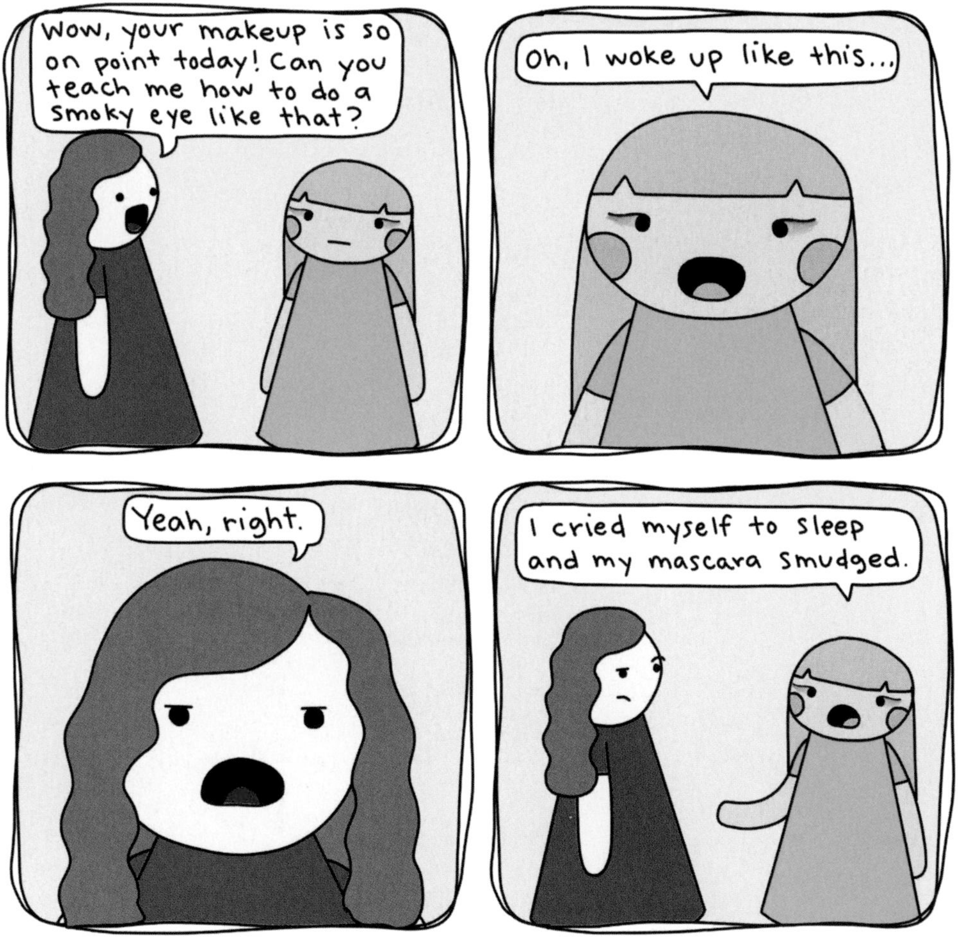
Wow, your makeup is so on point today! Can you teach me how to do a smoky eye like that?
Oh, I woke up like this...
Yeah, right.
I cried myself to sleep and my mascara smudged.

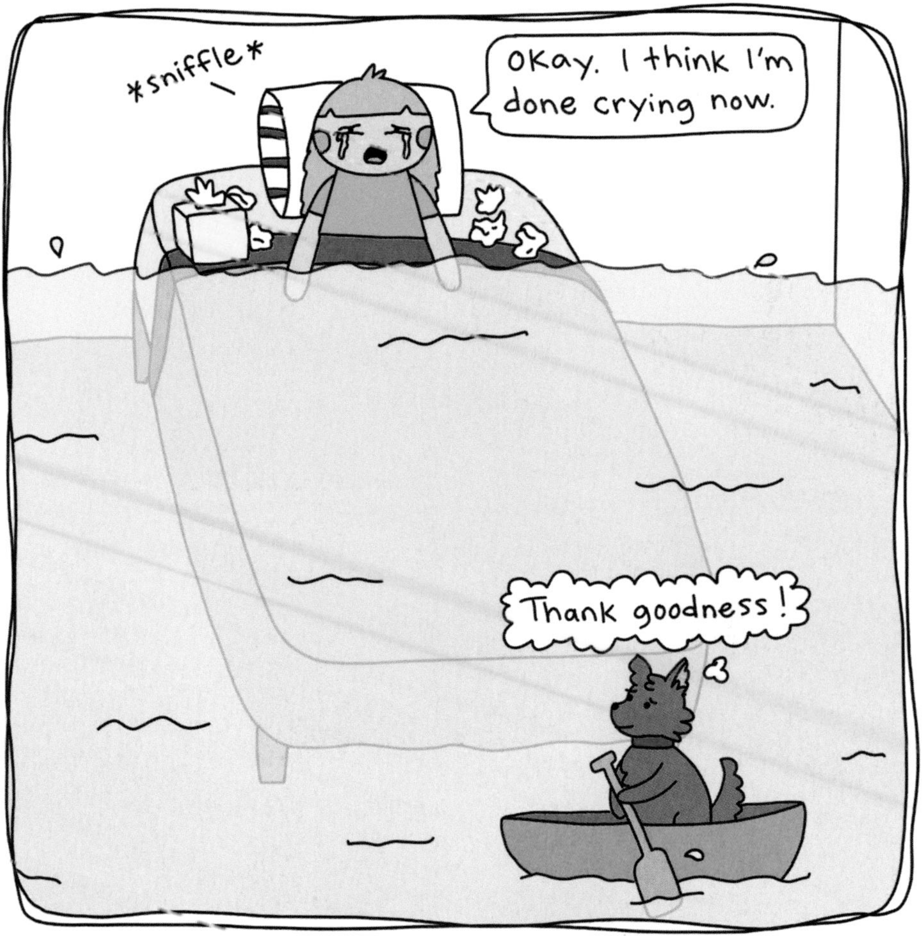
sniffle
Okay. I think I'm done crying now.
Thank goodness!

BAD ADVICE FOR A SAD PERSON

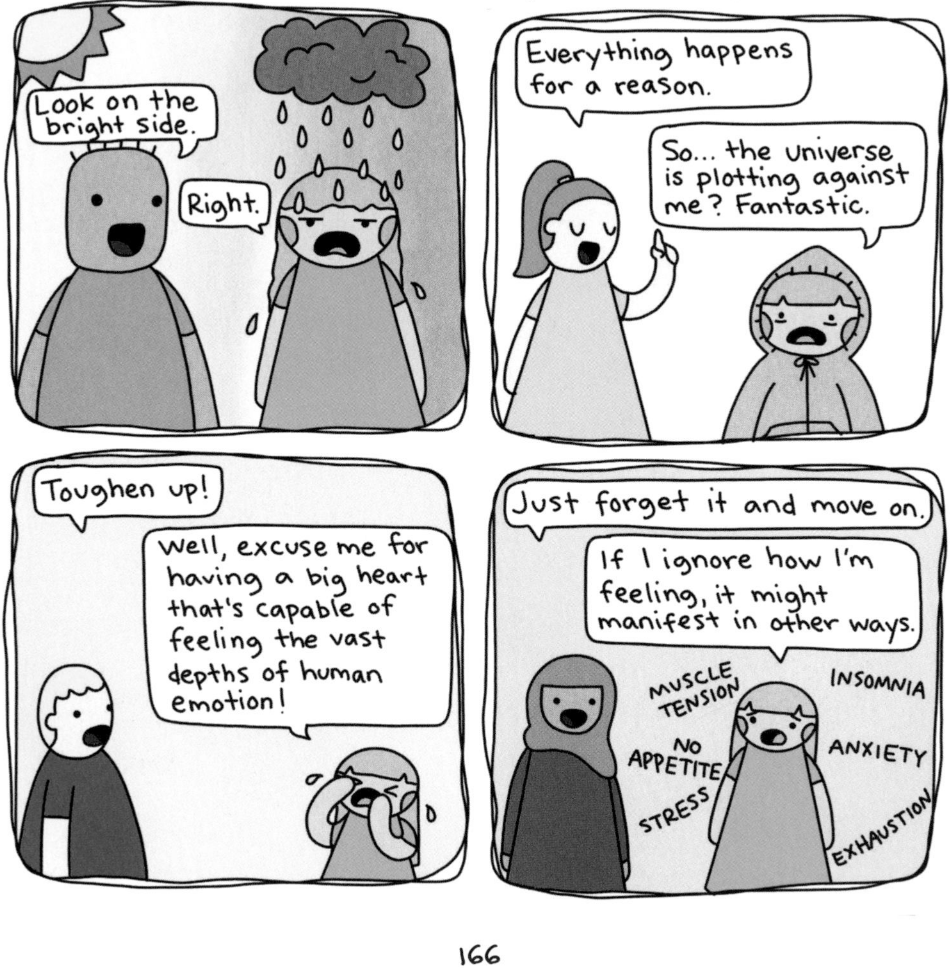
Look on the bright side.
Right.
Everything happens for a reason.
So... the universe is plotting against me? Fantastic.
Toughen up!
Well, excuse me for having a big heart that's capable of feeling the vast depths of human emotion!
Just forget it and move on.
If I ignore how I'm feeling, it might manifest in other ways.
MUSCLE TENSION
INSOMNIA
NO APPETITE
ANXIETY
STRESS
EXHAUSTION

HOW TO MEND A BROKEN HEART *

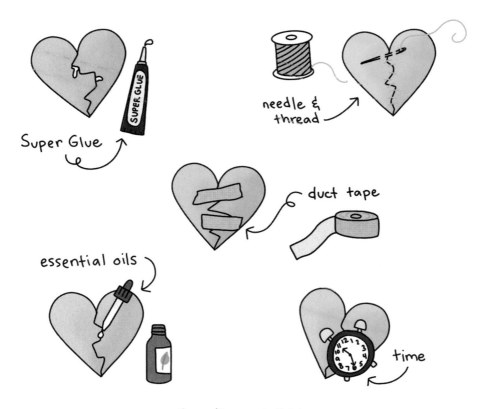

Super Glue

needle & thread

duct tape

essential oils

time

*results may vary

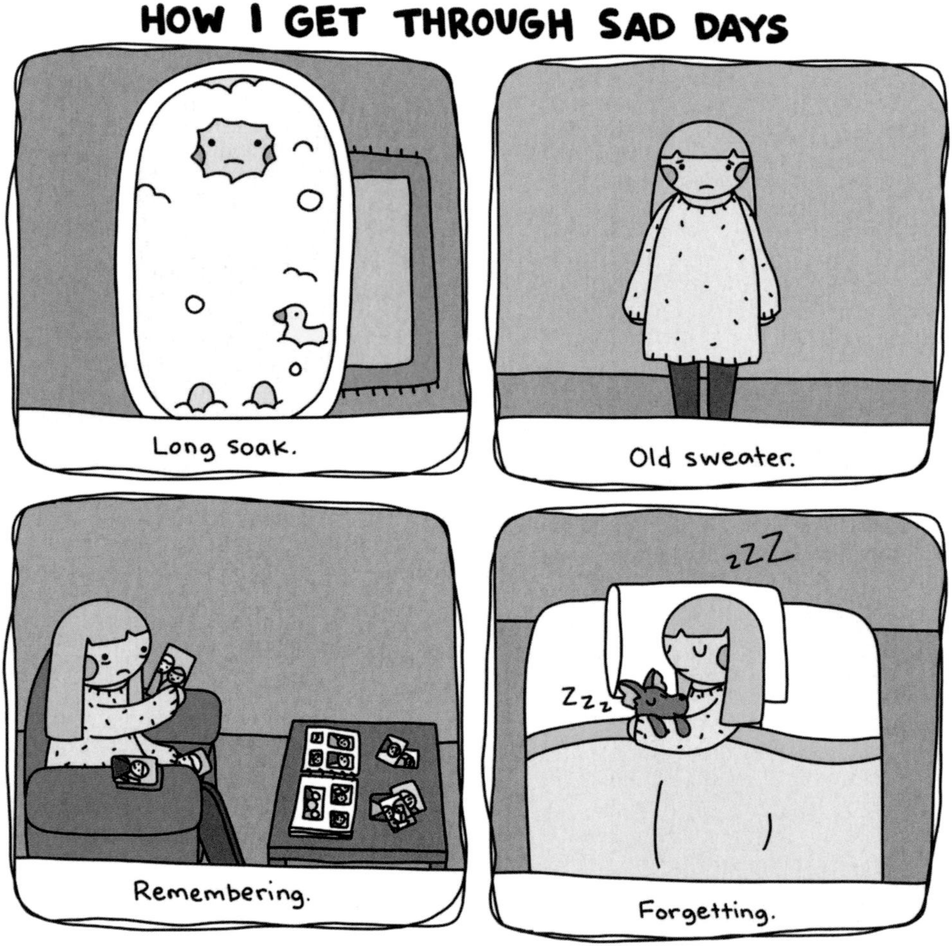
HOW I GET THROUGH SAD DAYS
Long soak.
Old sweater.
Remembering.
zzZ
Zzz
Forgetting.

STORMY WEATHER

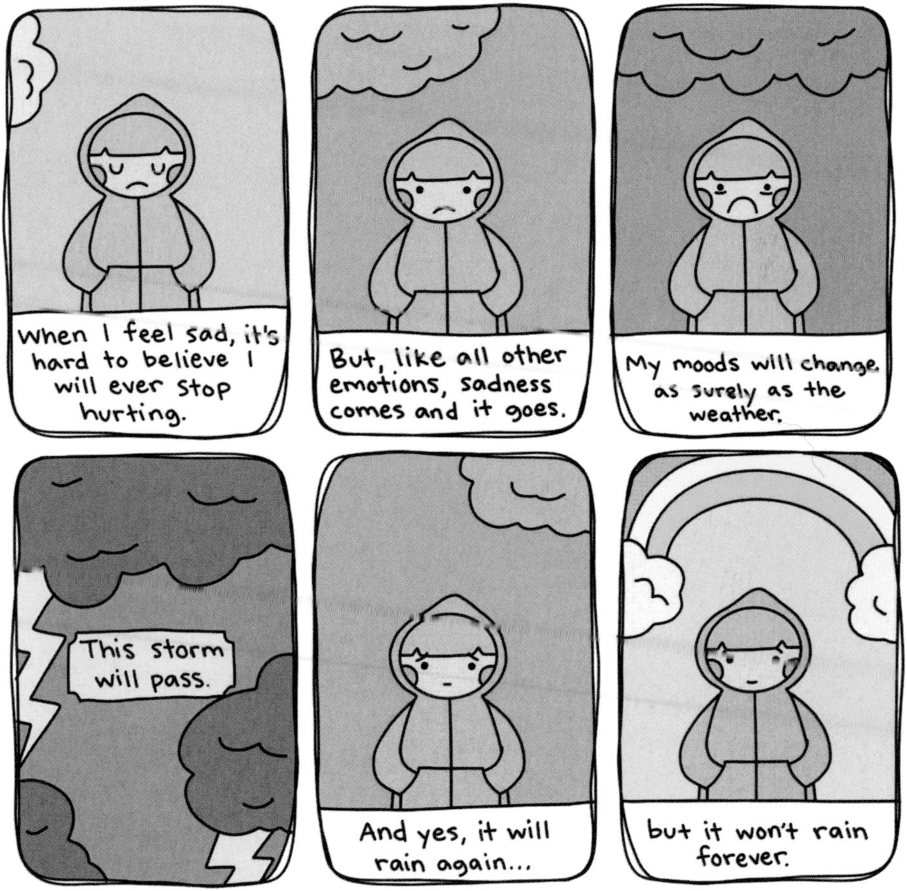
When I feel sad, it's hard to believe I will ever stop hurting.
But, like all other emotions, sadness comes and it goes.
My moods will change as surely as the weather.
This storm will pass.
And yes, it will rain again...
but it won't rain forever.

CHAPTER 15

TODAY I'M FEELING: CONFIDENT

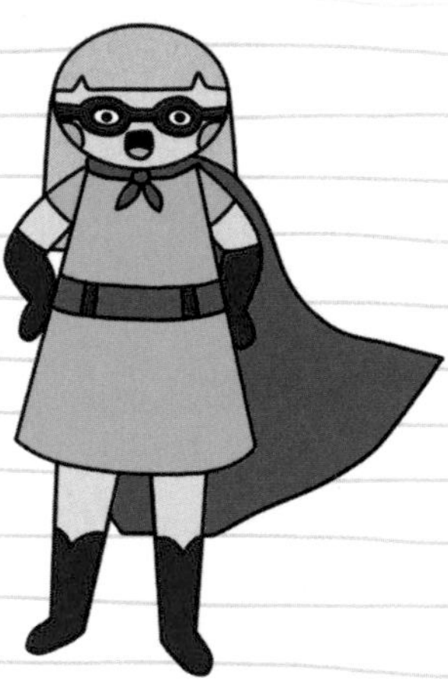

Some days I just feel like I've got it goin' on. Everything seems to be working out. I feel put-together and in control.

Even though I love those rare days, I've noticed that I have a tendency to self-correct my ego. I might be feeling confident about a project and think: *This is amazing!* and then immediately edit it to: *Well, it's okay.*

I've realized that's a waste of positive energy. Now when I have a high-confidence day, I try to make the most of it. I direct that confidence into doing challenging things. If I'm feeling good about myself, I'm gonna own it!

I just can't win...

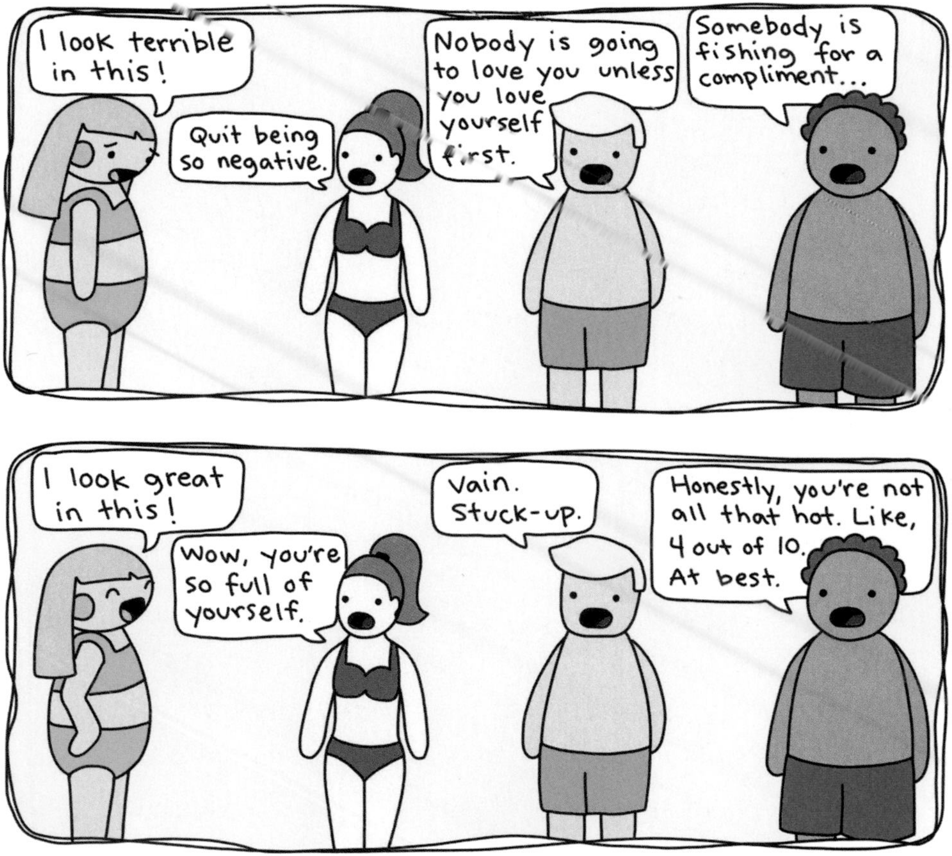
I look terrible in this!
Quit being so negative.
Nobody is going to love you unless you love yourself first.
Somebody is fishing for a compliment...
I look great in this!
Wow, you're so full of yourself.
Vain. Stuck-up.
Honestly, you're not all that hot. Like, 4 out of 10. At best.

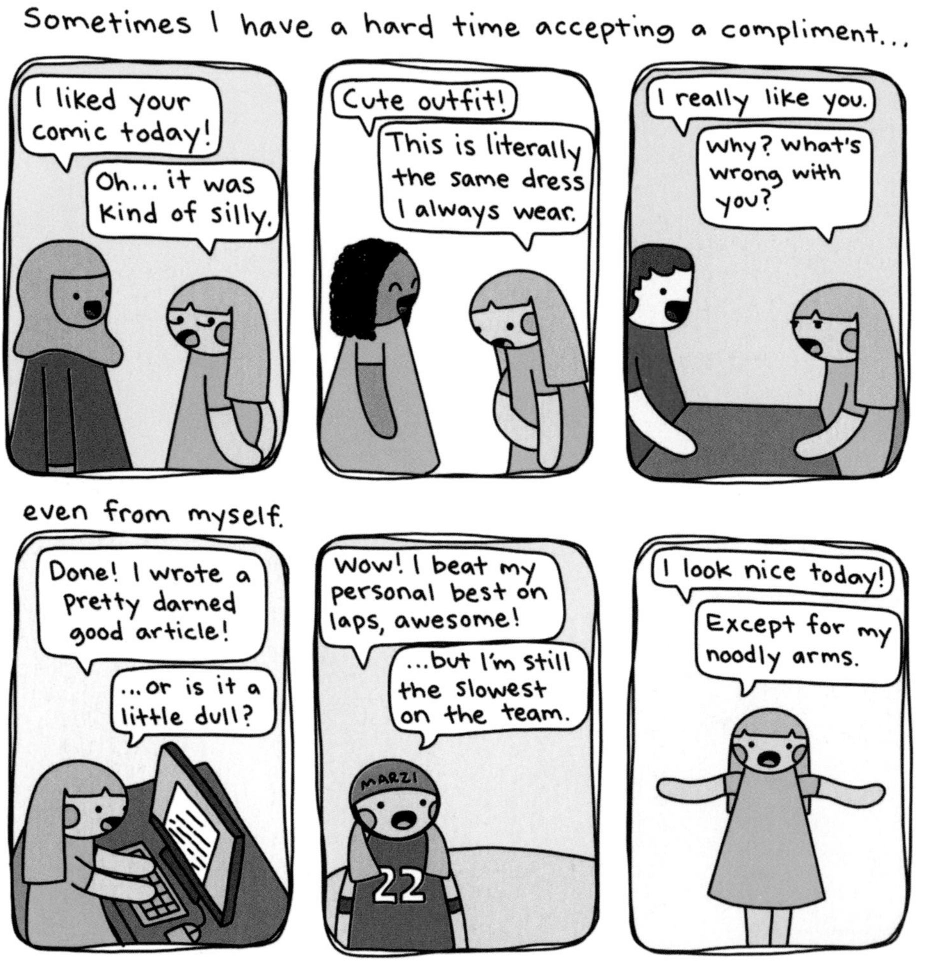
Sometimes I have a hard time accepting a compliment...
I liked your comic today!
Oh... it was kind of silly.
Cute outfit!
This is literally the same dress I always wear.
I really like you.
Why? What's wrong with you?
even from myself.
Done! I wrote a pretty darned good article!
...or is it a little dull?
Wow! I beat my personal best on laps, awesome!
...but I'm still the slowest on the team.
MARZI
22
I look nice today!
Except for my noodly arms.

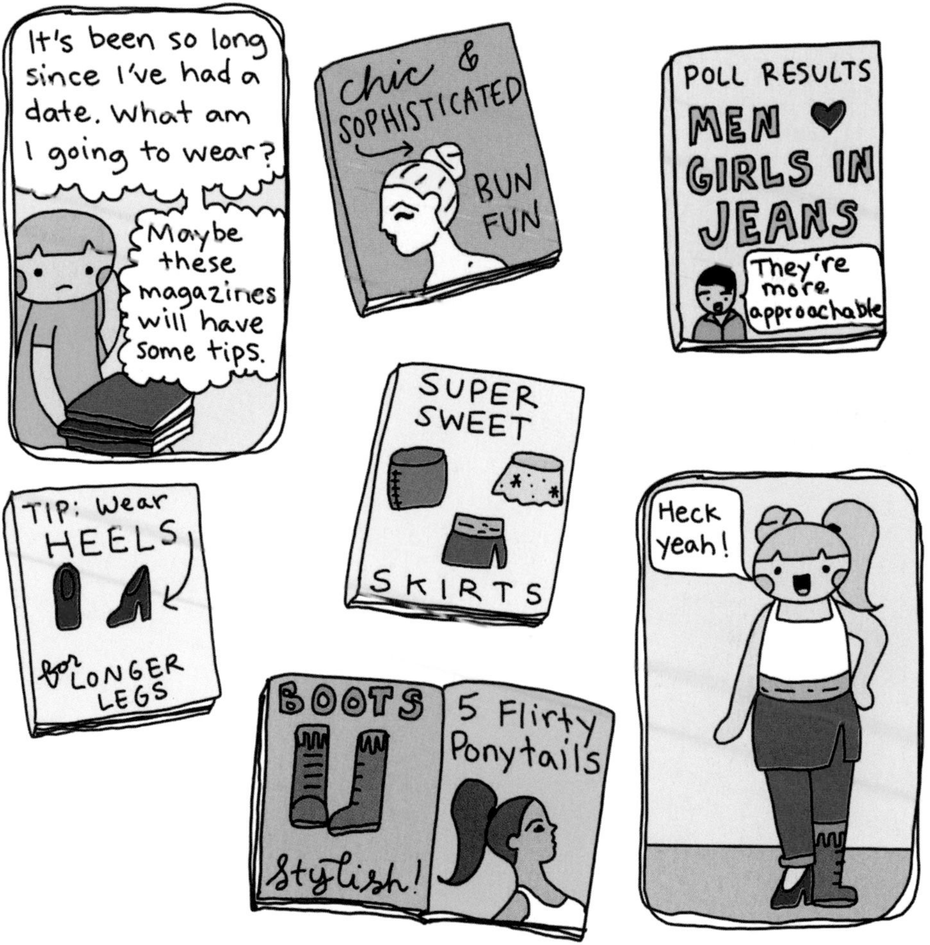
It's been so long since I've had a date. What am I going to wear?
Maybe these magazines will have some tips.
Chic & SOPHISTICATED
BUN FUN
POLL RESULTS
MEN ♥ GIRLS IN JEANS
They're more approachable
TIP: Wear HEELS for LONGER LEGS
SUPER SWEET SKIRTS
BOOTS
Stylish!
5 Flirty Ponytails
Heck yeah!

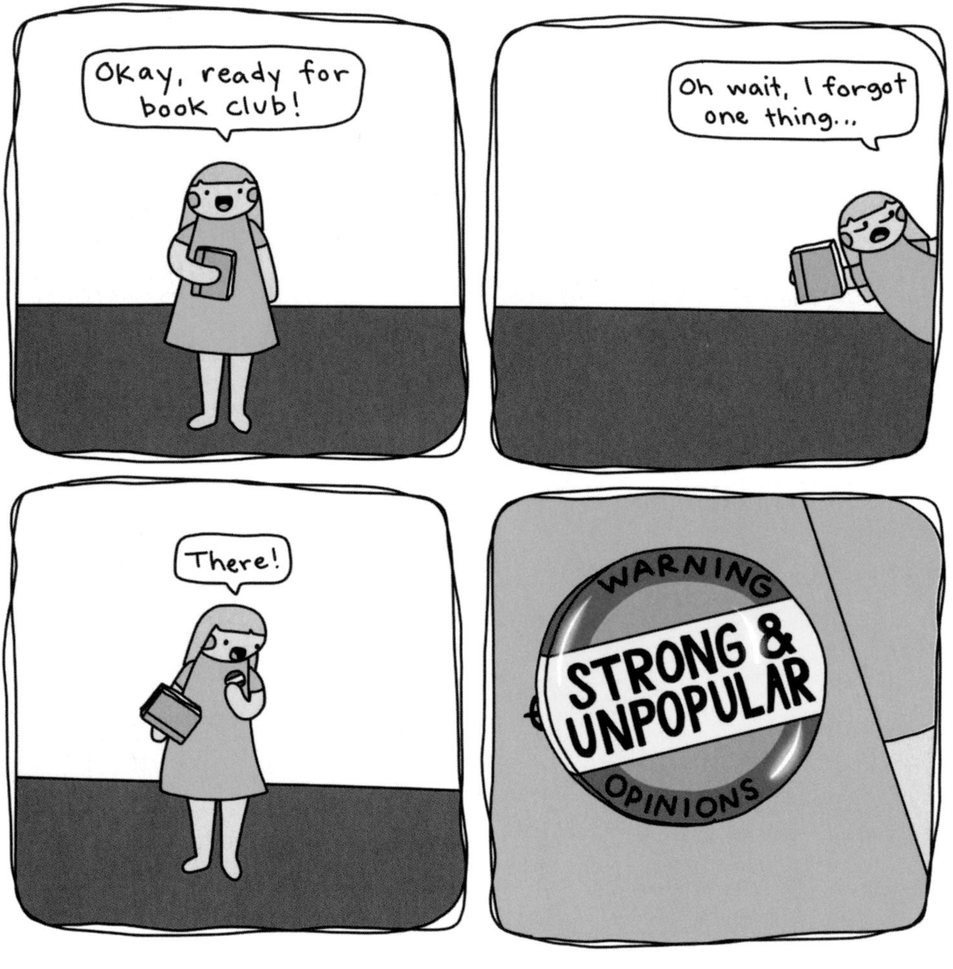
Okay, ready for book club!
Oh wait, I forgot one thing...
There!
WARNING
STRONG & UNPOPULAR
OPINIONS

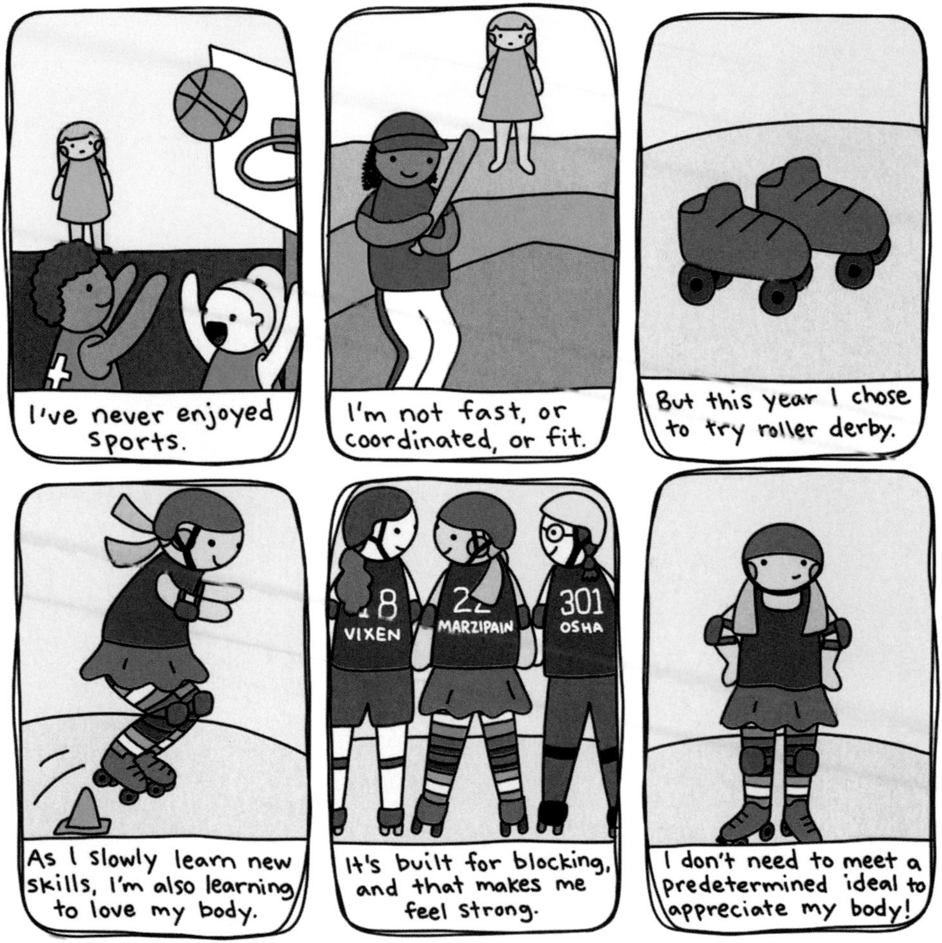
I've never enjoyed sports.
I'm not fast, or coordinated, or fit.
But this year I chose to try roller derby.
As I slowly learn new skills, I'm also learning to love my body.
18
VIXEN
22
MARZIPAIN
301
OSHA
It's built for blocking, and that makes me feel strong.
I don't need to meet a predetermined ideal to appreciate my body!

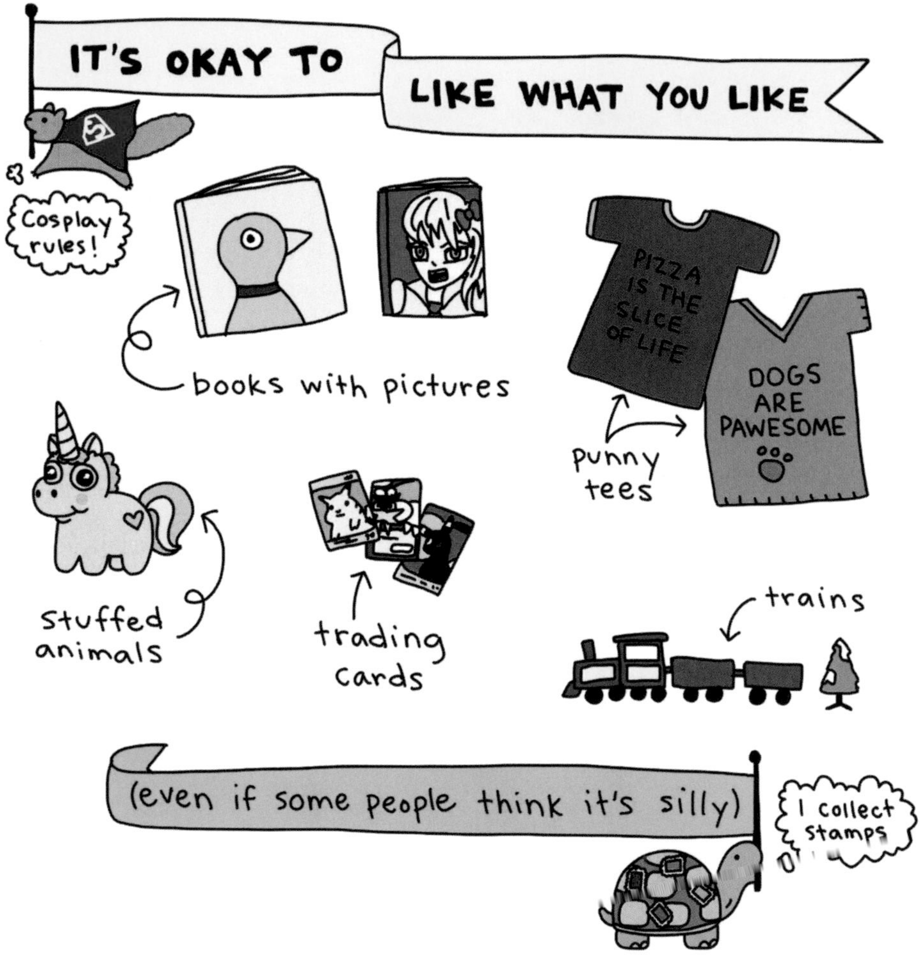
IT'S OKAY TO
LIKE WHAT YOU LIKE
Cosplay rules!
books with pictures
PIZZA IS THE SLICE OF LIFE
DOGS ARE PAWESOME
punny tees
stuffed animals
trading cards
trains
(even if some people think it's silly)
I collect stamps

SUCCESS

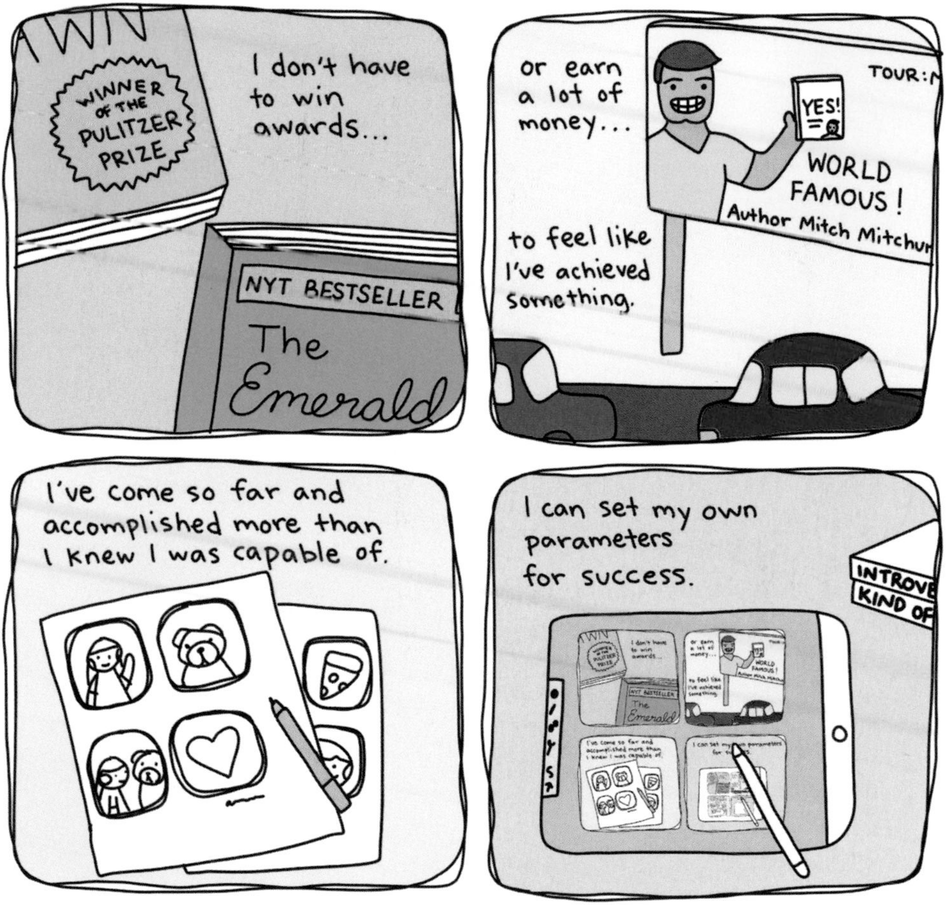
WINNER OF THE PULITZER PRIZE
I don't have to win awards...
NYT BESTSELLER
The Emerald
or earn a lot of money...
YES!
TOUR:
WORLD FAMOUS!
Author Mitch Mitchu
to feel like I've achieved something.
I've come so far and accomplished more than I knew I was capable of.
I can set my own parameters for success.

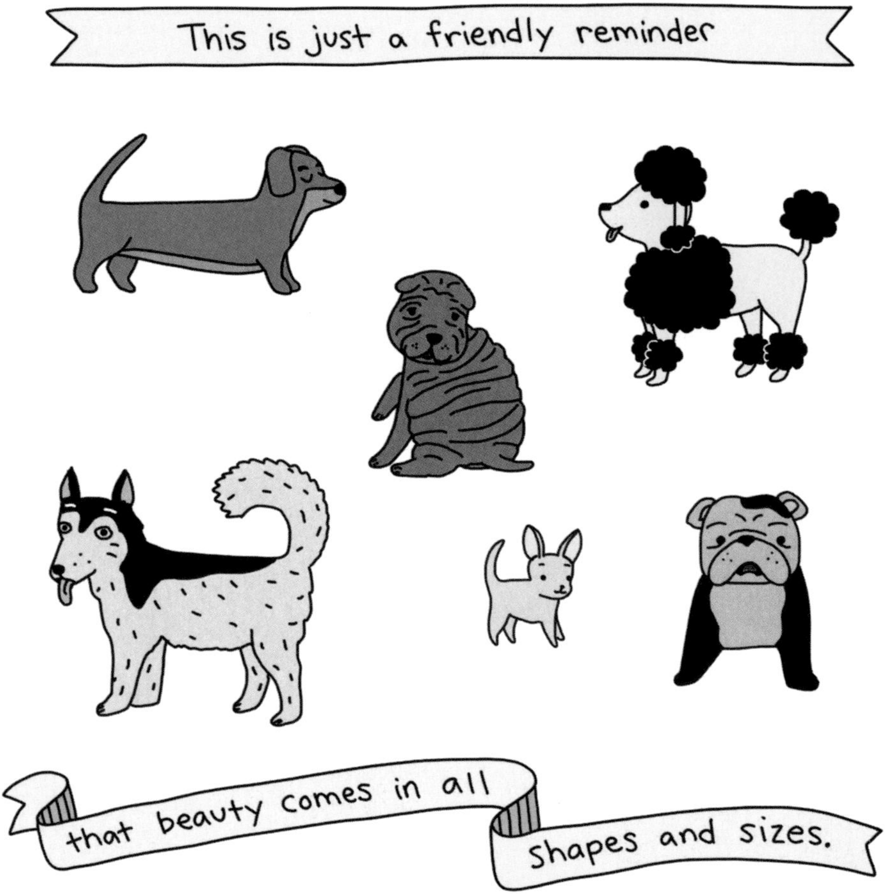
This is just a friendly reminder
that beauty comes in all
shapes and sizes.

I'm learning to make the shift from "I deserved that..."

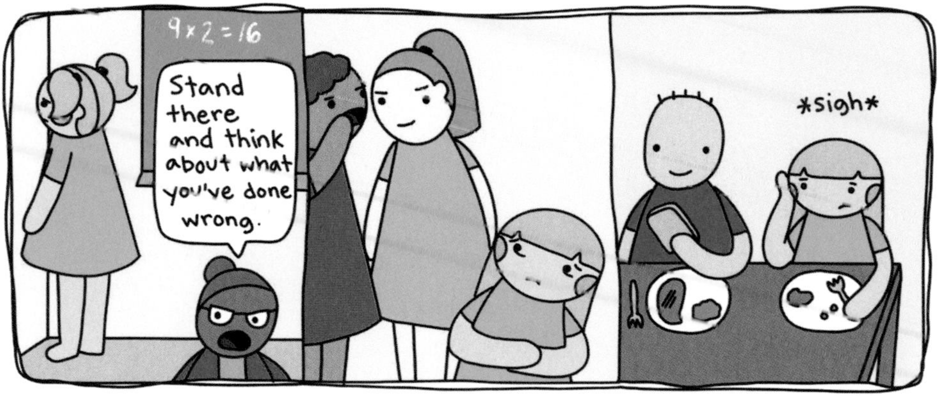
9×2=16
Stand there and think about what you've done wrong.
sigh

to "I deserve better."

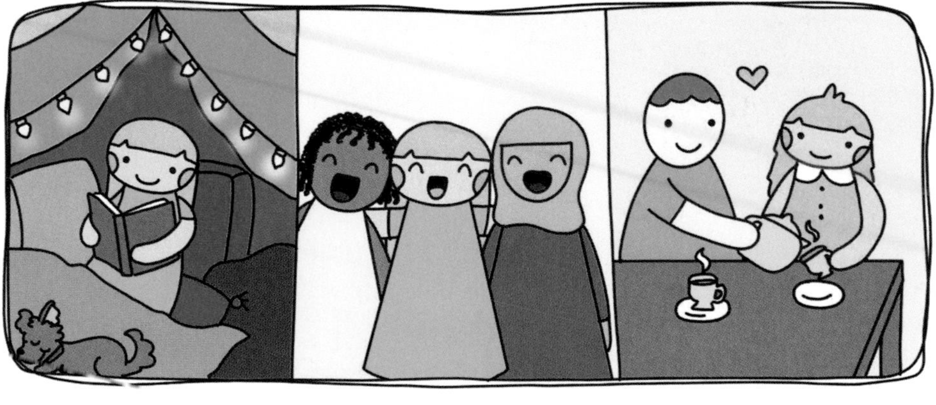

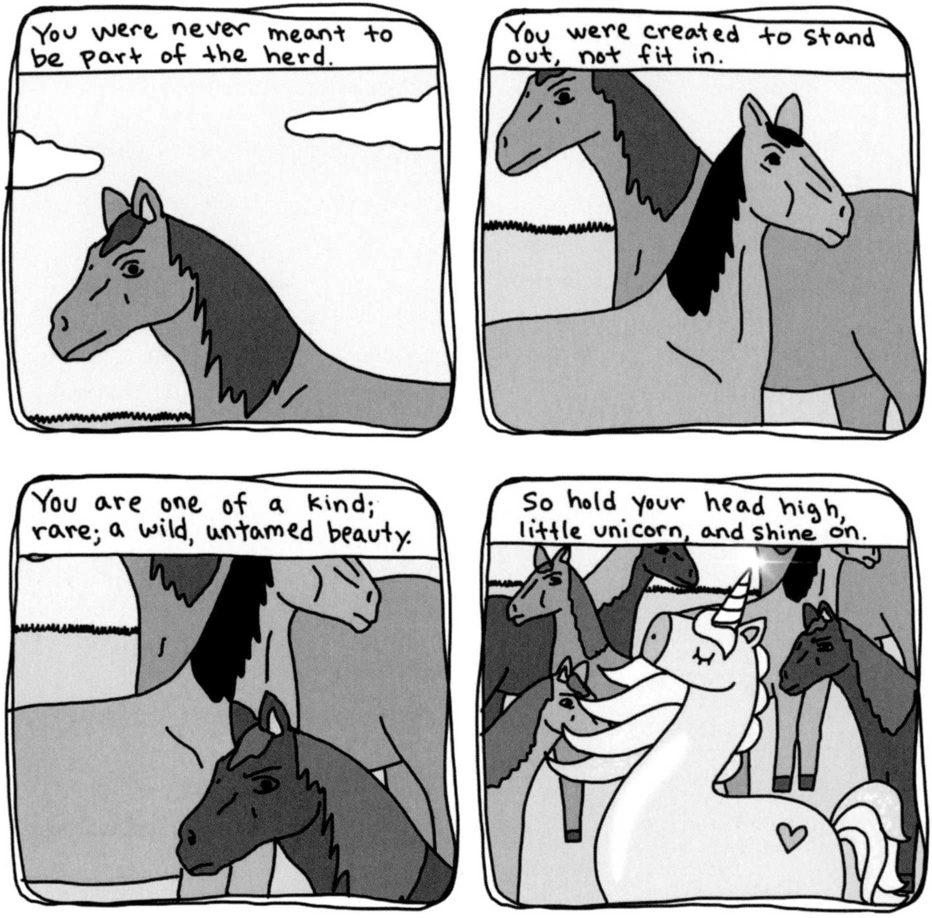
You were never meant to be part of the herd.
You were created to stand out, not fit in.
You are one of a kind; rare; a wild, untamed beauty.
So hold your head high, little unicorn, and shine on.

CHAPTER 16

TODAY I'M FEELING:

HOPEFUL

I've always thought of hope as one of the bravest

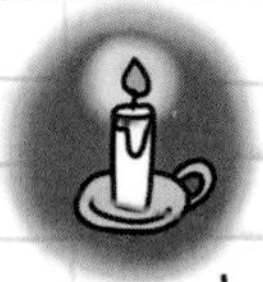

emotions. It's tenuous and precious; a small, flickering flame in the midst of a storm.

I used to be more wary of hope. It seemed risky! After all, if I kept my expectations low, I wouldn't be disappointed. I failed to realize that my feelings about hope were linked to my feelings about myself. Thoughts like these didn't leave much room for hope:

Only bad things happen to me.

I am a victim.

I don't deserve good things.

I didn't find hope until I found a glimmer of self-love. Because ultimately, hope is the belief that:

Good things can, and will, happen for me.

I'm a creator.

I deserve something better.

WHY I'M AFRAID TO HOPE

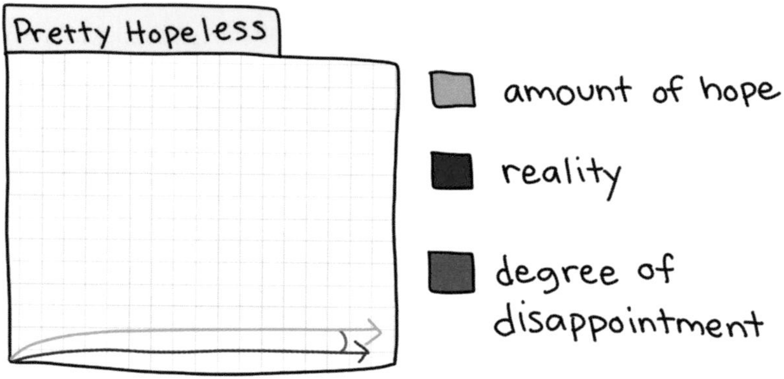
Pretty Hopeless
amount of hope
reality
degree of disappointment

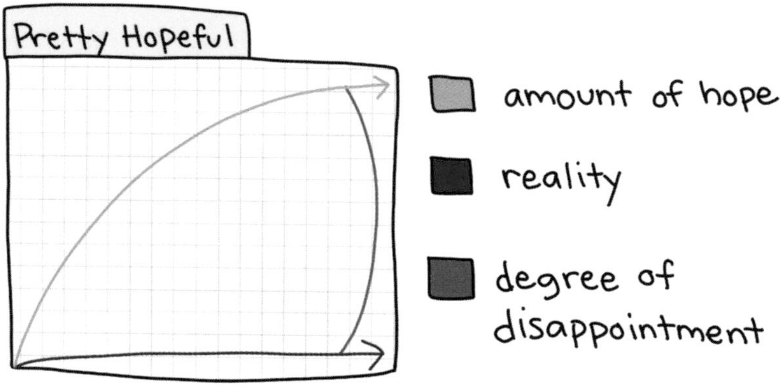
Pretty Hopeful
amount of hope
reality
degree of disappointment

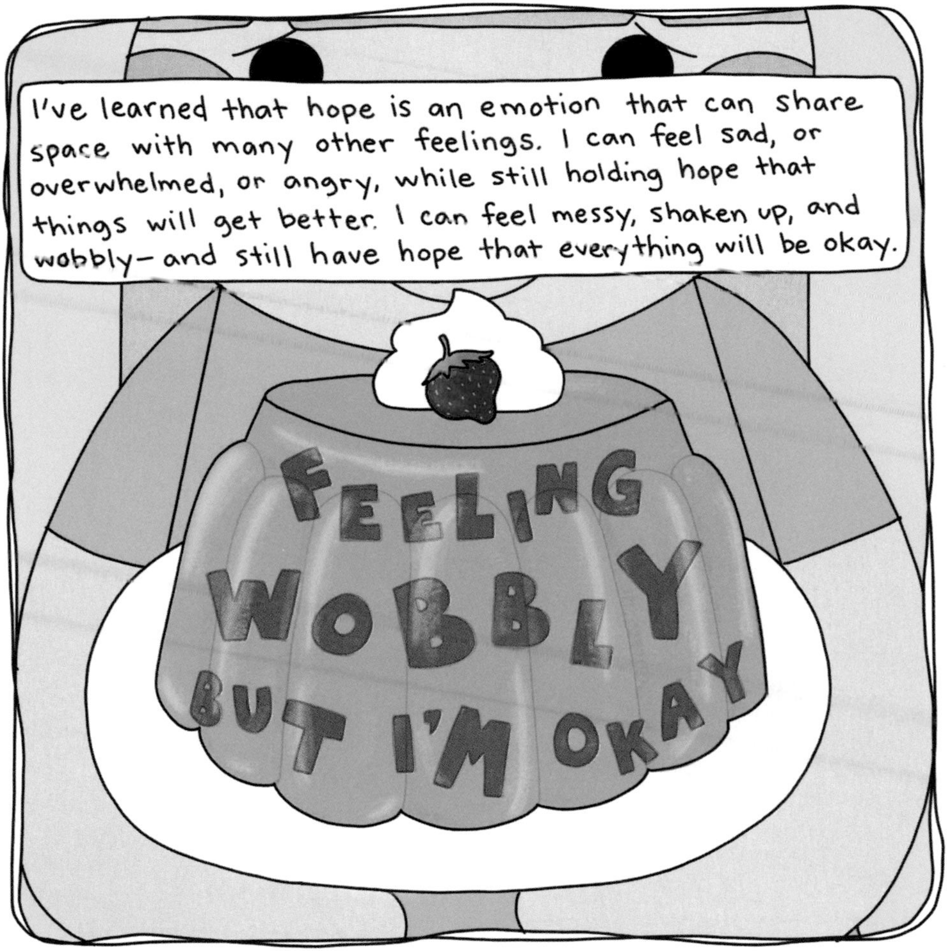
I've learned that hope is an emotion that can share space with many other feelings. I can feel sad, or overwhelmed, or angry, while still holding hope that things will get better. I can feel messy, shaken up, and wobbly—and still have hope that everything will be okay.
FEELING WOBBLY BUT I'M OKAY

AN ABRIDGED LIST OF MY SECRET HOPES

○ I hope velour tracksuits make a comeback!

I still have hope that I'll finally learn my 12 times table.

$$\begin{array}{r} 12 \\ \times\ 9 \\ \hline ? \end{array}$$

○ I hope I can someday create a dog ranch retirement community, where senior dogs and senior citizens can enjoy their golden years together.

I hope I'll get to tour the Jelly Belly factory.

TOP SECRET

○ I hope he feels the same way I do.

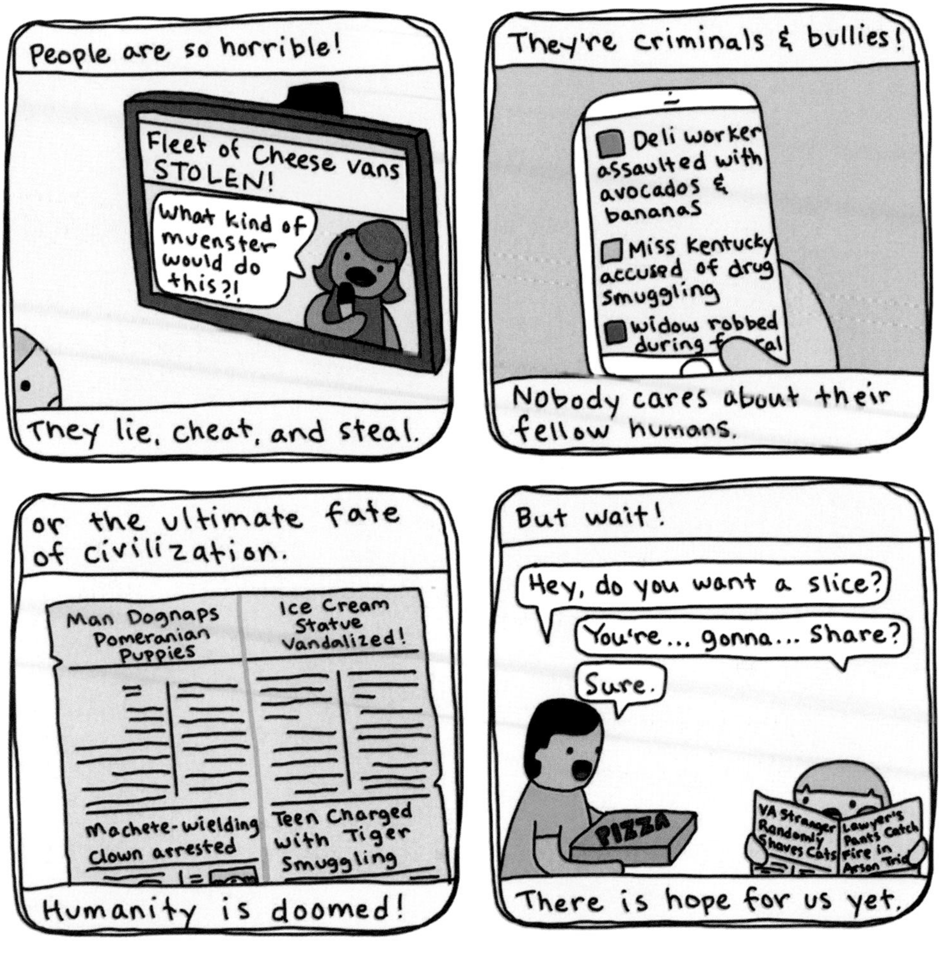
People are so horrible!
Fleet of Cheese vans STOLEN!
What kind of muenster would do this?!
They lie, cheat, and steal.
They're criminals & bullies!
Deli worker assaulted with avocados & bananas
Miss Kentucky accused of drug smuggling
widow robbed during
Nobody cares about their fellow humans.
or the ultimate fate of civilization.
Man Dognaps Pomeranian Puppies
Ice Cream Statue Vandalized!
Machete-wielding Clown arrested
Teen Charged with Tiger Smuggling
Humanity is doomed!
But wait!
Hey, do you want a slice?
You're... gonna... share?
Sure.
PIZZA
VA Stranger Randomly Shaves Cats
Lawyer's Pants Catch Fire in
There is hope for us yet.

THINGS THAT ALWAYS MAKE ME FEEL HOPEFUL

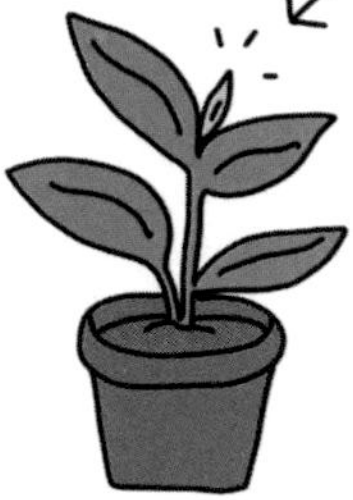

New leaves on my houseplants

"My" song playing on the radio

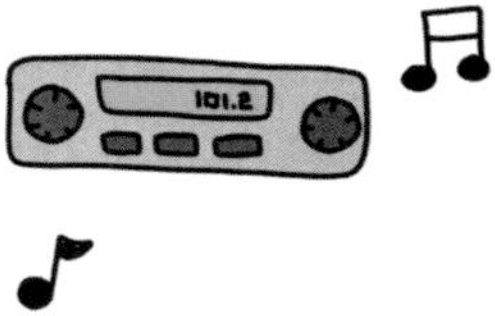
101.2

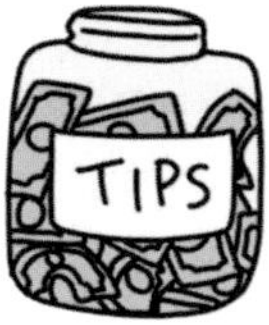
TIPS

A full tip jar at the coffee shop

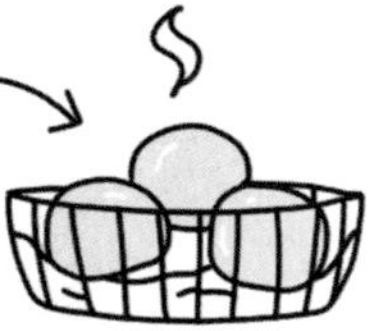

The waiter asking if I'd like more bread

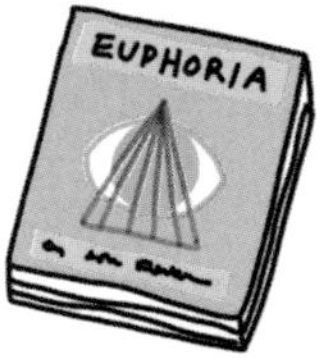
EUPHORIA

A brand-new novel with a crisp book jacket

My therapist recently told me that his schedule was changing. It wouldn't work out.

Even though our relationship was a professional one, it felt a lot like breaking up.

We'd both invested a lot of time and energy establishing trust, so this felt like a big loss.

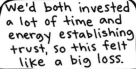

The idea of starting over with a new therapist was overwhelming.

When I posted on Instagram about it, a follower sent me a message.

I'm reading this really cool book and the amazing author made some self-care tips, I think you should check it out.

I was ready to run out and buy the book!

But when I clicked on the photo,

SELF-CARE IDEAS

it was a page from my own book.

It was a reminder that I've done hard things before...

and I came out the other side stronger and wiser. It gave me hope in myself again.

187

TIMES I DIDN'T GET WHAT I'D HOPED FOR

(but things still turned out okay)

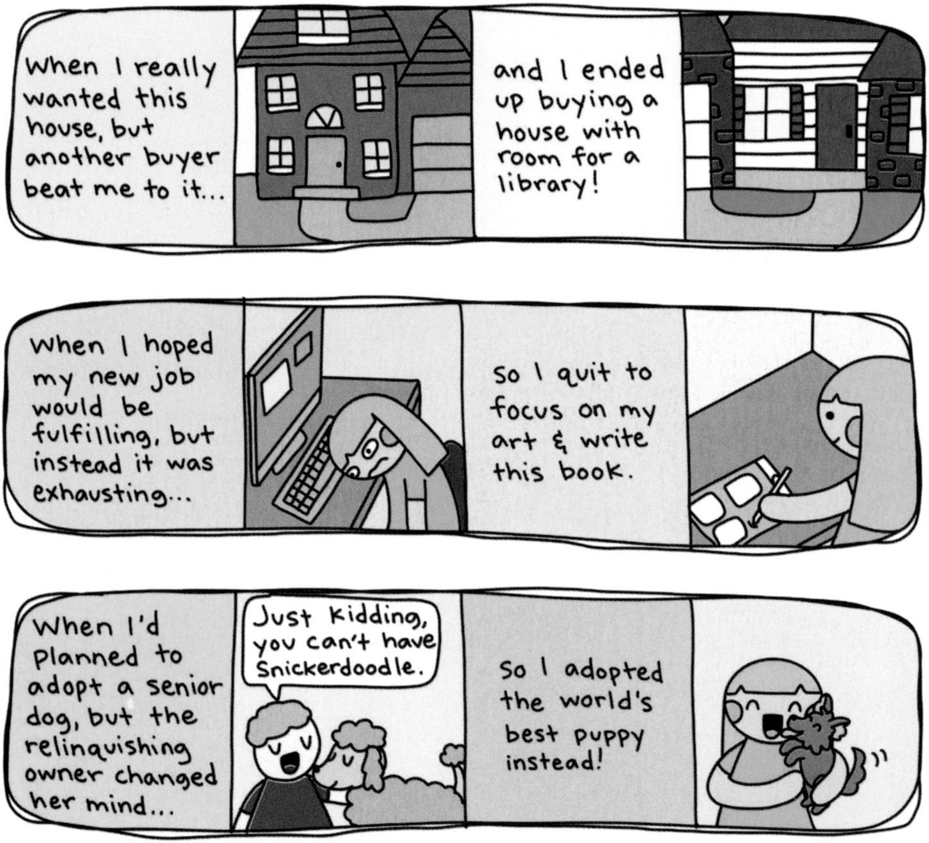

When I really wanted this house, but another buyer beat me to it...
and I ended up buying a house with room for a library!
When I hoped my new job would be fulfilling, but instead it was exhausting...
So I quit to focus on my art & write this book.
When I'd planned to adopt a senior dog, but the relinquishing owner changed her mind...
Just kidding, you can't have Snickerdoodle.
So I adopted the world's best puppy instead!

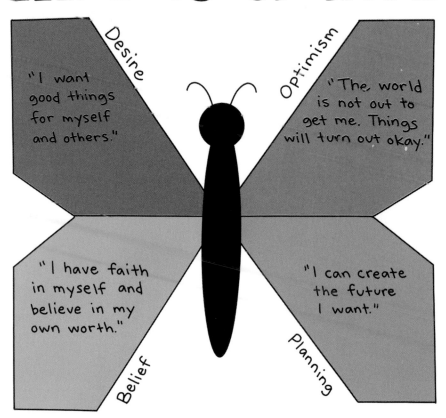

ELEMENTS OF HOPE

Desire
"I want good things for myself and others."

Optimism
"The world is not out to get me. Things will turn out okay."

Belief
"I have faith in myself and believe in my own worth."

Planning
"I can create the future I want."

THINGS I'VE HOPED FOR
THAT HAVE ACTUALLY HAPPENED

surviving high school

winning a crane game

my fave band getting back together

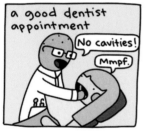

a good dentist appointment

No cavities!

Mmpf.

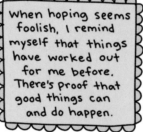

When hoping seems foolish, I remind myself that things have worked out for me before. There's proof that good things can and do happen.

the plane staying airborne

finding a way to express myself

a Taco Bell being built in my town

falling in love

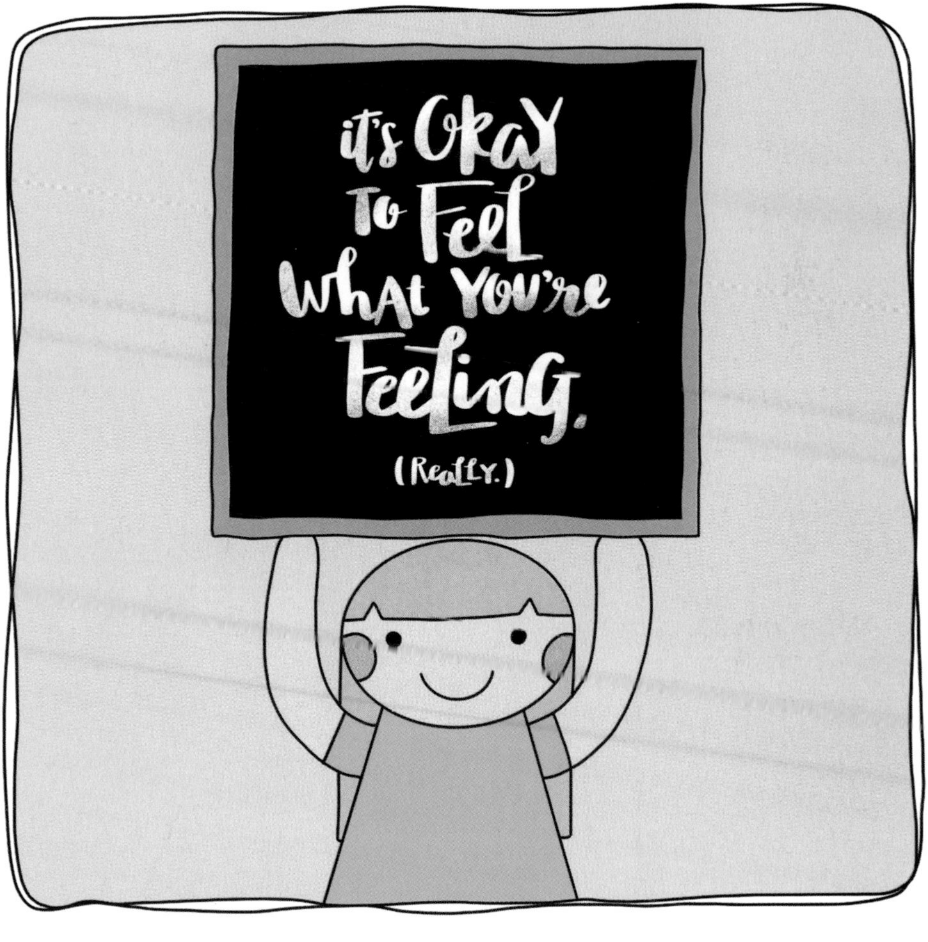
it's OKAY TO FEEL WHAT YOU'RE FEELING.
(REALLY.)

ABOUT THE AUTHOR

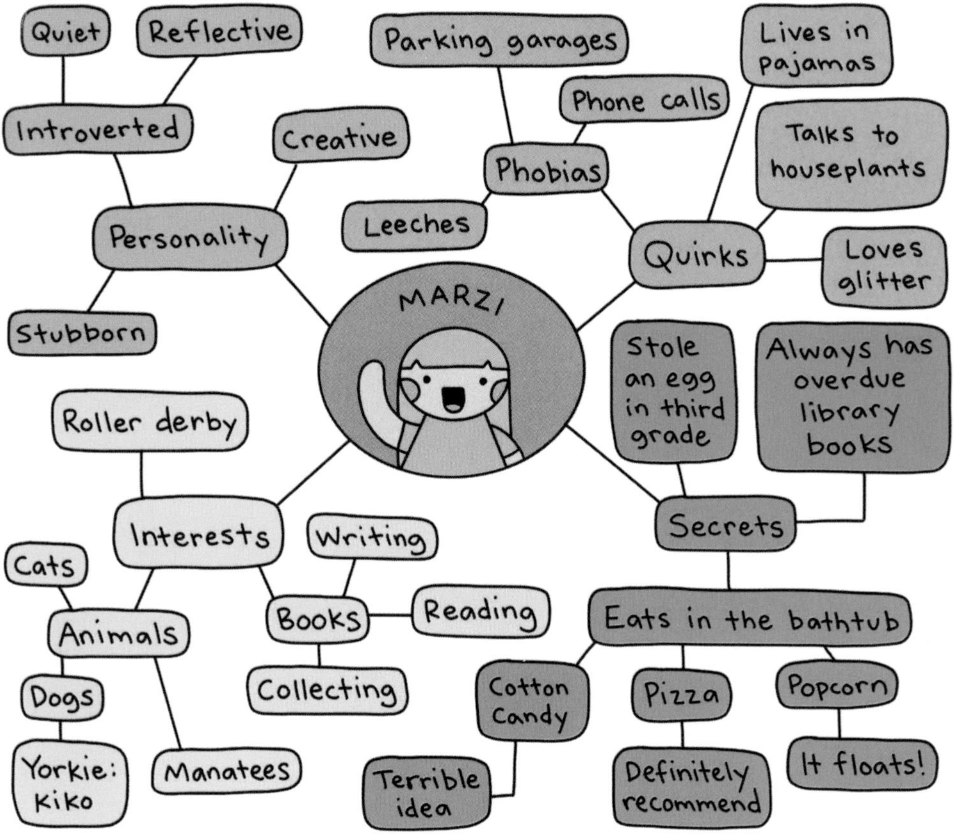

MARZI
Personality
Introverted
Quiet
Reflective
Creative
Stubborn
Phobias
Parking garages
Phone calls
Leeches
Quirks
Lives in pajamas
Talks to houseplants
Loves glitter
Secrets
Stole an egg in third grade
Always has overdue library books
Eats in the bathtub
Cotton Candy
Terrible idea
Pizza
Definitely recommend
Popcorn
It floats!
Interests
Roller derby
Animals
Cats
Dogs
Yorkie: Kiko
Manatees
Books
Writing
Reading
Collecting